Sport, Health and Drugs

In order to understand the complex relationships between modern sport and other aspects of society, it is necessary to strip away our preconceptions of how sport ought to operate and to examine, in as detached a manner as possible, the way in which sport actually operates.

For the first time, a sociological perspective is brought to bear on a topic which has received much previous attention, largely from a medical or physiological perspective. Particular issues examined include:

- sport, health and public policy
- child abuse and sex abuse in sport
- conflicts in the role of club medical staff in professional football
- doping in sport
- sports medicine and the development of performance-enhancing drugs
- case study of doping in cycling and the 1998 Tour de France.

Sport, Health and Drugs is a valuable and unique addition to the existing literature. Interview transcripts, case studies and press cuttings are used to ground theory in *reality*. Students and lecturers alike will find this an immensely readable and challenging resource.

Ivan Waddington is a Director at the Centre for Research into Sport and Society, University of Leicester, UK. He has long established expertise in both the sociology of sport and the sociology of health and has published widely on these topics. He was recently invited to present a paper to the European Commission's investigation into doping in sport.

Sport, Health and Drugs
A Critical Sociological Perspective

Ivan Waddington

London and New York

First published 2000 by E & FN Spon

Reprinted 2001 by Spon Press
11 New Fetter Lane, London EC4P 4EE

Simultaneously published in the USA and Canada
by Routledge
29 West 35th Street, New York, NY 10001

Spon Press is an imprint of the Taylor & Francis Group

Typeset in Sabon by
BC Typesetting, Bristol
Printed and bound in Great Britain by
Biddles Ltd, Guildford and King's Lynn

British Library Cataloguing in Publication Data
A catalogue record for this book is available from the British Library

Library of Congress Cataloging in Publication Data
A catalog record for this book has been requested

ISBN 0–419–25190–1 (hbk)
ISBN 0–419–25200–2 (pbk)

For my mother,
with love

Contents

Preface

The central themes of this book revolve around what have for many years been my two central areas of interest within sociology: the sociology of health and the sociology of sport. At an earlier stage of my career, I worked for several years in the Medical School at Leicester University, and later taught a course in the sociology of health within the Sociology Department at Leicester. My sociological perspective on health has benefited from many fruitful discussions over the years with David Field, Nick Jewson and Sydney Holloway and, more recently, Sue Dopson, to all of whom I express my thanks.

My interest in the sociology of sport began to develop from the late 1980s, when Eric Dunning and Patrick Murphy invited me to join them in teaching an MA programme in the sociology of sport. Since then, we have worked increasingly closely together; I have learnt a great deal from them, have argued with and on occasions been infuriated by one or other of them, but have always greatly valued their advice and support and, above all, their friendship. It was they, in the first instance, who encouraged me to write a book which examined aspects of sport from the perspective of the sociology of health.

I have also benefited from the support and advice of all my other colleagues in the Centre for Research into Sport and Society with whom I have been privileged to work since the Centre was formed in 1992. I have had many helpful discussions with Ken Sheard, whose excellent work on boxing also touches upon many health-related issues, and who kindly read and commented on parts of the manuscript. Dominic Malcolm, who also has an interest in doping in sport, has been kind enough to share his thoughts with me, and has read and commented on most of the chapters in the second part of the book. Sharon Colwell also read and commented helpfully on some of the chapters on doping. Martin Roderick has done sterling work interviewing current and ex-professional footballers for the research reported in Chapter 4. Margaret Milsom has provided, as always, superbly efficient administrative support, while Lisa Heggs provided invaluable help in relation to the presentation and organisation of the typescript in the form required by the publisher. To all of them I offer my warmest thanks, not only for their specific help in relation to this book, but also for making the CRSS such a stimulating and pleasant place to work.

I would also like to thank Ken Green, whose comments and advice have fed into the first two chapters; Peter Donnelly, who kindly provided me with draft versions of some of his research-in-progress; and William Upper, who provided me with a great deal of information relating to recent child abuse issues in Canada.

The research reported in Chapter 4 was partly funded by the Professional Footballers Association, and I would like to express my thanks to the PFA, and particularly to the Deputy Chief Executive, Brendon Batson, for their support. This research was also funded in part by a grant from the Research Committee of the Faculty of the Social Sciences at Leicester University, to whom I am also grateful. Finally, I would like to thank the Establishment Board of Leicester University, who granted me study leave during part of the 1998–99 academic year, when most of this book was written.

Introduction

The theoretical perspective which underlies this book is that of figurational or process sociology, which has grown out of the work of Norbert Elias (1897–1990). For the most part, this perspective has been used here implicitly in order to limit the more explicitly theoretical aspects of the book and thus make it as accessible as possible to those who have an interest in sport but who do not have a grounding in sociological theory. I have, therefore, not thought it necessary to describe in detail the central organising concept of figurational sociology – unsurprisingly, the concept of figuration itself – or the closely related concepts of interdependency ties and power balances or power ratios. Similarly, I have not thought it necessary to describe how Elias's concept of figuration helps us to overcome some of the problems associated with traditional and unhelpful dichotomies in sociology, such as those between the 'individual' and 'society', or 'social structure' and 'social change'. This has been done elsewhere (Murphy *et al.*, 2000, forthcoming). Readers who wish to find out more about Elias's general sociological work might usefully consult the excellent works by Mennell (1992) and van Krieken (1998), while those who wish to find out more about how figurational or process sociology and, in particular, Elias's work on civilising processes, have been applied to sport might look at any of the sport-related works by Elias and/or Dunning listed in the bibliography to this book. However, it may be helpful to say something about two aspects of Elias's work on which I have drawn explicitly and which provide two of the integrating themes for this book. These are the concepts of involvement and detachment, and Elias's view of the role of the sociologist as a destroyer of myths.

Throughout this book, I have sought to offer a relatively detached analysis of modern sport. I deliberately use the term 'relatively detached' rather than 'objective' because, following Elias, I believe the concepts of involvement and detachment have several advantages over the more commonly used terms 'objectivity' and 'subjectivity'.

Elias suggested that one of the problems with concepts like objectivity and subjectivity is that they tend to suggest a static and unbridgeable divide between two entities, 'subject' and 'object', and closely associated with this is the almost ubiquitous tendency, among those who use these terms, to describe research in all-or-nothing terms – that is, to describe it as either totally 'objective' or, conversely, as completely lacking in objectivity, that is, as being 'subjective' in an absolute sense.

Clearly such a conceptualisation is of little use, for – to stick with these terms for the moment – it is impossible to find an example of thinking which is absolutely 'objective', and it is extremely difficult to find examples, at least among sane adults, of thinking which is wholly 'subjective' in character. Equally, it is not possible in these terms adequately to describe the development of modern science, for this development was a long-term process, and there was not a single, historic, moment when 'objective' scientific knowledge suddenly emerged, fully formed, out of what had formerly been wholly 'subjective' forms of knowledge.

What is required, Elias argued, is a more adequate conceptualisation of our ways of thinking about the world, and of the processes as a result of which our present, more scientific, ways of thinking about the world have developed. Elias's conceptualisation of the problem in terms of degrees of involvement and detachment is, it might be held, more adequate than conventional arguments for the following reasons:

1   it does not involve a radical dichotomy between categories such as 'objective' and 'subjective', as though these were mutually exclusive categories;
2   this conceptualisation is processual – that is, it provides us with a framework with which we can examine the development, over time, of more scientific (or what Elias called more object-adequate or alternatively more reality-congruent) knowledge.

It is important to emphasise that Elias emphatically denies the possibility that the outlook of any sane adult can be either wholly detached or wholly involved. Normally, he notes, adult behaviour lies on a scale somewhere between these two extremes. Thus the concepts of involvement and detachment 'do not refer to two separate classes of objects . . . what we observe are people and people's manifestations, such as patterns of speech or of thought . . . some of which bear the stamp of higher, others of lesser detachment or involvement' (Elias, 1987: 4). Clearly, therefore, Elias is not suggesting that it is possible for us to obtain 'ultimate truth', or complete detachment.[1] It is certainly not my claim to offer in this book anything remotely resembling 'ultimate truth' – whatever that might be – or complete detachment; what I do hope to offer is a relatively detached perspective which helps to advance, in some small way, our understanding of some key aspects of the relationships between sport, health and drugs.

But how can we differentiate between attitudes or knowledge which reflect a relatively high degree of involvement and those which reflect a higher degree of detachment? Why should we, as sociologists, seek to achieve a higher degree of detachment in our work? And what are the processes which, over a long period of time, have gradually enabled people to think, first about the 'natural' world, and then, more recently, about the 'social' world, in more detached terms? These questions can be best explored via a consideration of Elias's essay 'The Fishermen in the Maelstrom' (Elias, 1987: 43–118).

Elias begins his essay by retelling an episode from Edgar Allan Poe's famous story about the descent into the maelstrom. Those who are familiar with the story will recall that two brothers who were fishermen were caught in a storm and were slowly being drawn into a whirlpool. At first, both brothers (a third brother had already been lost overboard) were too terrified to think clearly and to observe accurately what was going on around them. Gradually, however, the younger brother began to control his fear. While the elder brother remained paralysed by his fear, the younger man collected himself and began to observe what was happening around him, almost as if he were not involved. It was then that he became aware of certain regularities in the movement of objects in the water which were being driven around in circles before sinking into the whirlpool. In short, while observing and reflecting, he began to build up an elementary 'theory' relating to the movement of objects in the whirlpool. He came to the conclusion that cylindrical objects sank more slowly than objects of any other shape, and that smaller objects sank more slowly than larger ones. On the basis of his observations and of his elementary 'theory', he took appropriate action. While his brother remained immobilised by fear, he lashed himself to a cask and, after vainly encouraging his brother to do the same, leapt overboard. The boat, with his brother in it, descended rapidly into the whirlpool. However, the younger brother survived, for the cask to which he had lashed himself sank much more slowly, and the storm eventually blew itself out before the cask was sucked down into the whirlpool.

The story of the fishermen points up very clearly a kind of circularity which is by no means uncommon in the development of human societies. Both brothers found themselves involved in processes – a storm and the associated whirlpool – which appeared wholly beyond their control. Not surprisingly, their emotional involvement in their situation paralysed their reactions, making it difficult for them to analyse what was happening to them, or to take effective action to maximise their chances of survival. Perhaps for a time they may have clutched at imaginary straws, hoping for a miraculous intervention of some kind. After a while, however, one of the brothers began, to some degree, to calm down. As he did so, he began to think more coolly. By standing back, by controlling his fear, by seeing his situation (as it were) from a distance – in other words, by seeing himself and his situation in a rather more detached way – he was able to identify certain patterns within the whirlpool. Within the generally uncontrollable processes of the whirlpool, he was then able to use his new-found knowledge of these patterns in a way which gave him a sufficient degree of control to secure his own survival. In this situation, we can see very clearly that the level of emotional self-control, of detachment, and the development of more 'realistic' knowledge which enables us more effectively to control both 'natural' and 'social' processes are all interdependent and complementary.

This same kind of circularity can also be seen in the reaction of the older brother, who perished in the whirlpool. High exposure to the dangers of a process tends to increase the emotivity of human responses. High emotivity of response lessens the chance of a realistic understanding of the critical process and, hence, of a realistic practice in relation to it. In turn, relatively unrealistic practice under the pressure of strong emotional involvement lessens the chance of bringing the critical process under control. In short, inability to control tends to go hand in hand with high emotivity of response, which minimises the chance of controlling the dangers of the process, which keeps at a high level the emotivity of the response, and so forth.

In so far, therefore, as we are able to control our emotional involvement with the processes we are studying, we are more likely to develop a more realistic or 'reality-congruent' analysis of those processes. Conversely, the more emotionally involved we are, the more likely it is that our strong emotional involvement will distort our understanding. It is this consideration which constitutes the primary rationale for Elias's argument that we should seek, when engaged in research, to maintain a relatively high degree of detachment.

It is hoped that the relevance of the above arguments to the analysis of sport is clear. Participation in sport, whether playing or spectating, has the capacity to arouse high levels of emotion and excitement; indeed, as Elias and Dunning (1986) have pointed out, it is precisely this capacity of sport to generate relatively high levels of (often pleasurable) excitement which accounts, at least in part, for its widespread popularity. However, it is important to recognise that the relatively high level of emotion which surrounds many sporting issues often has the effect of hindering, rather than helping, the development of a more adequate understanding of modern sport, and of the relationships between sport and other aspects of the wider society. One obvious example concerns the use of performance-enhancing drugs in sport, which is the focus of the second half of this book; drug use in sport typically generates a great deal of emotion, and this in turn has often been associated with a tendency to substitute moral opprobrium and condemnation for relatively detached analysis and understanding. However, the former – however emotionally satisfying – constitutes a poor basis for policy formation. The problems of involvement and detachment in relation to doping are examined in more detail in Chapter 5.

Closely associated with the issues of involvement and detachment is Elias's concern with what he saw as the role of the sociologist as 'a destroyer of myths'. The importance which he attached to this is perhaps indicated by the fact that, in his *What is Sociology?* (1978a), he devoted a whole chapter to this issue. Elias argued that, if we study the development of science,

> it is soon discovered that the cause of science has been advanced in certain societies by small groups struggling against untested, pre-scientific systems of thought. To other and usually far more powerful groups, these latter beliefs appear quite obvious. Scientifically thinking groups are generally groups which criticise or reject the dominant and commonly accepted ideas of their society, even when these are upheld by recognised authorities, for they have found that they do not correspond to the observable facts. *In other words, scientists are destroyers of myths.* By factual observation, they endeavour to replace myths, religious ideas, metaphysical speculations and all unproven images of the natural processes with theories – testable, verifiable and correctable by factual observation.
>
> (Elias, 1978a: 52)

If the search for a relatively detached understanding of the complex relationships between sport, health and drugs constitutes one underlying theme of this book, then a second, closely related theme derives from a commitment to the role of the sociologist as a destroyer of myths. This commitment, it is important to emphasise, does not arise from any desire to undermine the values or beliefs of others, but is a necessary corollary of trying to develop more adequate explanations, for this necessarily involves subjecting ideologies to critical analysis.

Sport, perhaps more than most areas of social life, is deeply embedded in a whole variety of ideologies. Amongst the more obvious and commonplace ideologies associated with sport are the following: sport is good for one's health, both physical and mental; sport teaches the value of fair play; sport teaches people to work co-operatively; sport teaches us how to be magnanimous in victory and how to accept defeat gracefully; sport helps to break down barriers of race/ethnicity, class and gender; sport helps to build international friendship and understanding. However, the reality – as opposed to the ideology – is that while sport *may*, under certain circumstances, have these consequences, it may also, under different circumstances, have consequences which are the almost exact opposite of those so often claimed for sport. Thus sport *may* be used to break down barriers of race or ethnicity – the use of sport to bring people together in post-apartheid South Africa is a good example. It may, however, express and reinforce racial/ethnic or other divisions, as in the case of the organisation of sport in South Africa under apartheid (Jarvie, 1985), or as where sport is organised along sectarian religious lines, as in Northern Ireland (Sugden and Bairner, 1993). Sport *may* be used as a means of increasing international understanding; witness President Nixon's so-called 'ping-pong' diplomacy with the Chinese in the 1970s (Monnington, 1986). But it may also express and reinforce international divisions and tensions; witness the way in which sporting competition between the USA and the former Soviet Union became an adjunct to the economic, political and military rivalry of the superpowers during the Cold War (Guttmann, 1992: 85–102). Sport *may* teach people how to win gracefully, but it may also teach them to win at any cost, even if this involves the use of violence or cheating. And while sport *may* enhance a country's international reputation, it may also – for example, in the case of soccer hooliganism – do a great deal to damage a country's reputation, as English people will know only too well (J. Williams *et al.*, 1989).

In order to understand the complex relationships between modern sport and other aspects of society, it is necessary to strip away our pre-conceptions of how, in our view, sport *ought* to operate and to examine, in as detached a manner as possible, the way in which sport actually operates. In this context, it is suggested that those whom Lapchick (1989) has described as 'true believers' – that is, those whose commitment to sport is such that it leads them to suspend all critical faculties when examining sport – do neither themselves nor the sports which they claim to love any favours.

It is this commitment to the role of the sociologist as a destroyer of myths which explains the sub-title – *A Critical Sociological Perspective* – of this book. Most conventional approaches to understanding the relationship between sport and health and sport and drugs are based upon and reflect a series of untested, taken-for-granted assumptions and it is one of the central objectives of this book to subject these taken-for-granted assumptions to critical analysis. In the opening chapter, for example, it is suggested that the conventional approach to understanding the relationship between sport and health – an approach which, it should be noted, underpins much public and semi-public policy in this area – is, at best, greatly oversimplified and, at worst, simply misleading. For example, it is argued that much public policy is based on a confusion between physical activity, exercise and competitive sport; these are, it is suggested, very different kinds of activities, not least in terms of the differing patterns of social relations which charac-terise each, and these differences have important implications for the health consequences of the different kinds of activities. In Chapter 2, the taken-for-granted assumption that policies for the development of sport are self-evidently valuable and should be promoted by government is again questioned. It is suggested that such policies are often characterised by con-fusion in relation to policy goals – for example, are they aimed at improving the health of the population, producing future Olympic champions or reducing crime? – and that this confusion often results in a situation in which the achievement of one policy goal might undermine the achievement of other goals.

In Chapter 3, some of the health dangers associated with children's sport, and in particular the risks associated with child abuse and sex abuse, are examined, while in Chapter 4 it is suggested that the roles of the club doctor and club physiotherapist, particularly in elite-level or professional sport, are extremely problematic, for they raise a whole series of questions about whether the primary loyalty of club medical staff is to the club which employs them, or to the individual player-as-patient.

The second part of the book is concerned exclusively with doping in sport. Again the perspective is one which is critical of much of the existing literature and policy in this area. For example, it is suggested that, if we wish to understand why athletes use performance-enhancing drugs then we have to move away from a focus on the individual drug-using athlete – a perspective which is a characteristic of most official thinking in this area – and focus instead on the network of relationships among athletes, their coaches and their team doctors. The relationship between sports physicians and the development and use of performance-enhancing drugs is, it is argued, particularly problematic. Thus, while part of the ideology surrounding sports medicine suggests that sports physicians are in the front line of the fight against doping in sport, the reality, it is argued, is that sports medicine is actually one of the primary contexts within which performance-enhancing drugs have been developed and disseminated within the sporting community.

The book concludes with another critical analysis, this time of existing anti-doping policy in sport. It is suggested that a relatively detached analysis of the effectiveness of existing policy would have to suggest that – to put it at its most charitable – existing policy has not worked very well. In this context, the question is raised as to whether it is appropriate to move away from those anti-doping policies – policies which have been based on a 'law and order' approach in which the emphasis has been placed on the detection and punishment of offenders – which have been pursued since the 1960s, and which have largely failed – and whether we need to look at alternative policies, particularly those which are being used in anti-drugs campaigns within the wider society. Particularly relevant in this context, it is argued, are harm reduction policies, and it is suggested that sports administrators who have a genuine concern with the health of athletes should be prepared to examine such schemes with an open mind.

Given the critical perspective adopted throughout this book, it is probable that many people within the world of sport will find much with which to disagree. This may be no bad thing in terms of our understanding of sport, for disagreement and debate are legitimate aspects of science, and one means by which science develops. However, the fact that this book adopts a critical perspective in relation to existing patterns of sporting activity and sports provision should not be taken as an indication that I am in any way anti-sport. Nothing could be further from the truth. Not only does sport form the focus of my professional life, both in terms of teaching and research, but I have, since early childhood, enjoyed both playing and watching a variety of sports. Nor should it be thought that this critical perspective is aimed specifically at highly professionalised and highly commercialised sport, and that it reflects a nostalgic longing for some idealised, long-lost version of amateur sport. Again, nothing could be further from the truth, for my personal preferences, in terms of spectatorship, are English Premier League football and professional cycling.

In conclusion, it should be stressed that it is not my objective in this book to argue either that sport is good or bad; rather, my objective is to enhance our understanding of sport, and of the relationships between sport and other aspects of society. My primary objective is therefore an academic one – to enhance our understanding of these issues – though it should be noted that a better understanding of the organisation and consequences of sporting participation is a precondition for more effective policy formation and implementation, whatever our policy goals may be. It is hoped, therefore, that this book will have some value not merely in academic but also in policy formation terms.

Part I
Sport and health

1 Sport, health and ideology

There is a large and expanding literature on the relationship between physical activity and health. Almost all of this literature has been written from a physiological perspective and has typically been concerned with issues such as the relationship between physical activity and cardiovascular functioning, or the way in which exercise can help to control obesity. However, very little has been written about the relationship between exercise, sport and health from a distinctly *sociological* perspective. The central object of this chapter, which in some respects sets the scene for the remainder of the book, is to try to develop a properly sociological approach to understanding some of the key issues in the relationships between exercise, sport and health. More specifically, the objects of this chapter are: (1) to outline and to examine critically the widely accepted idea that sport and exercise have beneficial consequences for health; (2) to examine the different patterns of *social relations* associated with sport and exercise; and (3) to examine some of the *physiological* consequences of these social differences, in terms of the rather different impacts which sport and exercise can have on health.

SPORT, EXERCISE AND THE ETHOS OF THE HEALTHY BODY

There are probably few ideas which are as widely and uncritically accepted as that linking sport and exercise with good health. What is particularly striking about this ideology is its near universal acceptance across a range of societies for, in developing and developed societies, in capitalist and communist societies and in democratic and totalitarian societies, there is a broad consensus that 'sport is good for you'.

The ideology linking sport and health has a long history. In nineteenth-century Britain, the birthplace of many modern sports, an ideology of athleticism which linked sport with health, both physical and 'moral', was developed in the Victorian public schools (Mangan, 1981), while the promotion and maintenance of the health of schoolchildren has long been an area of concern to physical educators. Colquhoun and Kirk (1987: 100), for example, note that when physical education was introduced as a subject in the elementary school curriculum in the early twentieth century, it 'had the express purpose of improving the medical, physical and hygiene provision for children in schools'. Throughout the inter-war period, *The Health of the School Child*, the annual report of the Chief Medical Officer of the Board of Education, regularly made reference to the importance of physical education for the health of schoolchildren, and the idea that sport and exercise are associated with health is widely known and accepted by British schoolchildren today; a study for the Sports Council (1995: 128) noted that 'the health and fitness message seems to be well known by children. Virtually all of them, 92 per cent agreed that it was important to keep fit. . . . In addition, most children, 82 per cent, agreed that they felt fit and healthy when they did sport and exercise.' Not surprisingly, the idea that sport is health-promoting and even life-enhancing is one which is frequently stressed by those involved in sport; to quote the former Olympic gold medalist Sebastian Coe: 'Sport is an integral part of a healthy lifestyle in today's society' (foreword to Mottram, 1988).

Such views have been endorsed over many years in a variety of official and semi-official health publications in Britain. In 1988, *The Nation's Health,* a report from an independent team (Smith and Jacobson, 1988), noted that regular and moderate exercise has a number of health benefits, while *The Allied Dunbar National Fitness Survey* (Sports Council and Health Education Authority, 1992) and the Department of Health in its *Health of the Nation* (1992) similarly noted a number of health benefits associated with regular physical activity. More recently, the Health Educa- tion Authority (1997: 2–4) has suggested that 'the health benefits of an active lifestyle for adults are well established' while the same organisation, in its *Young and Active?* policy framework (1998) has also drawn attention to the health benefits of physical activity for young people. In similar fashion, the English Sports Council, in its strategy document *England, the Sporting Nation* (1997: 3), points to what it calls the 'well rehearsed' health benefits of sport.

Such statements are not confined to Britain. In *Targeting Sporting Change in Ireland*, a strategic plan drawn up by the Sport Section of the Irish Department of Education (1997), it is noted that there 'is serious concern across all levels of Irish society at the lack of general fitness and involvement in physical activity', and the document goes on to suggest that there are 'major health benefits to be gained in Ireland through increased participation in sport and physical activity' (1997: 6). In the United States, an authoritative report from the American College of Sports Medicine and the Center for Disease Control recommended that adults should take 30 minutes of moderate activity on most days of the week (Wimbush, 1994), while the Surgeon General's report, *Physical Activity and Health*

(US Department of Health and Human Services, 1996: 10), argued that 'significant health benefits can be obtained by including a moderate amount of physical activity on most, if not all, days of the week'. In Canada, a discussion paper prepared for Health Canada and Active Living Canada (Donnelly and Harvey, 1996) noted that the most comprehensive examination of Canadian data had similarly identified several significant health benefits of physical activity.

Such views are not limited to capitalist societies, or to countries in the developed world. Riordan, for example, has pointed out that governments in developing societies frequently place considerable stress on the development of sport, not only for the consequences which sport can have for nation-building and national integration but also for the effects it can have on hygiene and health; indeed, Riordan (1986: 291) argues that 'of all the functions of state-run sport in modernising societies, that to promote and maintain health must take first place', and he goes on to point out that 'in many such states sport comes under the aegis of the health ministry'. Elsewhere, Riordan (1981: 18) has pointed out that, following the Bolshevik Revolution in October 1917, the new Soviet Government saw regular participation in physical exercise as 'one – relatively inexpensive but effective – means of improving health standards rapidly and a channel by which to educate people in hygiene, nutrition and exercise'. Similarly, following the victory of the communists in China in 1949, emphasis was placed 'on the need to promote national sports, expand public health and medical work, and safe-guard the health of mothers, infants and children'. This policy, which dates from 1950, was endorsed by Mao in June 1952 when he called upon the Chinese people to 'promote physical culture and sport, and build up the people's health' (Clumpner and Pendleton, 1981: 111).

However, it might be noted that although the ideology linking sport and health is very widespread, the view that sport is good for health has only relatively recently come to be applied to women as well as men, for, during much of the nineteenth century, women were actively discouraged from taking part in vigorous exercise, which was often seen as *damaging* to their health. Patricia Vertinsky (1990: 39), in describing the situation in late nineteenth-century Britain, writes: 'The widespread notion that women were chronically weak and had only finite mental and physical energy because of menstruation had a strong effect upon the medical profession's and consequently the public's attitude towards female exercise and sport.' She argues that, 'Not infrequently, medically defined notions of optimal female health . . . have justified the practice of viewing female physiological functions as requiring prescribed and/or delimited levels of physical activity and restricted sporting opportunities' (ibid., p. 1).

Sheila Fletcher (1987: 145) has similarly noted that women's growing participation in cycling, swimming, golf and hockey in the late nineteenth century was met with resistance from eugenists such as Dr Arabella Kenealy who, in 1899, argued that women were in danger of neutering themselves by over-indulgence in athletics. The resistance to women's full participation in sport has similarly been documented for nineteenth-century New Zealand (S. Crawford, 1987), Canada (Lenskyj, 1987) and America (Vertinsky, 1987).

THE IDEOLOGY OF 'HEALTHISM' AND VICTIM-BLAMING

It is perhaps not surprising that those involved in what is sometimes called the 'fitness industry' have generally supported the idea that sport and exercise are health-promoting, though it might be noted that such people have frequently conflated the concepts of fitness, health and beauty as a means of more effectively marketing their services. Perhaps of rather greater importance however, since they directly affect every schoolchild in many countries in the developed world, have been recent developments in school physical education which have promoted the role of regular physical activity in achieving and maintaining health. In this context, Colquhoun (1991: 5) has written of an 'explosion' of interest from the physical education profession in teaching health-related issues, an explosion which, he suggests, is indicated by the burgeoning number of professional articles and curriculum guides in several countries, especially Britain, Australia, Canada and the USA.

This is, of course, not a new role for physical education, which, as we saw earlier, has had an association with health and medicine reaching back to the introduction of physical education in the primary school curriculum in Britain. However, Kirk and Colquhoun have suggested that 'the recent re-emergence of health matters to occupy a place of central importance in school physical education marks a new moment in both the production of physical educators' views of their professional mission and in the production of a new health consciousness in society at large' (1989: 417).

Colquhoun and Kirk (1987) have identified several processes which, they suggest, have influenced this re-orientation of physical education towards health-related issues, including a growing societal interest in health matters, the prevalence of heart disease and the spiralling costs of medical care. To these might be added the fact that many physical education teachers, perhaps conscious of the relatively low status of their subject *vis-à-vis* what are often considered more 'academic' subjects, have been more than happy to draw upon the prestige associated with medicine and science to provide what they hope will be a more secure and 'intellectual' basis for their subject.

However, Colquhoun (1991) has suggested that this emerging ideology of health-based physical education (HBPE) is not unproblematic, for it presents a very partial and distorted view of the causes of health and illness.

Drawing upon R. Crawford's (1980) concept of 'healthism', Colquhoun argues that HBPE is premised upon and helps to disseminate the idea that our health is largely under our own control. More specifically, he argues that 'by focusing on individual lifestyle as the major determinant of an individual's health, health based physical education (HBPE) conforms to the practices of conventional health education and has therefore been severely restricted in its potential for emancipation, social justice, equality and social change. Indeed, the political issues which accompany HBPE have not yet been fully exposed' (1991: 6).

The ideology of healthism, it is argued, serves to focus attention on individual responsibility for our own health and, simultaneously, to divert attention away from wider social processes – for example, poverty, unemployment, industrial pollution, or the poor quality or lack of accessibility of health services – which may be associated with high levels of illness. By thus shifting responsibility for health away from manufacturers, governments and other powerful groups, the ideology of healthism diverts attention away from the key issues in the politics of health. As R. Crawford (1980: 368) has noted, it perpetuates the misleading – or, at best, greatly oversimplified – idea that we can, *as individuals,* control our own existence. Moreover, our assumed ability individually to control our lives gradually becomes transformed into a moral imperative to do so for, suggests R. Crawford (1984), we live in an era of a new health consciousness where to be unhealthy has come to signify individual moral laxity. Thus slimness signifies not only good health but also self-discipline and moral responsibility, whereas fatness, in contrast, signifies idleness, emotional weakness and moral turpitude. In this sense our bodies, whether slim or obese, signify not merely our health status for they also become, quite literally, the embodiment of moral propriety or laxity. Within this context, those who fall ill are increasingly likely to be seen not as unfortunate and innocent victims of processes beyond their control but, rather, as people who, through their moral laxity and lack of self-discipline, have 'brought it on themselves'. The Victorian differentiation between the 'deserving' and the 'undeserving' poor is, in some respects, in the process of being replicated in the differentiation between the 'deserving' and 'undeserving' sick.

SPORT AND HEALTH: COMMERCIAL LINKS

One area which casts doubt on the assumed close relationship between sport and the promotion of healthy life-styles is that of sports sponsorship and, in particular, the widespread sponsorship of sport by the manufacturers of two of the most widely used drugs in the western world: alcohol and tobacco. In relation to the former, concern has been expressed about sponsorship of sport by breweries. Dealy (1990), for example, has drawn attention to the health problems associated with alcohol abuse and with the widespread practice of under-age drinking in the United States and has expressed concern at the close relationship between the National Collegiate Athletic Association (NCAA) and the breweries.

It is, however, the relationship between sport and the tobacco industry which has been the cause of greatest concern. Taylor (1985) has pointed out that from the 1970s, business sponsorship of sport grew rapidly in Britain with the tobacco companies being by far the biggest spenders. Sports sponsorship, he notes, has been a relatively cheap and highly cost-effective means of advertising for the tobacco companies, not least because in Britain it has enabled them to circumvent the 1965 ban on the advertising of cigarettes on television, for cigarette manufacturers have continued to reach large television audiences via the televised coverage of such popular sporting events as the Embassy Snooker World Championships, Benson and Hedges Cricket and the Silk Cut Rugby League Challenge Cup. Sponsorship of sporting events by tobacco companies has for many years been widespread; sports which have been sponsored by tobacco companies in Britain include motor-racing, power-boat racing, cricket, speedway, snooker, darts, bowls, horse-racing, tennis, rugby union, rugby league, basketball, badminton, show-jumping, motor-cycling and table tennis.

Sponsorship of sporting events by tobacco companies is, of course, not confined to Britain. In 1982 Dr Thomas Dadour introduced into the Western Australian parliament a Bill to ban all forms of cigarette advertising and promotion. The Bill was narrowly defeated. Had it been passed, one of the first casualties would have been the advertising at the Australia vs. England test match, which was sponsored by Benson and Hedges who had been the Australian Cricket Board's main sponsor for more than ten years. The following year, the state Government of Western Australia introduced another Bill similar to Dr Dadour's. This Bill was also defeated following intensive lobbying by, amongst others, those associated with the cigarette-sponsored sports under threat (Taylor, 1985: 48–9). In a perhaps even more revealing incident in 1995, the highly successful Swedish yacht *Nicorette,* which is sponsored by a company which manufactures products designed to help people give up smoking, was banned from the Cape to Rio race, which is sponsored by the tobacco giant Rothmans. The captain of the *Nicorette* protested against the decision (which was reversed some two weeks later) by saying that 'Rothmans is scared of his boat and the healthy lifestyle it seeks to promote'. Given the close relationship which is often claimed between sport and healthy life-styles, many people may find it more than a little incongruous that the organisers of a sporting event should not only accept sponsorship from a cigarette manufacturer but that they should also ban an entry sponsored by a manufacturer of products which are explicitly designed to help people give up smoking (*The Times,* 14 September 1995; *Guardian,* 27 September 1995).

The widespread sponsorship of sporting events by tobacco companies would not, at least in the context of the present argument, be of any significance were it not for the fact that, by the early 1980s, cigarette smoking was estimated to be responsible for more than 300,000 premature deaths a year in the United States, and nearly half a million deaths a year in Europe. The US Surgeon General has described cigarette smoking as 'the chief, single, avoidable cause of death in our society, and the most important public health issue of our time', while in Britain the Royal College of Physicians, in their report *Smoking and Health Now*, referred to the annual death rate caused by cigarette smoking as 'the present holocaust' (Taylor, 1985: xiv, xvii). More recently the British Government, in its consultation paper *Our Healthier Nation* (1998: 20), has pointed out that smoking 'is the biggest cause of early deaths in England. It is estimated to account for nearly a fifth of all deaths each year – 120,000 lives in the United Kingdom cut short or taken by tobacco.' Without labouring the point, one might reasonably suggest that the ideology which associates sports with healthy life-styles sits uneasily with the widespread acceptance of sports sponsorship by breweries and, even more so, by tobacco companies.

There are, however, clear signs that the relationship between sporting organisations and the tobacco companies will, at least in Britain, have to change in the next few years. Within three weeks of the Labour Party's general election victory in May 1997, the new Health Secretary in the incoming Labour Government announced that the Government intended to legislate to ban the sponsorship of sports events by tobacco companies. It is interesting to note that, rather than reporting this decision as good news in terms of health policy, some papers chose to report it as bad news for sport: *The Times*, for example (20 May 1997) reported the story on its front page under the headline 'Cigarette adverts ban could kill top British sports events', and it began its report by saying that 'Top sports events could be forced out of Britain or left impoverished if a Government pledge to outlaw the sponsorship of sport by cigarette manufacturers goes ahead'.

The Government had originally proposed that all sponsorship of sporting events would be required to end by the year 2003, but it subsequently decided that Formula One motor-racing should be given an extra three years – until 2006 – to find alternative sponsors. The draft legislation, which was announced in June 1999, also gave a similar extension to the snooker world championship, organised by the World Professional Billiards and Snooker Association (*The Times*, 18 June 1999).

EXERCISE AND HEALTH

There is now a substantial body of data from both epidemiological and clinical studies which indicates that moderate, rhythmic and regular exercise has a significant and beneficial impact on health. In Britain, the Royal College of Physicians of London (1991: 28) concluded that:

There is substantial evidence that regular aerobic exercise such as walking, jogging, dancing or swimming is beneficial to general physical and psychological health. Regular exercise appears to be particularly effective in prevention of coronary disease and osteoporosis and of some value in the management of obesity and diabetes.

More recently, the Health Education Authority (1996: 1) has summarised the health benefits of regular physical activity as follows:

- lower levels of all-cause mortality;
- reduced risk of developing coronary heart disease, stroke, hypertension and non-insulin-dependent diabetes mellitus;
- better control of obesity;
- possible protection against some cancers;
- decreased levels of moderate depression and anxiety;
- maintenance of healthy bones and possible prevention of osteoporosis;
- benefits for those with existing diseases, particularly for those with controlled hypertension, hyperlipidaemia, mild depression and chronic anxiety.

Studies in North America point to similar conclusions, and suggest that regular exercise is associated with reduced mortality from all causes, from cardiovascular disease and from cancer of combined sites (Paffenbarger *et al.*, 1986; Blair *et al.*, 1989), while a review of four population surveys (two carried out in Canada and two in the United States), suggests a positive association between physical activity and lower levels of anxiety and depression (Stephens, 1988). The report of the US Surgeon General (US Department of Health and Human Services, 1996) claimed to bring together, for the first time, what has been learnt about physical activity and health from decades of American research, and produced a list of health benefits very similar to those identified above by the Health Education Authority in Britain.

It might be noted that some of these health benefits are very substantial. The British Medical Association, for example, has noted that insurance statistics indicate that men with only moderately high blood pressure can expect to live about fifteen years less than men with low blood pressure, and it noted that regular exercise 'is potentially a major non-pharmacological method of lowering blood pressure' (BMA, 1992: 18). Similarly, one of the studies in the United States (Paffenbarger *et al.*, 1986) indicates that death rates among men whose work or leisure involves regular exercise are between one-third and one-half lower than those among men whose lives are more sedentary.

At first glance, studies like those cited above might seem to indicate that the health-based arguments in favour of sport and exercise are overwhelming. Donnelly and Harvey (1996: 5) have noted, tongue-in-cheek, that the 'numerous, almost miraculous claims for the benefits of physical activity lead one to wonder why it has not been patented by an innovative company', but, more seriously, they go on to point out that the widespread nature of these claims should serve as a warning against their too easy and uncritical acceptance, and that the context of the claims needs to be examined carefully. In this context, there are some important provisos to be borne in mind when considering studies on the relationship between exercise and health. The first is that these studies do not suggest that *all* exercise is beneficial; rather, they indicate that exercise *of a particular kind, amount and intensity* has a beneficial impact on health. *The Nation's Health* (Smith and Jacobson, 1988: 126), for example, refers quite specifically to the beneficial effects of what it calls 'moderate, rhythmic and regular exercise', which it goes on to define as exercise such as that involved in brisk walking, running or swimming for 20–30 minutes about three times each week. The British Medical Association (1992: 14) similarly suggested that the 'recommended amount of exercise from a health perspective is about twenty to thirty minutes of moderate exercise three times a week'. It noted that the exercise that is most frequently suggested is brisk walking, and added that the level of activity which produces significant health benefits 'is related to the initial level of fitness: for the middle-aged sedentary individual, this may correspond to walking, cycling slowly or gentle swimming' (1992: 14). The precise activity which is considered to constitute 'adequate' exercise varies from one study to another, but activities mentioned in this context include 'energetic getting about' and manual work around the house and garden (Morris *et al.*, 1980), dancing (BMA, 1992) and regular climbing of stairs (Paffenbarger *et al.*, 1986), while the US Surgeon General (US Department of Health and Human Services, 1996) recommends as examples of moderate activity washing and waxing a car, washing windows, gardening and raking leaves.

It is important to emphasise, therefore, that what these studies have documented is a beneficial effect on health of 'moderate', or even gentle, forms of exercise; as Morris *et al.* noted, the activities which were defined in their study as constituting adequate exercise were 'by no means extreme', and they added, of the 17,944 men who took part in their study, that 'our men are no athletes' (1980: 1210). The British Medical Association similarly noted that several studies, and 'particularly those from North America, have suggested that only rather low levels of activity are necessary to confer some degree of protection against heart disease both in terms of the intensity of effort and of the total amount of exercise taken' (BMA, 1992: 19).

This is an important point to note for, quite clearly, one cannot assume that the health benefits associated with moderate exercise will simply be duplicated – still less can one assume that they will be increased – by exercise which is more frequent, of longer duration and of greater intensity, for exercise of this kind, as we shall see later, may generate substantial health 'costs' in terms of additional stresses or injuries (for example, those associated with 'overuse'). In short, to suggest that a 30-minute gentle swim three times a week is good for one's health does not mean that running 70 miles a week as a means of preparing for running marathons is good for one's health in an equally simple or unproblematic way. Indeed, it might be noted that one of the American studies, which found that death rates generally went down as levels of physical activity increased, also found a reversed trend at the highest levels of physical activity. The authors note that this result may have been associated with methodological difficulties in the study, though they also recognise that it may reflect 'actual increased hazards associated with vigorous activities' (Paffenbarger *et al.*, 1986: 606). It might also be noted that one study in New Zealand (Sullivan *et al.*, 1994) – significantly, it was a study of competitive athletes, many of whom were ranked in the top 10 per cent nationally in their age group and might therefore be expected to have engaged in relatively intensive training – found a strong positive association between exercise and a large number of symptoms, including anxiety related to competition, stitches, lightheadedness, muscle cramps, wheezing, chest pressure, 'spots in front of eyes', retching and incontinence of urine and stool, while it was negatively associated with only a few symptoms, including headaches, abdominal bloating, sneezing and depression.

The second proviso concerning the studies cited above is that most relate primarily to physical activity or to exercise, rather than specifically to sport. Although sport and exercise are overlapping categories, there are nevertheless important differences between them, and these differences have important implications for their health consequences. It is to these issues that we now turn.

EXERCISE AND SPORT

Most sociological definitions of sport include the element of physical exertion as an essential component (Edwards, 1973; Guttmann, 1978; McPherson *et al.*, 1989). However, if all sport necessarily involves physical exercise, it is not the case that all physical exercise involves sport, for what is usually considered a further necessary component of sport – the competitive element – is frequently more or less absent from many forms of physical exercise. Moreover, since sport is inherently competitive, it must involve more than one person, for while one can exercise alone, one cannot play sport alone, since one needs an opponent. This relatively obvious difference between sport and exercise has important implications for their potentially very different health consequences.

As we have seen, most of the studies cited earlier were concerned with the health consequences of 'moderate, rhythmic and regular' exercise. One important difference between sport and exercise is that non-competitive exercise involves a rather different pattern of social relations than does sport and, associated with this, the former is much more likely than is the latter to involve physical movements of a rhythmic nature and, of critical importance, the intensity of the exercise is likely to be, to a much higher degree than in the case of sport, under the control of the individual participant. Consider, for example, the situation of a person who regularly takes a brisk walk, or goes jogging or swimming, as a means of 'keeping fit', or perhaps as a means of weight control. When such activities are undertaken alone, as they frequently are, the precise nature of the physical movement – that is, the action of walking, jogging or swimming – as well as both the duration and the intensity of the exercise, are to a high degree under the control of the individual involved in the exercise. Thus, for example, a person jogging or swimming alone can determine for how long to continue the exercise, and at what pace. Where exercise of this kind is undertaken in a small group of perhaps two or three friends, as is also common, the duration and intensity of the exercise are likely to involve a level of activity agreed upon by all participants and with which all participants are reasonably comfortable. It is important to note that this is *not* the situation in the case of sport.

As we noted earlier, sport cannot be played alone for it must involve two or more opposing players. This, together with the fact that sport involves not only co-operation but also, and in a highly institutionalised form, competition, means that sport, and particularly team sport, is usually a considerably more complex social activity than is non-competitive exercise. Consider, for example, a game of soccer or rugby or American football. The game involves a complex interweaving of the actions of a substantial number of players, together with the relationships between players and match officials, club coaches and many others, including, at the elite level, large numbers of fans. Even if we considerably oversimplify the situation by confining our analysis solely to the interactions between the players, it is clear that we are dealing here with a social phenomenon of some complexity. Elias and Dunning (1986: 193) drew upon the example of Association Football (soccer) to illustrate what they called the 'dynamics of sport groups'. They wrote:

> From the starting position evolves a fluid figuration formed by both teams. Within it, all individuals are, and remain throughout, more or less interdependent; they move and regroup themselves in response to each other. This may help to explain why we refer to this type of game as a specific form of group dynamics. For this moving and regrouping of interdependent players in response to each other *is* the game.
>
> It may not be immediately clear that by using the term 'group dynamics' in this context we do not refer to the changing figurations

of the two groups of players as if they could be considered in separation, as if each had dynamics of its own. That is not the case. In a game of football, the figuration of players on the one side and that of players on the other side, are interdependent and inseparable. They form in fact a single figuration. If one speaks of a sport-game as a specific form of group dynamics, one refers to the overall change in the figuration of the players of both sides together.

One aspect of the complex structure of sports such as football is that each match tends to develop what is often called a 'game pattern'. Though there is sometimes a tendency to speak of this game pattern as though it were something separate from the players, it is important to remind ourselves that it is in fact nothing other than the complex interweaving of the actions of a large number of players. However, it is also important to note that, as the game pattern becomes more complex – for example, as we move from a two-person game such as tennis to a multi-person game such as soccer – it becomes increasingly beyond the ability of any single player to control this game pattern and, indeed, from the perspective of any single player, this game pattern may appear to have a life of its own.

An associated aspect of the complex structure of many sports is that, in comparison with non-competitive exercise, any individual player is much less able to control their own movements and the pace and intensity at which they are required to play. Thus while the lone jogger and walker can determine their own movements with minimal reference to others, the movements of, for example, a soccer or rugby or ice-hockey player can only be understood in relation to the movements of other players on their own and the opposition side. Moreover, as a means of beating opposing players, players frequently initiate moves, or respond to the moves of others, involving rapid changes of pace and direction. In most sports, this gives rise to a pattern of movement which is the very opposite of rhythmic, for it often involves sharp and intensive bursts of activity, interspersed with short periods in which individual players may be able to take a 'breather'. It is important to emphasise, first, that the frequency and intensity of these bursts of intensive activity are, at least in complex games, largely beyond the ability of any single player to control; second, that players are almost inevitably constrained by the moves of their opponents to engage in activities which are anything but rhythmic; and third, that many of these movements, such as those involved in rapid acceleration and deceleration, or the twisting or turning movements involved in rapid changes of direction, impose considerably greater stresses on the body than do the much more rhythmic movements involved in non-competitive walking, jogging or swimming. These considerations, however, do not exhaust the health-related differences between sport and exercise. The competitive character of sport, in particular, requires further elaboration.

SPORT AND COMPETITION

Dunning (1986a) has pointed out that the growing competitiveness of modern sport is a long-term trend which may be traced back over two or more centuries. This process has, however, been particularly marked in the post-1945 period, and has been associated with, amongst other processes, the increasing politicisation and commercialisation of sport, both of which have had the effect of greatly increasing the importance of, and the rewards associated with winning, while downgrading the traditional value associated with taking part (Waddington and Murphy, 1992). This trend towards the growing competitiveness of sport has not, however, been without significant health 'costs' for athletes, most particularly in the form of more stress injuries and overuse injuries, and increased constraints to continue competing while injured (for a detailed example, see the situation in relation to professional football in England, described in Chapter 4).

A common sight in many sports is that of the trainer or physiotherapist running on to the field of play to treat an injured player, often by the application of an aerosol spray to a painful area, thereby enabling the player to continue. However, as Donohoe and Johnson (1986: 94) have pointed out, one of the functions of pain is to '"warn" us that we need to rest the damaged area', and they suggest that most athletes and coaches 'fail to recognize the damage that can be caused by suppressing pain'. This issue is part of the more general concern about overuse and recurrent injuries, a growing problem which is clearly associated with the increasing constraints on sportsmen and women to compete and more particularly to win with, one suspects, often scant concern for the potential longer-term health risks. Donohoe and Johnson (1986: 93) have noted that to 'succeed in modern sport, athletes are forced to train longer, harder, and earlier in life. They may be rewarded by faster times, better performances and increased fitness, but there is a price to pay for such intense training.' Part of the price of such intense training and of the readiness – often encouraged by coaches and medical advisers – to continue training and competing despite injury, is unquestionably paid in the form of overuse and recurrent injuries, which now constitute a serious problem in sport, and not just at the adult elite level. As Donohoe and Johnson (1986: 93) have noted, the 'long-term effects of overuse injuries are not known, but some concerned doctors have asked whether today's gold medallists could be crippled by arthritis by the age of 30', and they cite world-class competitors who have, in their words, 'been plagued by a succession of overuse injuries'. In this respect, the preliminary results from an ongoing study at Coventry University are very revealing. Of 284 former professional football (soccer) players who completed a questionnaire from the University's Psychosocial Rheumatology Research Centre, 49 per cent had been diagnosed with osteoarthritis, a percentage which is five times as high as that in similarly aged males in the general population. Of all the respondents 15 per cent were now registered disabled while a third of ex-players had, since retiring from professional football, undergone surgery for football-related injuries (Hicks, 1998).

Examples of athletes with painful and potentially serious injuries who have continued to compete are almost innumerable. In her autobiography, Olga Korbut, the former Olympic gold-medal-winning gymnast, described how, following the 1972 Munich Olympics, the successful Soviet gymnastics team was taken on a tour of what was then West Germany. She wrote: 'During that tour of Germany, the lumbago in my back began to hurt more and more. The novocaine injections took away the pain for a while, but I needed time to rest and heal. By the end of the tour, I walked as though I had a stake in my spine.' She added that 'My strongest memories of that entire period are fatigue, pain, and the empty feeling of being a fly whose blood has been sucked out by a predatory spider' (Korbut, 1992: 81–2).

It would be very wrong to imagine that such incidents only occurred under the now defunct communist systems of Eastern Europe, for examples of athletes playing on despite painful and potentially serious injuries are commonplace and there is considerable evidence to indicate that, particularly at the elite level, there are considerable constraints on players to play through pain and injury 'for the good of the team'. As Roderick (1998: 65) has noted, an important aspect of sporting culture at the elite or professional level involves a 'culture of risk', which 'normalizes pain, injuries, and "playing hurt"'. Consider, for example, the following extract from a pre-match team talk to the Wigan Rugby League team by their coach, John Monie:

> There's just one more thing I want to enforce. It doesn't matter what's wrong with you when you're injured, I want you on your feet and in the defensive line. . . . I don't care if the physio's out there and he wants to examine you and all that stuff. That's not important. What's important is . . . you've got twelve team-mates tackling their guts out, defending like anything inside the 22 and we've got the physio telling a guy to see if he can straighten his knee out.
>
> I don't care what's wrong with you . . . if the opposition's got the ball, I want you on your feet and in the defensive line. . . .
>
> There are no exceptions to that rule. So from now on, the only reason you stay down hurt and get attention from the sideline is because there's a break in play or you're unconscious – no other reasons will be accepted.
>
> (Hanson, 1991: 77)

Monie's team talk may perhaps be regarded as the English equivalent of the American view that 'you play unless the bone sticks through the meat' which, as Young (1993: 382) has noted, has long been used to rationalise injury in the NFL. Although it may not always be expressed in such blunt

terms, it is clear that, particularly at the elite level, there is a common expectation – which is shared by many players – that whenever possible players
should continue to play through injury 'for the good of the team', even if
this means playing with pain-killing injections. Hanson reported, for example, that Wigan Rugby League players frequently played after having been
given pain-killing injections. Before the Rugby League Cup Final at
Wembley in 1990, so many players had pain-killing injections that the club
doctor, Dr Zaman, came into the dressing room 'clutching a collection of
used syringes and needles' and asked of a Wembley official, 'Do you have
a box for sharps [used needles]?' (Hanson, 1991: 193). Don Strock, former
quarterback with the Miami Dolphins, has described how players would
group around 'injured teammates during a game to screen from spectators
the use of pain-killing injections, then hide the needles under the carpet-
like synthetic "turf"' (cited in Young, 1993: 376).

It is clear that experiences of this kind are commonplace among elite
players. Some aspects of the culture of 'playing hurt' within professional
football (soccer) in England are examined in Chapter 4; for the moment,
we might note that a survey of 725 professional soccer players carried out
by the magazine *Four Four Two* (October 1995) revealed that 70 per cent
of players had been asked to play when not fully fit. As Young *et al.*
(1994: 190) noted:

> Overt and covert pressures are brought to bear on injured athletes to
> coerce them to return to action. These may include certain 'degradation
> ceremonies' . . . such as segregated meal areas, constant questioning
> from coaches, being ostracized at team functions, or other special treat-
> ment that clearly identifies the injured athlete as separate.

An example of this kind of ostracism was provided by the former Liverpool
Football Club manager, Bill Shankly, regarded by many as one of the
greatest-ever soccer club managers. Shankly refused to speak to any player
who was unavailable to play because of injury (*On the Line*, 1996).
Young *et al.* (1994: 190) argued that 'Pressure placed on the player to
return to action before full recovery is in one sense intended to enhance the
team's ability to win, but in the process, the long-term health of the athlete
is often given little consideration.'

Although such pressures on players to tolerate and to play through pain
may in some respects be associated with particular conceptions of masculinity (to be examined later), it is also clear that there are broadly similar
constraints on women athletes to continue competing despite pain and
injury and that many women athletes respond in a broadly similar way to
their male counterparts. For example, in comparing their research in
Canada on female athletes' experience of pain and injury with their earlier
research on the experience of male athletes, Young and White (1995: 51)
write that 'If there is a difference between the way male and female athletes

in our projects appear to understand pain and injury, it is only a matter of degree . . . it is clear that both men and women adopt similar techniques to help to displace the centrality of pain in their sports lives'. An example of the way in which pain is denied is provided by the example of D, one of the elite women athletes interviewed by Young and White:

> The first time my injury occurred, I ignored it assuming it would go away, as did my previous aches and pains. Bruising, swelling, and muscle pain are integral aspects of basketball. Once the pain persisted, it became annoying. It never occurred to me at the age of 14 that my body was breaking down and needed a rest. I simply pushed harder because my injury was causing me to fall behind in my progress.
>
> (1995: 51)

Young and White add that:

> Years of denial and persistence have seriously weakened D's knees and ankles, and surgery to repair cartilage tears has left her legs badly scarred. At the time of writing, D remains in pain, is unable to play her sport, and uses painkillers almost daily.
>
> (1995: 52)

D's reference to injuries during her teenage years suggests that the problem of overuse and recurrent injuries is not confined to adults and, as we shall see in the next chapter, there is what is, in health terms, a worrying trend towards earlier and more intensive athletic involvement for younger and younger children.

Given the highly competitive character of much modern sport, it is not surprising to learn that overuse and recurrent injuries are very common. Lynch and Carcasona (1994), for example, have noted that a study of 123 male players in a Danish soccer club found that 37 per cent of all injuries were overuse injuries, while a Swedish study of 180 senior male soccer players found that 31 per cent of injuries were caused by overuse. FIFA's report on soccer's 1994 World Cup, held in the United States, indicated that 12 per cent of all treatments of players were for chronic injuries or ailments which predated the World Cup Finals (Nepfer, 1994: 190). It would, however, be quite wrong to think that such injuries only occur at the elite level, for there is little doubt that in most western countries sport at *all* levels has become increasingly competitive and this has given rise to large numbers of recurrent injuries at the non-elite, as well as the elite, level. A large-scale survey carried out in England and Wales for the Sports Council found that one-third of all injuries resulting from participation in sport or exercise were recurrent injuries. On the basis of this study, the Sports Council estimated that in England and Wales there are 10.4 million incidents a year resulting in recurrent injuries (Sports Council, 1991: 25). Quite clearly, we are not dealing with a phenomenon which is confined to elite sport, but one which is extremely widespread.

SPORT, VIOLENCE AND AGGRESSIVE MASCULINITY

Many sports, unlike most forms of non-sporting exercise, involve physical contact and are, in effect, mock battles. This is perhaps most evident in the case of combat sports, in some of which – for example, boxing – a central object is to inflict physical damage on one's opponent. Clearly, however, the use of violence is not confined to combat sports, for though the level of physical violence permitted in sport has, in general, shown a long-term decline as sports have become more 'civilised' (Dunning and Sheard, 1979; Dunning, 1990), the use of physical violence to a greater or lesser degree remains a central characteristic of modern sport. In this regard, Dunning (1986b: 270) has noted that:

All sports are inherently competitive and hence conducive to the arousal of aggression. Under specific conditions, such aggression can spill over into forms of open violence that are contrary to the rules. In some sports, however – rugby, soccer, hockey and boxing are examples – violence in the form of a 'play-fight' or 'mock battle' between two individuals or groups is a central and legitimate ingredient.

Many sports have, in present-day societies, become enclaves for the expression of physical violence, not in the form of unlicensed or uncontrolled violence, but in the form of socially sanctioned violence as expressed in violently aggressive 'body contact'; indeed, in the relatively highly pacified societies of the modern West, sport is probably the main – for many people the only – activity in which they are regularly involved in aggressive physical contact with others.

The link between sport, aggression and violence provides an important key to understanding why sport is a major context for the inculcation and expression of gender differences and identities, for sport constitutes perhaps the most widely available arena for the legitimate expression of masculine aggression and for the display of traditional and dominant notions of masculinity involving physical strength and courage. Thus, Young *et al.* (1994: 176), drawing upon their interview data with Canadian adult male athletes, noted that the use of force and violence and the tolerance of risks, pain and injury are valued by many male athletes as masculinising, while the sporting performances of women, gay men and men pursuing alternative versions of manliness are, by contrast, trivialised. In similar fashion, Sheard and Dunning (1973), in their essay on the rugby club as a type of 'male preserve', noted that many of the songs traditionally sung in rugby clubs stress and reinforce masculinity by mocking, not only women, but also gay men.

Young *et al.* (1994) pointed out that these traditional and dominant concepts of masculinity involve, as a central proposition, the idea that 'real' men play sport in an intensely confrontational manner. In the more violent contact sports, this may mean that bodies are used as weapons for, as Messner noted:

> In many of our most popular sports, the achievement of goals (scoring and winning) is predicated on the successful utilization of violence – that is, these are activities in which the human body is routinely turned into a weapon to be used against other bodies, resulting in pain, serious injury, and even death.
>
> (1990: 203)

In such a context, players are expected to give and to take 'hard knocks', to injure and to be injured and, when injured, to 'take it like a man'. A prime example is provided by American football which, though considerably less violent than it was in the late nineteenth century, remains, by comparison with most sports, relatively violent; it is significant that proponents of American football list among what they see as the positive features of the game its bellicosity and its similarities to actual warfare and the pain and self-sacrifice which it requires, while injury becomes what Guttmann (1978: 121) called 'a certificate of virility, a badge of courage'. For many players and fans alike, relatively violent sports such as American football and rugby are, precisely because of their violent character, arenas *par excellence* for young men to demonstrate their masculinity. Not surprisingly, injury rates associated with such sports are considerably higher than those associated with most other sports and very much in excess of those associated with non-competitive exercise. In relation to American football, for example, Guttmann pointed out that:

> The percentage of players incurring injuries severe enough to cause them to miss at least one game a season is over 100 percent; this means not that every NFL player is injured at least once each season, but that those who are not injured are more than offset by those who are injured several times. The average length of a playing career has dropped to 3.2 years, which is not long enough to qualify a player for inclusion in the league's pension plan.
>
> (1988: 161–2)

Studies from England and Wales (Sports Council, 1991) and New Zealand (Hume and Marshall, 1994) similarly indicate that injury rates in rugby are substantially above those in any other sport.

THE EPIDEMIOLOGY OF SPORTS INJURIES

Sports injuries are extremely common and, quite clearly, the risk of injury has to be taken into account in any attempt to assess the health 'costs' and 'benefits' of sport and exercise. The largest and most comprehensive study of the number and cost of sports injuries in Britain was carried out by Sheffield University Medical School for the Sports Council (1991). The study, which related to England and Wales, provides a great deal of relevant information and is worth examining in some detail.

A postal questionnaire, which asked about participation in sports and exercise and injury experiences in the previous four weeks, was sent to a sample of 28,857 people, selected at random from the lists of family (primary care) physicians. The response rate was 68 per cent. Of the 17,564 usable responses, 7,829 respondents (45 per cent) had taken part in vigorous exercise or sport; 1,429 had been injured, and they reported a total of 1,803 injuries (1991: 2).

From these data, it was possible to provide estimates of the annual incidence of sports injuries in England and Wales. On this basis, it was estimated that there were 19.3 million incidents resulting in new injuries and a further 10.4 million incidents resulting in recurrent injuries, making a total of no fewer than 29.7 million injuries a year. The direct treatment costs of new and recurrent injuries were estimated at £422 million, with costs of lost production (due to days off work) estimated at £575 million, giving a total annual cost of sporting injuries of £997 million (1991: 25, 31). In the light of these data, one can understand why one text on sports injuries (Vinger and Hoerner, 1982) is sub-titled 'The Unthwarted Epidemic'.

Three years after this major study, a team from Sheffield University Medical School (Nicholl *et al.*, 1994) undertook a survey to ascertain the direct health-care costs and benefits associated with exercise. The health benefits of exercise (such as avoidance of certain chronic illnesses such as cardiovascular disease and osteoporosis) were weighed against the costs of treatment of exercise-related injuries. It was found that, whereas there were clear economic benefits associated with exercise for adults aged 45 and over, for younger adults (aged 15–44), the costs avoided by the disease-prevention effects of exercise (less than £5 per person per year) were more than offset by the medical costs resulting from participation in sport and exercise (approximately £30 per person per year). Put another way, for every 15–44-year-old who regularly participates in exercise, there is a net cost to the British taxpayer of £25 per year. The authors concluded, 'there are strong economic arguments in favour of exercise in adults aged 45 or over, but *not* in younger adults' (1994: 109, emphasis added). A Dutch study which produced similar findings to those of Nicholl *et al.* noted that 'this is an amazing result, and it contrasts heavily with statements of people who use the supposed health effect of sport as an economic argument to promote sport' (Reijnen and Velthuijsen, 1989, cited in Nicholl *et al.*, 1994).

As was noted earlier, injury risks vary markedly from one sport to another with, not surprisingly, the highest risks being associated with contact sports. The Sports Council study (1991: 33) found, for example, that rugby was by far the most dangerous sport, in terms of risk of injury, with an injury rate of 59.3 per 100 participants per four weeks. The second most dangerous sport was soccer (39.3) followed by martial arts (36.3), hockey (24.8) and cricket (20.2). A study in New Zealand (Hume and Marshall, 1994) similarly found that rugby union had the highest injury rate, while other high-risk sports included horse-riding, soccer, cricket, netball, rugby league, basketball and snow-skiing. That there is a close association between physical contact and injury risk is clear; Lynch and Carcasona (1994: 170–1) cite a study of youth outdoor and indoor soccer in the United States which found that 66 per cent of injuries in the outdoor league and 70 per cent of injuries in the indoor league resulted from physical contact.

Not surprisingly, the Sports Council study in England and Wales found that the activities with the lowest risks of injury were the non-contact and rhythmic (and largely non-competitive) activities involved in 'keep fit' (6.5 incidents per 100 participants per four weeks) and swimming and diving (2.9). However, even relatively rhythmic and non-contact activities may be associated with substantial injury risks. Heil (1993: 5) noted that it has been estimated that in the United States, a third of the nation's 15 million joggers sustain a musculoskeletal injury each year and nearly a half of habitual runners experience lower extremity injury, while there are also 1,000 spinal injuries each year as a result of swimmers diving into water.

Although the majority of sporting injuries are relatively minor, a substantial number are more serious. The Sports Council study (1991: 18–19) found that 25 per cent of new injuries and 31 per cent of recurrent injuries required treatment by a family doctor, hospital or other health professional, while 37 per cent of new injuries and 43 per cent of recurrent injuries involved some restriction on activities. This restriction was usually on the injured taking part in sports or exercise, though 7 per cent of all injuries resulted in the participants taking time off work; in all, 11.5 million working days a year are lost in England and Wales as a result of sports injuries. A study in New Zealand (Hume and Marshall, 1994) found that 15 per cent of consultations at the Dunedin Hospital Emergency Department were for sports injuries, which also accounted for 9 per cent of all injury hospitalisations in New Zealand, and 17 per cent of all injuries compensated by the Accident Compensation Corporation. Both the risk of injury, and also the risk of serious injury, increase in more violent contact sports. In this context Young (1993: 377), writing of American football, has argued that:

No workplace matches football for either the regularity or severity of injury . . . football injuries may include arthritis, concussion, fractures, and, most catastrophically, blindness, paralysis and even death . . . a review of heat stresses such as cramp, exhaustion and stroke related to amateur and professional football . . . reported 29 player deaths between 1968 and 1978 . . . the 1990 season represented the first in over 60 years without a player death.

CONCLUSION

What conclusions, then, can we draw about the relationships between exercise, sport and health? Do the data support the widely taken-for-granted assumption that 'sport is good for one's health'? Three points would seem to emerge from the data reviewed in this chapter. The first is that no simple generalisation can adequately encapsulate the complexity of the relationships between sport, exercise and health. The second, related point is that it is clearly necessary to differentiate between exercise and sport, for they involve, as we have seen, rather different patterns of social relationships and, associated with this, they are likely to have rather different consequences for health. The third point is that we also need to differentiate between types and levels of sport, with the distinctions between contact and non-contact sport and between elite and mass sport being particularly important.

If we make these distinctions, it may be possible to reconcile what, at first sight, may appear to be radically incompatible findings. Thus, on the one hand, there does seem to be overwhelming evidence indicating that regular, rhythmic and moderate exercise has a significant and beneficial impact on health. On the other hand, Young (1993: 373) may also be correct in his claim, which appears to relate primarily to North America, that:

By any measure, professional sport is a violent and hazardous workplace, replete with its own unique forms of 'industrial disease'. No other single milieu, including the risky and labor-intensive settings of miners, oil drillers, or construction site workers, can compare with the routine injuries of team sports such as football, ice-hockey, soccer, rugby and the like.

In general, it is probably reasonable to suggest that in the case of rhythmic, non-competitive exercise where body movements are, to a relatively high degree, under the control of the individual participant, the health benefits substantially outweigh the health costs. However, as we move from non-competitive exercise to competitive sport, and as we move from non-contact to contact sport, so the health costs, in the form of injuries, begin to mount. Similarly, as we move from mass sport to elite sport, the constraints to train longer and more intensively and to continue competing through pain and injury also increase, with a concomitant increase in the health risks. The health-related arguments in favour of regular and moderate exercise may be overwhelming, but such arguments are considerably less persuasive in relation to competitive sport, and very much less persuasive in relation to elite, or professional, sport. In the next chapter, we examine some of the implications of these conclusions for public policy in relation to sport and health.

2 Sport, health and public policy

Some policy issues and problems

In Chapter 1, it was argued that the widespead and largely uncritical accept-ance of the ideology linking sport and health has had the effect of obscuring, rather than helping to clarify, our understanding of the complex relationships between physical activity, exercise, sport and health. The central object of this chapter is to build on the analysis in the last chapter in order critically to examine public policy in the areas of physical activity, exercise, sport and health.

In this context it is useful to differentiate at the outset between two broad kinds of public policy. The first of these is policy of the kind which has been associated with the work of the Health Education Authority (HEA) in the United Kingdom, and the Surgeon General in the United States. Such policies are firmly embedded within a public health framework and have relatively clearly stated goals which are concerned with improving the health of the community; in this context, encouraging people to adopt more active life-styles is seen, not as a desirable end in itself, but as a means of improving public health.

In contrast to policies which are orientated primarily towards public health concerns are policies like those which have emanated from the Sports Councils in the United Kingdom, or from government departments which have an interest in promoting sport. A good example of the latter, to be examined in some detail later, is the *Sport: Raising the Game* policy statement which was produced by the Department of National Heritage (DNH) in July 1995. Such policies, it is important to note, have their origins not within the public health policy community, but within the sports policy community, and those who are responsible for developing and implement-ing such policies are not orientated primarily towards public health issues, but towards the promotion of sport *per se*. In relation to the latter, there is, of course, no doubt that many (though not all) people find participation in sport intrinsically enjoyable and rewarding. However, in the battle for public funding, in which sport has to compete with many other services which might generally be thought to have a more pressing claim on public funds – for example, health, education or pensions – the fact that many people enjoy sport might be thought to constitute a relatively poor basis for a claim for public expenditure.

Within this context, the widely accepted view that 'sport is good for health' might be seen to provide a more persuasive justification for public funding for sport. Perhaps not surprisingly, many people within the sporting policy community have, by uncritically conflating the concepts of physical activity, exercise and sport, been able to claim for sport health benefits which are certainly associated with many forms of physical activity but whose relationship to competitive sport is, as we saw in the previous chapter, much more problematic. Moreover, those within the sporting community have also been able to call upon a number of other ideologies – for example, that the provision of sporting facilities fosters community development, reduces crime, helps to break down barriers of race/ethnicity and enhances the country's international prestige – to advance their claims for public expenditure on sport. My primary concern here is with the health-related issues, though it should be noted that, as was pointed out briefly in the Introduction to this book and as the recent review by Long and Sanderson (1998) makes clear, the evidence to support most of these claims is, at best, very skimpy.

Of more immediate significance within the present context, however, is the fact that, largely because of the way in which sport has become linked with a whole variety of pro-sport ideologies, the goals of public policy in relation to sport have – much more so than in the case of the policy goals deriving from the public health policy community – become diffuse and unclear. More specifically, health-related concerns have often been subordinated to other goals of sporting policy, and have sometimes resulted in the development of policies whose impact on health may actually be a *negative* one. These issues are best explored via an examination of the two rather different forms of public policy identified at the beginning of this chapter: public health policy and policy for sport. It is recognised, of course, that there is some overlap between the activities of the public health and the sports policy communities – for example, the *Allied Dunbar National Fitness Survey* (1992) was funded by the HEA, the Department of Health and the Sports Council – but nevertheless the central thrusts of public health policy and sports development policy are sufficiently different to justify this distinction.

PUBLIC HEALTH POLICY AND PHYSICAL ACTIVITY

Although the health benefits of physical activity have long been extolled, it has only been in the last few years that bodies concerned with public health issues have begun to formulate clear guidelines about what was considered, in terms of health benefits, an appropriate amount of physical activity. The early recommendations – most notably, the 'position stand' of the American College of Sports Medicine (1990) – focused on cardio-respiratory endurance and specified sustained periods of *vigorous* physical activity involving large muscle groups. However, in more recent years, the recommended level of physical activity has been scaled down, largely as a result of two developments. First, more recent research has indicated that it is not necessary to engage in very vigorous activity to derive substantial health benefits, for there are major health gains to be obtained from exercise of *moderate* intensity. Second, there was a growing realisation that pro-grammes involving vigorous physical activity were, for many people, simply unrealistic, and that programmes involving more moderate levels of activity were associated with improved adherence; in these respects the latter were, in terms of public health policy, more effective.

In line with these developments, the executive summary of the US Surgeon General's report, *Physical Activity and Health* (US Department of Health and Human Services, 1996: 1) lists as its key finding the fact that:

> people of all ages can improve the quality of their lives through a life-long practice of moderate physical activity. You don't have to be train-ing for the Boston Marathon to derive real health benefits from physical activity. A regular, preferably daily regimen of at least 30–45 minutes of brisk walking, bicycling, or even working around the house or yard will reduce your risks of developing coronary heart disease, hyper-tension, colon cancer, and diabetes.

It is worth emphasising that the primary concern of the report is with physical activity rather than sport; indeed it is striking that almost all of the examples of moderate physical activity recommended in the report are either life-style activities such as washing and waxing a car, washing windows or floors, gardening, dancing, pushing a stroller, raking leaves or shovelling snow, or non-contact, rhythmic exercises such as water aerobics, swimming laps, bicycling gently, jumping rope, stair-walking, walking and shooting baskets. The only competitive sports which figure in the list of recommended examples of moderate activity are playing basketball for 15–20 minutes and playing volleyball for 45 minutes; all the other major competitive sports in the United States are conspicuous by their absence from this list of recommended activities! The emphasis on life-style activ-ities, rather than competitive sport, is further reinforced by the observation that, in the United States, the 'most popular leisure-time activities among adults are walking and gardening or yard work' (1996: 14).

The Children's Lifetime Physical Activity Model (Corbin *et al.*, 1994) reflects a similar emphasis on life-style activities of moderate intensity, rather than competitive sports. The model suggests that children should, as an optimum, participate three or more times a week in a volume of activity involving the expenditure of at least 6–8 kcal/kg/day. This level of activity is, as Harris and Cale (1997: 59) pointed out, 'one that inactive children can achieve with a modest commitment to childhood games and activities, or lifestyle activities such as walking or riding a bicycle to school or performing physical tasks around the home'.

Within Britain, the evolution of public health policy in relation to physical activity has followed a broadly similar pattern to that in the United States. In September 1993, the Government established a Task Force to develop a national strategy for promoting physical activity and, in the following year, the HEA convened an international symposium which was charged with the responsibility of identifying the most effective health education messages for promoting physical activity. The symposium report (*Moving On*, HEA, 1995) suggested that, in relation to physical activity, public health policy should, first, seek to reduce the proportion of the population who are sedentary and, second, to increase the proportion of the population engaging in regular physical activity of a moderate intensity. The report did recommend that policy should also be orientated towards increasing the proportion of the population engaging in regular vigorous physical activity, though particular stress was laid on the first two objectives. The third objective, it was pointed out, represented the more traditional goal of exercise programmes, while the first two objectives 'represent a shift in thinking towards the promotion of physical activity of a more moderate intensity' (HEA, 1995: 4). This led to the main physical activity recommendation: that adults should take 30 minutes of moderate intensity physical activity, such as a sustained brisk walk, on at least five days of the week.

Particular concern was expressed about the large number of people – nearly a third of all adults, and 55 per cent of those aged 65 or older – who take part in no physical activity on a regular basis, and who have at least a two-fold increase in mortality risk. In this context, the HEA (1995: 8) noted that 'The greatest public health benefits are likely to be gained from encouraging an increase in moderate activity. Therefore, sedentary individuals and those who are active on an irregular basis are the priority audiences to be reached.'

Since its *Moving On* (1995) policy statement, the HEA has produced a series of policy documents about physical activity and health; these include *Promoting Physical Activity in Primary Health Care* (1996), which was targeted at primary health-care teams, *Young and Active?* (1998), a policy framework for young people, and the three-year campaign, *Active for Life*, which was launched in 1996. In all of these policy documents the emphasis has consistently been placed on encouraging people to engage in physical activity of *moderate* intensity. For example, the publicity material for Phase Three of the *Active for Life* campaign, which ran from April 1998 to March 1999, pointed out that 'Being active doesn't have to be hard work; everyday activities like dancing, cycling, walking and swimming can improve health'.

Moreover – and like the report of the Surgeon General in the United States – HEA policy revolves centrally around the concept of *physical activity* and, within that policy, competitive sport does not figure centrally. The *Young and Active?* policy statement (1998: 2), for example, provides definitions of key concepts underlying the policy. These key concepts include physical activity, exercise, physical fitness, physical education and health-related exercise but, significantly, *not* sport. It might also be noted that in that same policy document the HEA, in pointing to the health benefits of physical activity, notes that some of these benefits (for example, in terms of enhanced self-esteem) 'can be limited by an over-emphasis on competitive performance' (HEA, 1998: 2). In its earlier *Moving On* policy statement, the HEA also recognised that negative perceptions of what it called 'sporty image' constitute one of the barriers to more widespread participation in health-enhancing physical activity.

In considering these HEA policy statements, two points are clear. The first of these is that these policies are unambiguously and very firmly embedded in a public health framework and express public health concerns. That this is so is, for example, clearly illustrated by the nature of the groups which have been specifically targeted by the HEA campaigns. Thus while the three-year *Active for Life* campaign is aimed at the whole population of England aged 16–74 years, it echoes the thrust of the public health priorities of the earlier *Moving On* policy in that it particularly targets more sedentary population groups, which it identified as:

- young women aged 16–24 years;
- middle aged men and women aged 44–55 years;
- older people aged over 50 years.

The earlier *Moving On* policy also suggested that people with disabilities and those from low-income groups were also particularly likely to be sedentary. These target groups, it hardly needs saying, have been identified on the basis of their health needs, rather than on the basis of any likely contribution they might be able to make to the nation's sporting achievements.

The second, equally clear, point is that competitive sport is, at best, marginal to HEA policy. What is important is physical activity; in terms of their impact on health, physical activities such as heavy DIY, gardening, heavy housework or dancing are just as valuable as gentle swimming or doubles tennis. In this context, it might be suggested that what HEA policy *is* about – that is, public health – is thrown into sharper relief by what it is *not* about – namely, competitive sport. HEA policy, for example, is emphatically *not* about improving levels of sporting performance; there is nothing in the HEA documents which corresponds in any way with the English Sports Council's 'sports development continuum' described as a 'framework for helping individuals to achieve their personal best [which] is expressed as a continuum moving from foundation, through participation and performance, to [sporting] excellence' (English Sports Council, 1997: 5). HEA policy, in contrast, is *not* about achieving personal bests. It is *not* about identifying talented young athletes. It is *not* about producing future Olympic champions. And it is *not* about enhancing Britain's international reputation through sporting performance. It *is* about improving health and saving lives, and it is this which accounts for the fact that two of the three major target groups – middle-aged and elderly people – involve those who, in sporting terms, will generally be some way past their personal bests.

SPORTS DEVELOPMENT POLICY

Within Britain the Government, both directly through the Ministry of Sport and indirectly through government-funded organisations such as the Sports Councils, takes an active part in promoting the development of sport. That such policies are valuable, and that they effectively promote a number of desirable objectives, seem to be generally taken for granted. But are the goals of such policies clear? And if these policies have several goals, are those goals mutually compatible, or might the achievement of one goal undermine the achievement of other goals? And, in particular, what is the relationship between sports development policies and health promotion?

In order to try to resolve some of these problems, it may be useful to look at some examples of sports policy, and the claims which are made in those policy statements on behalf of sport. The English Sports Council (1997: 3), in its *England, the Sporting Nation* strategy document, claims that:

> The benefits of sport are well rehearsed – national identity and prestige, community development, personal challenge, as well as economic and health benefits. Sport is a central element in the English way of life.

The document went on to claim that sport 'has a natural synergy with tourism, the environment, our heritage and culture'.

Two years previously the then Prime Minister, John Major, a keen sportsman who was closely and personally identified with the Government's *Sport: Raising the Game* policy (Department of National Heritage, 1995), wrote in the Preface to that policy document that sport:

> enriches the lives of the thousands of millions of people of all ages around the world who know and enjoy it. Sport is a central part of Britain's National Heritage.
> . . . Sport is a binding force between generations and across borders. But, by a miraculous paradox, it is at the same time one of the defining characteristics of nationhood and of local pride. We should cherish it for both those reasons.

. . . Competitive sport teaches valuable lessons which last for life. Every game delivers both a winner and a loser. Sports men (*sic*) must learn to be both. Sport only thrives if both parties play by the rules, and accept the results with good grace. It is one of the best means of learning how to live alongside others and make a contribution as part of a team. It improves health and it opens the door to new friendships.

(1995: 2)

In the light of such sweeping claims, it is appropriate to ask a number of questions about the goals of public policy for sport (Waddington and Murphy, 1998). Are such policies, like those of the HEA, orientated primarily towards public health goals? In other words, is the primary goal to encourage mass participation in sport with a view to improving the health of the nation? Or is the primary goal to encourage participation in sport in order to have a broader base from which future world or Olympic champions can be selected and trained? Or is the goal to encourage people to participate in sport because this is felt to be a useful means of teaching what may be held to be desirable values; for example, the values of fair play, of respect for one's opponent, of sporting behaviour, and of accepting defeat gracefully? Or is the goal to develop local communities? Or is it to encourage young people, in particular, to play sport as a means of diverting them away from crime or vandalism? In the latter context, it might be noted that in Britain, the provision of sporting facilities as a means of accommodating disaffected working-class youth has been articulated in several policy statements since the early 1960s, and that policy was reinforced by the rise in youth unemployment and the serious urban riots in the 1980s (Carrington and Leaman, 1983).

It is important to clarify these questions, not least because the way in which they are answered determines what other questions we need to ask. For example, if sports development policies derive primarily from health considerations, then we need to locate such policies within the context of the kind of issues examined in some detail in Chapter 1. If, on the other hand, the primary concern is to provide a wider base from which will be selected elite athletes whose sporting achievements in international competition will reflect favourably upon Britain's international standing, then we need to ask questions about the relationship between sport, politics and international relations. And if the primary goal is to provide non-criminal outlets for the energies of disaffected youth, then we need to ask questions about sport as a means of social control. The way in which we answer these questions may also indicate which government department (or departments) should have major responsibility for sports development policies. Should it be the Ministry for Sport or the Department of Health, or Education, or even the Home Office? And what problems of cross-departmental co-ordination and control might this involve?

It is not possible, within this chapter, to examine all of these questions; my primary concerns are with health-related issues and it is upon these that I will focus. More specifically, I want to examine recent British Government policy in relation to sport and physical education, with particular reference to the *Sport: Raising the Game* policy which was introduced by the last Conservative Government in 1995, the general principles of which have been implicitly accepted by the Labour Government which has been in office since May 1997. As we noted earlier, there may be several reasons why governments adopt particular policies in relation to sport – for example, to produce future Olympic champions – but the question I wish to address here is as follows: does recent Government policy for sport and physical education make sense on *health* grounds?

SPORT, PHYSICAL EDUCATION AND PUBLIC POLICY IN THE UNITED KINGDOM

The most striking characteristic of Government policy in relation to sport and PE for school-age children from the mid-1990s has been the way in which the Government has sought not only, in its view, to re-establish the centrality of sport in schools, but also to prioritise certain kinds of physical activities while marginalising others. National Curriculum Physical Education (NCPE) has been taught in British schools since 1992 and features six activity areas: competitive games, athletics, swimming, gymnastics, dance and outdoor and adventurous activities. Within a couple of years of the introduction of the NCPE, however, powerful voices within the Government, most notably those of the then Prime Minister, John Major, and his Minister for Sport, began to make clear their unhappiness at what they perceived as a lack of sufficient emphasis on competitive sport (and especially team games) in the NCPE and they sought to re-prioritise sport and, in particular, 'traditional' team games, within NCPE (Penney and Evans, 1997). This resulted in two major initiatives: the revised NCPE (implemented in August 1995) and the Government's 1995 policy statement *Sport: Raising the Game* (DNH, 1995). As the latter document pointed out, 'in the revised National Curriculum the government has greatly increased the importance of competitive sport', while 'the focus of this Policy Statement [*Sport: Raising the Game*] is deliberately on sport rather than physical education' (1995: 7). The central thrust of government policy was thus quite clear; in the Prime Minister's words, it was 'to put sport [by which the Government meant competitive sport, rather than physical activities in general] back at the heart of weekly life in school' (DNH, 1995: 2).

As part of the policy of re-prioritising sport and team games within the PE curriculum, *Sport: Raising the Game* also announced that the Office for Standards in Education (OFSTED) was being asked to inspect and report on the quality and range of games offered as part of the PE curriculum, to monitor the provision of training to teach the main and traditional team sports in initial teacher training, and to ensure that all trainee teachers were made aware of the increased opportunities to gain coaching qualifications. The policy also sought to promote within schools a sporting culture which, among other things, would involve linking schools with sports clubs and rewarding those schools that place even greater emphasis on sport and team games in extra-curricular physical education. This attempt to encourage children to become more heavily involved with sport and sports clubs from an early age mirrors a growing trend – a trend which, as we note in the next chapter, has itself given rise to some concerns in terms of the health of young children – which Donnelly (1993) has identified as an increasingly prominent characteristic of children's sport: namely, an earlier and more intensive athletic involvement for younger and younger children.

The Government's attempt to prioritise competitive team sports for young people appears to have been widely and uncritically accepted both beyond, and also largely within, the subject community of physical educationists. Government and other official views of physical education often appear to consider competitive sport as the primary focus of physical education, an opinion more likely to be confirmed than challenged within the above-mentioned community. In 1995, the then Secretary of State at the Department of National Heritage, Stephen Dorrell, expressed his belief that the Government's commitment to putting sport back 'at the heart of school life', as the Prime Minister put it, 'is shared . . . by the great majority of the teaching profession' (Dorrell, 1995). By the mid-1990s, the views of the Prime Minister, the Secretary of State for National Heritage, the Minister for Sport, the Sports Council, sports governing bodies and many PE teachers, were in broad agreement in welcoming the Government's policy statement. Almond *et al.* (1996: 7–8), responding to *Sport: Raising the Game* on behalf of the Physical Education Association of the United Kingdom commented that the Association 'is extremely pleased with the public statements made by both the Prime Minister and the Government' and acknowledged that games would 'still have a major and significant role to play within the PE curriculum'.

As Penney and Evans (1997) pointed out, Government policy thus privileged defined 'activity areas' – specifically competitive sports and, in particular, traditional team games – over broader, permeating themes such as 'health-related exercise'. However, this renewed emphasis on sport and games within the PE curriculum has potentially significant consequences for the relationship between PE and health. It is to this issue that I now turn.

SPORT, PHYSICAL EDUCATION AND HEALTH

It is helpful to evaluate recent Government policy in the light of the concept of health-related exercise, which, as we noted in the previous chapter, has come to provide an increasingly important rationale for physical education in recent years.

The basic principle of health-related exercise is that, through an appropriately structured curriculum in physical education, young people can be introduced to forms of physical activity which will benefit their health and which, it is hoped, they will continue to practise not just in their school years, but also throughout their adult lives. There are, therefore, two key questions to be answered in relation to Government policy for sport and PE. First, is the increased emphasis on competitive sports and, in particular, team games, one which makes sense in terms of their likely health consequences for young people? And second, is the emphasis on competitive sports and team games likely to generate a continuing commitment to and involvement in physical activity by young people after they leave school?

The taken-for-granted relationship between sport, physical education and health is clearly illustrated in the comment of Alderson and Crutchley that 'the essential focus for physical education in schools should be sport'. To this they add that the role of physical educationists 'should be to prepare children for sport culture within our society so that they may make best use of it in relation to their personal development, their effective use of leisure time and their *physical and psychological well-being*' (1990: 54; emphasis added).

However, as we saw in Chapter 1, the health 'costs' associated with contact sports such as rugby, football and hockey are considerably greater than those associated with non-contact sports or with non-competitive exercise. In this context, it is important to note that those activities which the Government sought to prioritise, both within the revised NCPE and in its *Sport: Raising the Game* policy, are precisely those competitive sports, and often contact sports, in which the health 'costs' are greatest. On the other hand, those activities which are increasingly being marginalised within the PE curriculum – most notably, dance and outdoor and adventurous activities (Penney and Evans, 1994; Waddington *et al.*, 1997; Waddington *et al.*, 1998) – are those which offer substantial health benefits but with far fewer health 'costs'. This would not seem to be the most appropriate policy if the priority is to improve the health of young people.

In this regard, it should be noted that many of the injuries typically associated with sports in the PE curriculum have potentially serious ramifications for physically developing children. Helm (cited in Pool and Carnall, 1997: 10) has pointed out that at the age of about 12 (girls) and 14 (boys) 'the skeleton is at its most vulnerable to fracture. During these years the bones are growing rapidly and muscle cannot keep up, so there is a danger of dislocation and fracture.' In this context, Pool and Carnall have identified a number of injuries which are commonly associated with sports in the PE curriculum. These include fractured cheekbones, often sustained in sports such as hockey and lacrosse; torn cartilages and damaged hamstrings, tendons and ligaments, which are common in athletics, many team sports and indeed all contact sports involving extensive twisting, turning and rapid explosive movements; and spinal injuries, most common in games like rugby, particularly where opponents are mismatched in terms of size, strength and fitness, which is often the case in age-grouped school sport and representative teams. It is not perhaps unreasonable to suggest that, in many respects, the structure of school sport *appears routinely to court the risk of injury for growing youngsters.*

Moreover, the renewed prioritising of sport in the PE curriculum, together with concern about the low level of activity of some children, has led some teachers to adopt what Harris and Cale (1997: 61) call a 'hard line approach' which involves 'increasingly forcing pupils into "hard" exercise, such as arduous cross-country running or fitness testing'. If we are genuinely concerned about the health of young people, such an approach should be questioned. It is important to note that while PE teachers may be aware and generally accepting of the role they are encouraged to play in promoting physical activity for health, they also appear to be largely unaware of recent exercise recommendations and may not appreciate the implications for health-related physical activity (Harris and Cale, 1997). Whereas the Children's Lifetime Physical Activity Model (Corbin *et al.*, 1994) highlights the fact that exercise does not have to be strenuous to be beneficial to health and that 'moderate activity is associated with improved adherence in children . . . and a lower risk of injury' (Harris and Cale, 1997: 61), it appears that teachers may be reluctant to recognise and incorporate moderate rather than vigorous forms of activity into health-related exercise lessons and frequently promote vigorous physical activity 'at the expense of less strenuous forms of exercise' (Harris and Cale, 1997: 61).

Given this situation, it is not altogether surprising that children's and young people's perceptions of fitness and health are such that 'fitness tends to be associated with high levels of performance and uncomfortable physical exertion' and that fitness is often viewed 'in relation to sporting achievement rather than relative to everyday life activities' (Harris, 1994: 146). This, it might be noted, is in many ways almost the exact opposite of the view of health-promoting physical activity which organisations concerned with public health are seeking to promote. As we noted earlier, the HEA in its literature has stressed that being active does *not* have to be hard work, and that everyday life-style activities such as dancing or walking can improve health; the view that being active involves high levels of performance and uncomfortable physical exertion is likely, for many people – and perhaps particularly for girls – to generate negative perceptions of what more active life-styles involve.

Even among more critical observers, however, there remains an at least partial taken-for-granted acceptance of a positive relationship between sport and health. Thus, while acknowledging the tendency of physical educationists mistakenly to view vigorous exercise as necessary for health benefits, Harris and Cale still claim that it is 'desirable . . . that exercise . . . advice and guidance stresses to young people that *all forms and amounts* of exercise, performed safely, are beneficial and that any level of physical activity is better than none' (1997: 62; emphasis added). The point being made here, however, is that some forms of exercise, and particularly those likely to be experienced in sport (and especially in team games), are by their very nature difficult to perform safely and, particularly for young people, are as likely to result in health 'costs' as health benefits.

In the context of health-related exercise the second question, as we noted earlier, concerns the degree to which team games are an effective means of encouraging a continuing commitment, after young people leave school, to a physically active life-style. On this point, the evidence seems fairly clear. As Roberts (1996a: 105–6) noted, the emphasis which has traditionally been placed on team games in British schools has never been very effective in terms of encouraging the active involvement of more than a small minority of young people in playing sport after they leave school, and he argues that 'recent trends in young people's leisure styles suggest that if traditional games regimes are re-adopted in the 1990s they will be even less successful than earlier in the twentieth century'. This point is worth exploring in a little detail.

As Roberts points out, the *Sport: Raising the Game* policy is premised upon the idea that 'there had been a decline in school sport and that a rescue job was needed to promote physically active recreation among Britain's youth'. However, he adds that it is 'impossible to square the analysis in *Sport: Raising the Game* with the government departments' own research evidence', which indicated that, in the years up to 1994,

> young people were playing more sports in and out of school than in the past, that the drop-out rate on completion of statutory schooling had fallen dramatically, that social class and gender differences had narrowed, and that by the mid-1990s sports had higher youth participation and retention rates than any other structured forms of leisure.
> (1996a: 105)

In the light of these data, Roberts concluded that the *Sport: Raising the Game* policy 'prescribes a cure for a fictitious illness. School sport has been a recent success story, not a disaster zone, if success can be measured in terms of the number of pupils playing and continuing to play after leaving school' (1996a: 105). Significantly, however, this success story has little to do with the promotion of traditional team sports.

Roberts noted that the traditional team sports have, in recent years, increasingly been joined by other activities within the PE curriculum, which is now considerably broader than the traditional games regime (Roberts, 1996b: 50). This growing diversity of physical activities within school has been paralleled by that of physical activities provided outside of school by local authority multi-sport centres, and also by the private sector health and fitness industry. This pattern of provision, he suggested, has been associated with an increased level of participation by young people because 'the mode of delivery has coincided with the age group's preferred leisure styles' (1996a: 113). In this context, he argued that young people's leisure activities have become increasingly individualised as the 'life course' – most notably the transition from school to work, and to marriage and family life – has become destandardised, particularly in the period since the mid-1970s. In this regard, he notes that:

> Labour markets have become more flexible, occupational careers have become less secure, risks of unemployment have risen and work schedules have become more varied. Alongside these economic trends neighbourhoods have become less close-knit than they once were, families have become less stable, and researchers now recognise a variety of masculinities and femininities.
>
> (1996a: 106)

In addition, he suggested, gender and social class divisions within youth cultures have become less clear cut. One aspect of these changes is that young people's biographies – their experiences of education, training, employment and family life – have become increasingly individualised, and this growing individualisation has also been expressed in their preferences in relation to active leisure:

> In and out of school young people in Britain are now able to play their preferred sports in places and in groups that express their individuality. Sport has adapted to the splintering of young people's tastes. The new school menus contain items that appeal to males and females in all age bands. Both sexes can use sports to assert their independence (playing what they want, when they want, with whom they want), and display their preferred forms of masculinity and femininity. . . . Sports participation can be expected to rise in all adult age groups in Britain as the current cohort of young people carry their higher propensity to participate into later life stages.
>
> (Roberts, 1996a: 113)

However, Roberts suggests that the policy set out in *Sport: Raising the Game* – in particular, returning to the traditional games regime in schools and making sports clubs more prominent in community provisions – 'will almost certainly lead to a flight from sport by Britain's young people'. This is, he suggests, 'the only plausible interpretation that can be placed on the evidence, much of it from government sponsored research, on recent trends in sports promotion and delivery on the one hand, and young people's participation rates on the other' (Roberts, 1996a: 113).

Roberts' comments about the individualisation of the life-styles of young people are equally applicable to much of the adult population, and the shift in the pattern of leisure-time physical activity which he identified for young people has also been identified in relation to adults. For example, the English Sports Council (1997: 10) noted that among adults there has recently been a 'decline in partner and team sports' but that this decline 'has been matched by increased participation in fitness-oriented, non-competitive, individual, flexible lifestyle activities such as walking, swimming, cycling, keep fit and aerobics and weight training', and the Council went on to note, very much in the style of Roberts' argument, that 'future trends are likely to reinforce the emphasis on individuality and flexibility'. The trend away from competitive sports, and in particular team games, and towards fitness-orientated, non-competitive life-style activities, is one which may be welcomed in public health circles, and no doubt in hospital casualty departments up and down the country, but it appears to be rather less welcome to those who – like the very many people within the sport and PE community who openly welcomed the *Sport: Raising the Game* policy – would seem to be less concerned with health, and more concerned with developing sporting performance, with enhancing sporting excellence, and with winning international championships. It is surely no accident that while the *Sport: Raising the Game* statement was published by the Department of National Heritage, which includes the Ministry of Sport, had a preface written by the then Prime Minister and was sent out with a separate letter of support from the then Secretary of State for Education, there is, significantly, no indication of any input from the Department of Health.

POSTSCRIPT

Just as the manuscript of this book was being completed, the Education and Employment Secretary, David Blunkett, unveiled proposals for changes in the National Curriculum which would, if approved, run from September 2000. The proposals included one major change in relation to PE in schools. Although remaining compulsory in Key Stages 1–3 (5–14-year-olds), competitive games were no longer to be compulsory in Key Stage 4 (14–16-year-olds). Instead, 14–16-year-olds would, under the proposed changes, be allowed to choose any two from six activities: games, gymnastics, athletics, dance, swimming and water safety, or outdoor and adventurous activities. The press release from the DfEE (208/99, 13 May, p. 3) indicated that this 'increased flexibility is intended to ensure that older pupils retain an interest in fitness and exercise'. It included a statement from the Secretary of State to the effect that

> It is particularly important to ensure that 15 and 16 year olds retain their enthusiasm for sport and fitness and carry this through to later

life. *Many enjoy games, but some do not. Such pupils will be able to carry out other, equally challenging activities instead of games.*

(1999: 4; emphasis added)

This was a statement of some significance, for it represented the first step by the Labour Government away from the prioritisation of games within the PE policy which it had inherited from John Major's Conservative Government. It should also be noted that the changes proposed by David Blunkett will, if implemented, help to make the PE curriculum more consistent with the increasingly individualised life-styles, including active leisure patterns, of young people, as outlined in this chapter.

However, it should also be noted that all the key aspects of the previous Government's *Sport: Raising the Game* policy, including the emphasis on team sports, have not been repudiated by the Labour Government, and remain intact. In addition, the proposals from the Secretary of State were to be put out to consultation until late July 1999, and though the results of this consultation process are not known at the time of writing, the initial announcement created what the *Guardian* called 'a predictable storm', and it is clear that there is likely to be considerable opposition from some of those within the sports lobby (*Guardian*, 12 May 1999; *Guardian Education*, 18 May 1999).

3 Health-related issues in child sport

Child abuse and sex abuse

As we saw in the opening chapter, there are many health risks associated with participation in sport. Some of these risks are, at least to some extent, openly recognised. Most people who are involved in playing or promoting sport are, for example, aware of the fact that playing sport inevitably involves a risk of injury, even if most people considerably underestimate the real health costs, in terms of injuries, of sporting participation. There are, however, some health risks associated with participation in sport which are much less openly recognised and which are much less frequently discussed. Two such areas of risk are those associated with child abuse and sex abuse in sport, and it is these which form the central concern of this chapter.

When discussing child abuse, it is important to recognise that what is considered to constitute child abuse is associated with changing attitudes towards children and therefore varies from one society to another and from one historical period to another. In this context we might note, for example, that in modern Britain or the United States, views about the status and rights of children are very different from those which prevailed in seventeenth-century England, when children were considered to be inherently bad and therefore in need of strict discipline. This latter view was sufficient to justify what would now be considered extremely harsh – indeed, cruel – forms of chastisement of children (Gillham, 1994: 1).

It should therefore be noted that, as Cooper (1993: 2) has pointed out, 'Child abuse as we conceive of it is a modern phenomenon.' Some writers, like Cooper, suggest that child abuse was 'discovered' in the United States as recently as the early 1960s, most notably with Kempe's 1962 identification of the 'battered child syndrome', while others such as Reder *et al.* (1993: 8) have dated what they call the 'rediscovery' of child abuse a little earlier, and associate it in particular with the work of Caffey, a paediatric radiologist, in 1946.

It is also important to note that, as expectations about what constitutes 'proper' care of children have risen, so policy and practice have also changed; indeed the terms used to describe children's suffering have changed from 'child battering' through 'non-accidental injury' to 'child abuse'. This change of terms is significant for, as Cooper (1993: 2) noted, it reflects the fact that, in the last two decades, there has been a shift away from an exclusive concern with what might be regarded as 'basic abuse' – for example, failing to meet the physiological needs of the child for food, or inflicting excessive physical punishment – to what is sometimes called 'higher order' abuse, including emotional abuse and a variety of forms of sexual abuse.

This broad conception of 'abuse' can be illustrated by reference to the current legislative framework in the United Kingdom. The Children Act of 1989 identified two ways in which children might suffer: they may be 'in need' because they lack welfare services, or they may be at risk of 'significant harm' from the acts or omissions of their carers. The Act defines 'significant harm' very broadly; it can relate to a child's physical, intellectual, emotional, social or behavioural development, while ill-treatment encompasses sexual abuse and forms of abuse which are not physical (Cooper, 1993: 1–3). Drawing upon a broad conception of abuse like that involved in the concept of 'significant harm', the central object of this chapter is to review some of the data relating to patterns of child abuse in sport.

Writing of children's sport, Donnelly (1993: 96) has drawn attention to what he – and doubtless many others – would consider a disturbing trend. He writes:

> As children encounter opportunities for increasingly lucrative careers as professional athletes, parents are tempted to encourage their children to become heavily involved in professional sports at early ages. As evidenced by increasing demands for international success in sport as a justification for government and corporate spending on elite participation, and by a variety of attempts to establish schemes for the early identification of athletic talent, there is an obvious trend toward earlier and more intensive athletic involvement for younger and younger children.

This trend towards earlier and more intensive involvement of children in sport raises a number of health concerns, for children are, for a number of reasons, particularly vulnerable to a variety of forms of exploitation or abuse. In part, this vulnerability arises from the fact that, as we noted in Chapter 2, the bodies of young children are growing rapidly and this makes them particularly susceptible to certain kinds of injuries, particularly dislocations and fractures. In this context, it is important for those responsible for the medical care of child athletes to remind those in charge of their coaching programmes that the athletes in question are children, that particular care should be taken to ensure that they are not given training schedules which are appropriate for adults, and that they are not subject to overtraining.

Though such advice might seem obvious – indeed, it might even seem so obvious as to be unnecessary – it is the case that the increasingly competitive character of sport means that even children are sometimes subjected to very heavy training schedules which are inappropriate for young, growing bodies. In this context, Donnelly has noted that injuries characteristic of overtraining among young athletes have been widely reported in the literature (for example, Rowley, 1986), and he also notes that such injuries were reported by a majority of the forty-five recently retired, high-level athletes who were interviewed in his own study (Donnelly, 1993) and who spoke about their own experiences as young athletes.

The exploitation or abuse of children in sport can take many forms. It may involve the imposition on young athletes of extreme regimes in relation to diet and weight control. Such extreme regimes are particularly likely to be imposed on athletes such as young female gymnasts, for there are both sport-specific and gender dimensions to this problem. Where such strict diet and weight-control regimes are imposed, they are sometimes associated with harsh sanctions, including verbal abuse of young children – almost invariably girls – who fail to meet weight targets. In addition, young athletes – and particularly those whom it is felt may reach elite status – may be bullied and cajoled into continuing to train and compete through pain and injury, even at the risk of permanent damage to their health. On occasions, a young athlete may be subject to several different forms of abuse within the context of their relationship with the coach. Thus, for example, Kew (1997: 71–4) cites excerpts from a real-life account of a young female athlete who, over a five-year period and in the context of her relationship with her coach, was subjected to the following forms of abuse: control and surveillance over her life-style; overtraining and training with injuries; sexual harassment and sexual 'favours'; substance abuse; and psychological problems and burn-out, leading ultimately to the rejection of sport. Moreover, the abuse of young children in sport may not come merely from coaches; parents may invest a great deal of time, energy and money in seeking to develop the sporting careers of their children, and parents may, either openly or tacitly, acquiesce in the imposition of excessively harsh training regimes on their children in the hope of making them into champions.

The risks of abuse, and the kinds of abuse, almost certainly vary from one sport to another and indeed from one country to another. One of the most highly institutionalised patterns of abuse was that which developed under the former communist regime in East Germany and which has recently come to light with the prosecutions of four former East German swimming coaches and two doctors. All six formerly worked at the Dynamo Berlin Club, and have been charged with inflicting grievous bodily harm by administering drugs to nineteen minors between 1974 and the fall of the Berlin Wall in 1989. This practice was part of a state-sponsored doping programme on a massive scale which was authorised by the Central Committee of the Communist Party in October 1974 and which involved the routine administration of steroids and other drugs to athletes who included girl swimmers of 13 and 14 and, in some cases, children as young as 10 (*The Times*, 19 March 1998).

In the West, particular concern has been expressed in recent years about the abuse of young girls in gymnastics and figure skating. In this context, J. Ryan (1996: 3) suggested that in the United States these sports may be seen as involving 'legal, even celebrated, child abuse'. She writes:

> Both sports embody the contradiction of modern womanhood. Society has allowed women to aspire higher, but to do so a woman must often reject that which makes her female, including motherhood. Similarly, gymnastics and figure skating remove the limits of a girl's body, teaching it to soar beyond what seems possible. Yet they also imprison it, binding it like the tiny Victorian waist or the Chinese woman's foot. The girls aren't allowed passage into adulthood. To survive in the sports, they beat back puberty, desperate to stay small and thin, refusing to let their bodies grow up. In this way the sports pervert the very femininity they hold so dear. The physical skills have become so demanding that only a body shaped like a missile – in other words, a body shaped like a boy's – can excel. Breasts and hips slow the spins, lower the leaps and disrupt the clean, lean body lines that judges reward. 'Women's gymnastics' and 'ladies' figure skating' are misnomers today. Once the athletes become women, their elite careers wither.
>
> (J. Ryan, 1996: 6)

She adds (1996: 6–7) that the training and dieting schedules of these young athletes can create

> serious physical and psychological problems that can linger long after the public has turned its attention to the next phenomenon in pigtails. The intensive training and pressure heaped on by coaches, parents and federation officials – the very people who should be protecting the children – often result in eating disorders, weakened bones, stunted growth, debilitating injuries and damaged psyches.

It should be noted that Ryan is not suggesting that all gymnasts and figure skaters are subjected to regimes of this kind. Rather, she is describing the harsh regimes to which some young elite gymnasts and figure skaters in the United States are subject. Nor is she suggesting that young people should not take part in gymnastics or figure skating, or that all elite gymnasts and figure skaters emerge from their sports unhealthy and psychologically damaged. Rather, she is concerned to point to the vulnerability of young athletes, and to the need to ensure that the desire for sporting success does not expose young people to training programmes which can be both physically and psychologically damaging. As such, Ryan's book, *Little Girls in Pretty Boxes*, provides a timely reminder both of the vulnerability of young people and of the damage which can be done to young children if proper child protection practices are not followed.

CHILD SEX ABUSE IN SPORT

It is difficult to establish with any accuracy the frequency of child sexual abuse either within the wider society or specifically within sport. However, such data as do exist suggest that child sexual abuse is not an uncommon phenomenon. Bagley and King (1990) reviewed a large number of studies covering such diverse groups as students in New England and Canada, women in San Francisco, adults in Texas and parents in Boston as well as national prevalence studies of adults in Canada and the United Kingdom. Among New England students, 19 per cent of female and 9 per cent of male students reported having been sexually assaulted as children (under 16) by an older partner. In San Francisco, 38 per cent of women reported at least one experience of sexual abuse before the age of 18. In Texas, 11 per cent of female and 3 per cent of males reported having been sexually abused as children. In Boston, 15 per cent of female and 6 per cent of male parents reported incidents of childhood sexual abuse. In the national prevalence surveys, 18 per cent of women and 8 per cent of men in Canada reported having been the victims of 'unwanted sexual acts' (involving physical contact) before the age of 17, while in the British prevalence survey, 12 per cent of women and 8 per cent of men reported having been sexually abused before the age of 16.

Data on the prevalence of sex abuse in sport are even less reliable, but there is growing evidence that it is a danger of which those responsible for the health of child athletes should be aware. Donnelly and Sparks (1997) note that a survey of Canadian national team athletes found that 20 per cent had had sexual intercourse with a coach or other authority figure, while 8.6 per cent had experienced forced sexual intercourse (20 per cent of these being under the age of 16). A doctoral thesis by Marge Holman at the University of Windsor in Canada indicated that 57 per cent of Canadian university athletes had experienced sexual harassment (cited in Donnelly and Sparks, 1997). Probably the most infamous case of child sexual abuse in Canadian sport is that which has recently been revealed in ice hockey. In January 1997, Graham James, a former junior hockey coach to the Calgary Hitmen, Swift Current Broncos and the Moose Jaw Warriors of the Western Hockey League, was sentenced to three years in gaol after being convicted of sexually abusing two of his young players (*Ottawa Citizen*, 6 January 1997). The case was given extensive publicity in Canada and the United States, not just because of the importance of ice hockey, particularly within Canadian society, but also because it was subsequently revealed that one of the players who had been systematically abused by James was Sheldon Kennedy, who at the time of James's trial was playing in America for the Boston Bruins in the National Hockey League. Kennedy's decision to make it known publicly that he was one of the victims in the case triggered off a large number of phone calls from men calling sexual assault centres in Canada and requesting help in relation to their own history of being abused. Catherine Hedlin of the Edmonton Sexual Assault Centre in Alberta was quoted as saying, 'We've had at least fifty calls since the story broke, specifically about sports-related sexual abuse, and 80 per cent of those calls have been men.' She added that, 'When they call, they say, "When Kennedy spoke out, he made me realize I wasn't alone and that I could talk about it"' (*Ottawa Citizen*, 16 January 1997). Little more than a month after James was convicted, Canadian police were investigating fresh allegations that sexual predators had operated out of the Maple Leaf Gardens in Toronto – regarded by many as the shrine of Canadian hockey – during the late 1970s and early 1980s, and that arena employees had enticed boys with gifts of hockey sticks before abusing them in back rooms during games (*New York Times*, 23 February 1997). The Toronto police officer heading the investigation was quoted as saying that there were 'many, many victims' of the stadium's ring of paedophiles (*Daily Telegraph*, 22 February 1997).

Within the United Kingdom, a study of 149 Scottish athletes by Yorganci (1992) found that 54 per cent of respondents had either experienced, or knew someone who had experienced, at least one of the following forms of sexual harassment: demeaning language, including sexual innuendo; unwarranted invitations; intrusive physical contact; fondling the genital area; or pressure to have sexual intercourse with their coach or other performers. In Britain, there has recently been a series of successful prosecutions in relation to child sex abuse in several sporting contexts. In 1995 Paul Hickson, who was Britain's swimming coach at the Los Angeles and Seoul Olympics, was convicted of indecently assaulting and/or raping fifteen young female swimmers over a period of fifteen years. In August 1997, a man who ran an under-11s soccer club in Lincolnshire was sentenced to 28 months in prison for committing indecent acts with two boys aged 9 and 11; he fled the country while on bail, but was re-arrested after he returned to the country, when he was discovered coaching young players in Cambridgeshire (*Cambridge Evening News*, 19 December 1997). In March 1998, a martial arts coach in Cambridgeshire was convicted of indecently assaulting seven youngsters aged 11 to 15 (*Cambridge Evening News*, 25 March 1998). A TV documentary in 1997 revealed that young boys had been sexually abused at coaching schemes at two professional soccer clubs in England (*Dispatches*, Channel 4 TV, 23 January 1997); the person who was at the centre of these TV revelations, Barry Bennell, was gaoled for nine years in June 1998 after pleading guilty to twenty-three specimen charges relating to sexual offences (*Independent*, 2 June 1998). Five months later, the founder of Celtic Boys Club in Glasgow was gaoled for two years for abusing three young players (*Daily Telegraph*, 28 November 1998). At about the same time, a paedophile who set up a cycling club in Birmingham was convicted of indecently assaulting three child members whom he took on cycling trips (*Cycling Weekly*, 21 November 1998), while in early 1999 it was reported that in Newcastle, a police investigation had been launched and the City Council had suspended one of its male coaches following allegations of indecent assault of children at one of the council's sports centres (*Independent*, 8 January 1999).

Although such cases do not allow us to develop any precise estimate of the incidence of child sex abuse in sport, they do suggest, particularly when viewed in conjunction with studies such as that by Yorganci, that sexual harassment and/or abuse are sufficiently common to be matters of concern.

One striking feature of the pattern of child abuse which is revealed by cases such as those cited above is that, within the context of the sports club, young people are not only vulnerable to abuse but, more specifically, *they are also vulnerable to repeated abuse, often over very long periods of time.* In the case of the British Olympic swimming coach, noted earlier, the offences against young swimmers were committed over a period of fifteen years. In that of the offences against young boys in professional soccer, the offences took place over a fourteen-year period, while the martial arts instructor in Cambridgeshire committed his offences over a twenty-two-year period. In Canada, Sheldon Kennedy was abused by Graham James 300 times over a twelve-year period. The fact that coaches who abuse young players are often able to conceal their actions from others, and that they are able to continue the pattern of abuse over such long time periods, is indicative of the great power which coaches are frequently able to wield over young people in their care, and of the associated vulnerability of young people to abuse. This issue requires more detailed examination.

WHY ARE YOUNG CHILDREN VULNERABLE?

It is important to note that children are normally in a relatively weak (that is, relatively powerless) position in relation to those who run and/or coach in clubs for young boys and girls. This makes them particularly vulnerable to exploitation by unscrupulous people, and suggests the need for vigilance and for appropriate child protection measures wherever children are involved in sport. The vulnerability of young children to abuse is associated with a number of social processes, but the following aspects of adult–child relations in sport are of particular importance.

First, when children are coached by adults there is a clear power relationship implied in the adult–child relationship. Children learn from other contexts, such as the home and the school, that they are generally subject to the authority of adults and are expected to do as they are instructed by adults. As a consequence, children – and perhaps especially very young children – may find it difficult to disobey the instructions of adults who are entrusted with their care, even where the children may feel a deep sense of unease or unhappiness with those instructions. Moreover, as Donnelly and Sparks (1997) have noted, the young athlete may be further disempowered by, for example, the coach befriending their parents.

Second, the power differentials associated with the adult–child relationship may be reinforced by power differences associated with gender relations, such as where an adult male is coaching a young girl athlete. In relation to sexual abuse, most research has focused on male rather than female abusers because they number over 90 per cent of recorded cases (Brackenridge, 1994: 291). However, Brackenridge noted that there is a growing literature on abuse by females (see, for example, Moore, 1991), while recent data collected in Britain by the children's charity Kidscape suggest that sexual abuse by women may be more common than had previously been thought ('The Ultimate Taboo', Panorama, BBC1, 6 October 1997). Lenskyj (1990: 241) claimed that where both parties in a sport setting are female, 'the specific threat of sexual abuse is absent from these coach/athlete relationships' but, in the light of growing evidence of sexual abuse by women, Lenskyj's comment should be treated with a good deal of scepticism.

Third, the dependent position of the young athlete may be further reinforced by the fact that he or she may feel it necessary to please the coach because the coach may be seen as controlling access to desired goals, for example selection for local, regional or national teams or, in sports such as soccer, a favourable recommendation to a professional club. In this situation, the young person may feel that a refusal to co-operate with the coach, even where they have serious doubts about the propriety of what the coach is suggesting, may jeopardise their chances of receiving a favourable recommendation. The difficulties in which the young person may find him/herself in this regard are clearly illustrated by two comments (cited in Kew, 1997: 70) relating to the case of the Olympic swimming coach convicted of raping fifteen young girl swimmers. One of the victims who, instead of reporting the offender, tried mentally to block out the attacks, said:

> They would have taken my swimming away from me and that was really important to me. I just felt pathetic, ashamed, embarrassed and ugly.

The second comment is from the prosecutor in the court case:

It is a classic case of a person in authority, or in a position of trust, abusing that trust. Most endured his conduct over months and even years. They tolerated his behaviour in the knowledge that to displease him or to break the links would adversely affect their careers.

The power which the coach has by virtue of controlling access to desired goals – in this case, a favourable recommendation to a professional club – was also clearly brought out by the judge who sentenced Barry Bennell to nine years in prison for sexually abusing young boys in English professional soccer clubs. In sentencing Bennell, the judge said:

You preyed on adolescent and pre-adolescent boys whose sexual experience was nil. You had access to well known football clubs, football clothing and things of that kind. You could pinpoint young boys in the right direction and help them with their careers and wishes to become successful footballers. They were prepared to do almost anything you asked.

(*Independent*, 2 June 1998)

Fourth, in many sports (such as gymnastics) it may not only be legitimate but also necessary for the coach to touch the athlete's body. This provides opportunities for 'inappropriate' touching which young children may, for a variety of reasons, feel reluctant to report and which may also be difficult to prove to the standard required in a court of law.

RECENT POLICY DEVELOPMENTS

Recently there have been a number of policy developments which may be seen as symptomatic of, and a response to, the growing concern about child abuse in sport. These developments appear to have been, at least in part, a response to several high-profile prosecutions for child abuse. For example, in Canada, the conviction of Graham James appears to have been the catalyst for the development of policy in relation to child abuse in sport.[1] The *Ottawa Citizen* (26 January 1997) wrote: 'If there is a benefit to the sordid story of Graham James and the courageous revelations of victim Sheldon Kennedy, it is that Canada's sports organizations are refusing to let the problem of sexual harassment and abuse go away', while the executive director of the Canadian Association for the Advancement of Women and Sport (CAAWS) described the James case as a 'wake-up call'. In January 1997, thirty-five national sport organisations and governing bodies, under the leadership of the CAAWS, the Canadian Centre for Ethics and Sport, and Sport Canada, set up a collective working group with the task of producing a guide to assist those involved in sports organisations at all levels to develop policies and procedures to prevent and respond to abuse and harassment. The result was a very detailed manual, *Speak Out! . . . Act Now!* which was published on behalf of the collective by the Canadian Hockey Association (1997). A few months later, the CAAWS, in association with the Canadian Red Cross, produced another guide, *What Parents Can Do about Harassment and Abuse in Sport* (CAAWS, 1998).

In the United Kingdom, the National Society for the Prevention of Cruelty to Children (NSPCC) and the National Coaching Foundation combined in 1995 to publish *Protecting Children: A Guide for Sportspeople*. The following year, the National Coaching Foundation published its *Guidance for National Governing Bodies on Child Protection Procedures*, which was revised in 1997 (NCF, 1997). In October 1997, the Football Association announced the launch of a Coaches Association which would require all members to abide by its published code of child protection. And in February 1999, Bristol Rovers Football Club announced that it had appointed a child protection officer and had established a 'Child Safe' scheme, which had been developed in conjunction with the Avon and Somerset Police; the scheme had received the support of the Football Association, which was recommending the scheme to all clubs. The scheme had also been adopted by Bath Rugby Football Club and by Gloucestershire County Cricket Club (*Independent*, 15 February 1999). In swimming, the Amateur Swimming Association established a series of child protection procedures and a set of guidelines for coaches following the conviction of an Olympic swimming coach for a number of child sex abuse offences in 1995 and, most recently, it has launched, in conjunction with the NSPCC, a 24-hour helpline to aid young victims of sexual abuse (*Guardian*, 14 December 1998).

Within the United Kingdom, the most detailed code of practice in relation to the prevention of child abuse in sport is that which was produced in 1995 by the NSPCC and the National Coaching Foundation. This document runs to almost 100 pages, and sets out a number of guidelines for child protection procedures, among which the following are of central importance:

- all sports organisations must have a policy statement regarding child abuse which must be brought to the attention of all staff, whether employed or voluntary;
- work should be planned to help avoid situations in which abuse might occur (for example, by helping avoid situations where an adult is alone with a child);
- organisations should establish a system where children can talk to an independent person outside the club, who should be given clear instructions about what action to take if abuse is alleged or suspected;
- there should be agreed procedures for protecting children and these should be applied to all staff, whether employed or voluntary. These procedures should include ensuring that all staff have clear roles and

responsibilities, issuing guidelines regarding action to be taken if abuse is suspected, and a supervision and appraisal system which incorporates checks on relationships and observation of practice;

• the same recruitment, interview and selection procedures should be used for volunteers and paid employees – although appropriate recruitment and selection procedures, including police checks, cannot prevent abusers from being employed, they can reduce the risk;

• all staff should be trained in the prevention of child abuse, including recognition of the symptoms of abuse.

(NSPCC/National Coaching Foundation, 1995: 43)

Those involved in the organisation of sport for children have, on the whole, been slow to recognise and to respond to the dangers of child abuse. This may perhaps be because there is a commonsense perception of sport as a healthy activity and, within this context, it might seem for many people 'unthinkable' that anyone could deliberately abuse young children. However, a moment's reflection is enough to indicate that sports clubs which cater for young people are likely targets for paedophiles and others who might abuse children; such clubs not only attract large numbers of children and young people, but they also offer activities in which those young people will be clothed only in sportswear which may reveal much of their bodies, the children will be routinely involved in dressing, undressing and showering, and some sports may also offer legitimate opportunities for touching the bodies of young children. In this context, the Amateur Swimming Association in the United Kingdom has recently noted that almost 90 per cent of the 300,000 swimming club members are under the age of 16, and the Association has expresssed concern that the sport may attract paedophiles (*Guardian*, 14 December 1998).

Although, as we noted earlier, the risk of sexual exploitation and abuse appears to vary from one sport to another, it is also the case, as Jaques and Brackenridge (1999: 229) have pointed out, that 'many risks are . . . shared across sports' and they suggest that all sports should be considered as 'risk settings'. Given this situation, and given the growing evidence of child abuse in sport, it is clearly important that all sports clubs in which children are involved have a clear code of practice for those working with young children. Such a code, it should be noted, would be in the interests of both children and adults. An appropriate code would have the effect not only of protecting children from abuse but, and perhaps no less importantly, of protecting innocent adults against false allegations of abuse.

4   Doctors' dilemmas

Conflicts in the role of club medical staff in professional football

As we saw in the first chapter, elite or professional sport involves a relatively high risk of injury, and the injury risk is particularly high in contact sports. In this context, and in sports such as professional football (soccer), the quality of medical care provided by the club doctor and physiotherapists may be of considerable importance, for it may make the difference between an injury-hit squad, in which key players are unavailable for selection, and one which is relatively injury-free. The quality of the medical care may also have a significant impact on the recovery time of players who do get injured. Given this situation, it is perhaps surprising that we know very little about club doctors and physiotherapists, and the roles which they perform within their clubs. The central object of this chapter is to shed some light on what is a largely unexplored area; namely, the role of club medical staff in professional football.

Writing from the perspective of a team doctor in water sports, Newton (1990: 309) suggested that 'Essentially the profile of the team doctor is that of the old-fashioned family doctor'. Though many sports physicians have a background in general practice and though it is undoubtedly tempting to cite the example of the much-loved 'old-fashioned family doctor' as the model for the practice of sports medicine, this comparison is in some respects misleading. There are a number of important differences – and not simply in terms of the different kinds of medical problems with which they have to deal – between the role of the general practitioner and that of the sports physician. These differences – and particularly the differences in terms of managing potentially delicate problems in the doctor–patient relationship – are brought most clearly into focus by an examination of the role of the club doctor.

Although the pattern of interaction between doctor and patient is influenced by a number of processes, including those relating to the relative age, gender and social class of both doctor and patient, as well as the specific nature of the patient's medical problem, there are nevertheless certain fundamental assumptions which underpin all such relationships. Among the most important assumptions in this respect are the following: first, that the doctor uses his or her skill wholly and exclusively on behalf of the patient; second, that the doctor is not acting as an agent on behalf of anybody else whose interests may conflict with those of the patient; and third, because the doctor acts exclusively on behalf of the patient, he/she may be trusted with private or intimate information which will be treated confidentially and not divulged to others.

However, these assumptions – which underpin most doctor–patient interactions and which are central to the trust that is such an important part of relationships in general practice – may not be applicable in quite the same way, or to the same degree, in the work situation of the practitioner of sports medicine, and particularly in the work of the club doctor involved in professional or elite sport. This is an important problem which requires careful examination.

Writing in 1990, the then medical officer to the British athletes' team (Bottomley, 1990: 159) nicely pointed to this potential problem in the role of the club doctor. He noted that the 'team doctor, having been invited by the club or governing body of the sport in question, is acting as an agent of that club or body'. Clearly the club, which engages the doctor to act on its behalf, has a legitimate interest in the management of players' illnesses and injuries. But if the team doctor is acting as an agent of the club, how can he/she simultaneously act as the agent for, and on behalf of, the individual player? What happens if the interests of the club and the player do not coincide, as inevitably will be the case from time to time?

Roy and Irvin (1983: 30) pointed out that where members of the medical and related professions are employed by the team management, 'this may lead to an explicit expectation on the part of the management or coaching staff of loyalty to them', and they add that 'this arrangement may not always be in the best interests of the athlete'. For example, there is often in professional football, as we shall see, a clear and strong expectation that, wherever possible, players will continue to play through pain and injury 'for the sake of the team', and club medical staff may be subject to strong pressure to pass players fit to play, perhaps with the help of painkilling injections, before they have fully recovered from injury. Should the doctor (or physiotherapist) concur, thereby possibly risking further and perhaps more serious injury to the player? Or should they insist that the player is rested, thereby possibly incurring the disapproval of the manager? How do club doctors and physiotherapists balance the long-term health interests of the player-as-patient with the short-term interests of the club/manager in fielding the strongest team? And how do club medical staff deal with potentially delicate issues involving patient confidentiality?

Some of these complexities in the roles of the club doctor and other club medical staff are pointed up by Mellion and Walsh (1990: 1), who note that the team physician 'addresses the physical, emotional, and spiritual needs of the athlete in the context of the sport *and the needs of the team*' (emphasis added). They explicitly recognise that the team physician has 'a range of responsibilities that reflect the many relationships involved in the care of the team' and suggest that the club doctor's responsibilities 'to the athlete, the team, and the institution and its representatives must be balanced'.

Balancing these multiple responsibilities may, however, prove to be a difficult and delicate issue, though this is not always clearly recognised in the literature on the role of the sports physician. Brown and Benner (1984: 39), for example, assert quite simply that the 'role of the sports physician or other sports medicine professional is clear. The athlete's health and well-being are the first priorities, followed, not preceded, by the athlete's ability to compete and perform.' In similar vein, Horan (1990: 343–4), writing about the role of the club doctor in cricket, suggested that 'the interests of the club must not be allowed to override those of the player'. Expanding upon this point, he adds: 'Attempts at playing unfit players must be strongly resisted, and the doctor must have the final say.' Moreover, there is no explicit recognition of any special problems in relation to confidentiality, Horan simply asserting that when treating players, the 'normal confidentiality of the doctor–patient relationship must be preserved'. Writing from the perspective of the team doctor in Rugby union, Kennedy (1990: 315) echoes Horan's advice concerning playing players who have not yet fully recovered from injury. He notes that the players themselves will often ask for painkilling injections prior to playing, and is emphatic in his advice that this practice 'is to be avoided', adding that 'the request should not arise if the selectors and coach have agreed beforehand that an injured player should be rested until he is fully fit'.

The authors cited above would seem to suggest that any problems the club doctor might encounter can be resolved relatively easily by the application of a few straightforward rules: the interests of the player must be placed above those of the club; normal rules of confidentiality governing doctor–patient relationships should apply in the work of the club doctor; club doctors should not succumb to pressure, whether from the manager/coach or the player, to allow players to play with the help of painkilling injections, and should not agree to players playing before they have fully recovered from injury.

But to what extent do the simple guidelines outlined above by writers such as Brown and Benner, Horan and Kennedy help to resolve conflicts facing club doctors? To what extent do those authors describe, not how club doctors *actually* behave in the real world, but how, in an ideal world, they consider that club doctors *ought* to behave? How, in their day-to-day practice, do club doctors resolve the potential conflicts of interest between their responsibility to their employer (the club) and their responsibility to the individual player-as-patient? To what extent are club doctors subject to pressure to agree to players playing while injured? From whom do these pressures come? How effectively are club doctors able to resist these pressures? Are the long-term health risks of playing through injury explained to, and understood by, players? Or is relevant information withheld from, or simply not conveyed to, players? And how do club doctors deal with delicate issues involving doctor–patient confidentialty? For example, how much information about the players' health is communicated to the team coach or manager? Is such information confined to the players' injury status, or does it include information which the manager might want, but which would normally be considered confidential to the doctor–patient relationship, such as information relating to a player's life-style? And what do club medical staff do if they discover that a player has a problem in relation to excessive alcohol consumption or that a player is illegally using drugs? Are such problems handled within the confidentiality of the doctor–patient relationship, or do doctors feel constrained to inform the coach/manager? Although these questions have all been phrased in relation to the club doctor, they also relate equally, of course, to the role of the club physiotherapist.

A good deal of light was shed on these questions by a study recently undertaken by the Centre for Research into Sport and Society at Leicester University. The study, which was carried out on behalf of the Professional Footballers Association, examined the management of injuries in professional football and it focused, in particular, on the roles of the club doctor and the club physiotherapist (Waddington *et al.*, 1999). The study involved tape-recorded interviews of between 30 minutes and 1 hour with twelve club doctors and ten club physiotherapists. Twenty-seven players and ex-players were also interviewed about their experiences of injury and rehabilitation. The interviews were carried out in the second half of the 1997–98 season and the first half of the 1998–99 season. In addition to the interviews, a postal questionnaire was sent to ninety club doctors who were not interviewed; fifty-eight questionnaires were returned.

Doctors in the Premier League were more amenable to being interviewed, which almost certainly reflected their generally greater involvement in their clubs. However, this did mean that the sample of doctors who were interviewed was biased towards club doctors in the Premiership. Of the twelve interviews, seven were with doctors at clubs in the Premier League, two with doctors at clubs in the First Division of the Nationwide League, two with doctors at Second Division clubs, while one interview was with a doctor in a Third Division club. One of the Premier club doctors had also previously worked in a Second Division club. However, the bias towards doctors in Premier League clubs was offset by the data obtained in the postal questionnaire. Replies were received from thirteen doctors at Premier League clubs, thirteen doctors at First Division clubs, fifteen doctors at Second Division clubs and sixteen doctors at Third Division clubs. One doctor did not indicate the division in which his club played.

Of the club physiotherapists, three worked in Premier League clubs, two in First Division clubs, two in Second Division clubs and two in Third Division clubs. In addition, one physiotherapist had formerly worked in two football clubs (one Third Division club, one Premier League club) but now worked as a club physiotherapist in another sport.

UNDERSTANDING FOOTBALL CULTURE

In order to understand the role of club medical staff, it is necessary to understand something about the culture of professional football and the associated constraints within which club doctors and physiotherapists work. In this context, it is important to note that playing with pain, or when injured, is a central part of the culture of professional football. One of the characteristics which managers look for in players is that they should have what, in professional football, is regarded as a 'good attitude', and one way in which players can demonstrate to their manager that they have such an attitude is by being prepared to play when injured. A good illustration of what, from a manager's point of view, constitutes a 'good attitude' was provided by the Liverpool manager, Gerard Houlier. Interviewed in the *Sunday Times* (6 December 1998), Houlier said that the kind of players a manager wants are those who 'will fight for you once they are on that grass'. He added: 'I'll name you one – Jamie Carragher. What a professional. He might have a niggly injury, but he'll always be out there giving you some of this' (Houlier smashed a fist into his other palm by way of emphasis).

Being prepared to play while injured is thus defined as a central characteristic of 'the good professional'. A related aspect of football culture is that players who are unable to play as a result of injury and who can, therefore, make no direct contribution to the team on the field of play may be seen as being of little value to the club, and may be stigmatised, ignored or otherwise inconvenienced.

The idea that the player who cannot play because of injury is, at least for the duration of his injury, of little use to the club may be expressed in a variety of ways. As we noted in Chapter 1, the former Liverpool manager, Bill Shankley, would refuse to speak directly to players who were unavailable for selection as a result of injury. Perhaps surprisingly, such attitudes are still commonly to be found among managers. One player told us that some managers 'have a theory that injured players aren't worth spit basically. . . . "You are no use to us if you are injured".' However, some managers were more sympathetic; the same player said that 'some managers always go out of their way to talk to you as an injured player'. One club doctor to whom we spoke also pointed out that the relationship between the manager and injured players varies from one manager to another: 'I mean it depends a little bit on the manager . . . some managers obviously feel very uncomfortable with injured players, don't know what to say to them, feel as if they're being let down in some way.'

Many players referred to experiences with managers whose managerial style was summed up by one player as 'roll your sleeves up and get on with it . . . the old sergeant major jobs'. This player said that his current manager had been both sympathetic and helpful in relation to his injury problems, but that previous managers had been much less sympathetic: 'I am used to someone saying: "Are you not fit yet? What's the matter with you? I want you tomorrow. I want you Wednesday and then I want you Friday. Get your arse in gear."'

Another player described the attitude of one of his former managers towards injured players as follows: 'You're not meant to be injured. You should be playing. You get paid to play. He totally ignored you when you were in the treatment room. His attitude was: "You're no use to me anymore."'

He added that his present manager had a similar attitude:

> My present manager is like that. I've heard him speaking to one of the players. He said: 'You're no use to me now, so what's the point in talking to you and seeing how you are.' I've been injured three weeks now and he's asked me for the first time today how I am. Just as I'm getting back to fitness.

A similar point was made by one of the physiotherapists, who said that some managers took the view that 'At the end of the day, you're a non-producer, as they say, if you're injured. You're not playing Saturday and you're no good to anyone. Some managers put it that way.'

The special status of players who are injured and therefore unavailable for selection is expressed in a variety of ways, all of which have the effect of reminding injured players that, for as long as they are injured, they are of little use to the club. In his book *Left Foot Forward*, in which he described a year in his life as a Charlton Athletic player in the mid-1990s, Garry Nelson (1995) pointed out that, for example, players who were in the first team squad at Charlton and were available for selection would get four complimentary tickets for each game, but that players who were injured would only receive two complimentary tickets. More importantly, in most clubs injured players have a daily routine which is significantly different from – and which is often deliberately designed to be less comfortable than – that of players who are fit. The latter normally report for training at about 10.00 a.m. and finish training about 12.30 or 1.00 p.m., following which they will normally eat together at the club and then have the rest of the day free. Injured players, on the other hand, are normally required to report to the ground before players who are fit, and are kept at the ground long after the others have departed, often until about 4.30 p.m. Of course, part of the different routine of injured players is related to the fact that they cannot take part in normal training sessions and that they require physiotherapy or other treatment. However, the different routine for injured players cannot be explained simply in terms of their need for specialist treatment, for, in many clubs, the routine is deliberately designed to 'inconvenience' injured players and thus to act as a disincentive to them to remain on the injured list for one day longer than is absolutely necessary. For example, one physiotherapist who had worked in two football clubs but who now worked in another sport said:

> I've frequently had it said to me when I've worked at professional soccer clubs: 'Inconvenience the injured player. We don't want them too comfortable in the treatment room, sitting in the warm when the rest are out there in the cold.' There's this paranoia, I never could work it out, I don't know why it really exists.

Asked what this policy of 'inconveniencing' the injured player involved, he replied: 'Get them in earlier for training. Keep them after training has finished so that all of the fit players are going home and they have to stay behind for extra treatment.' A similar idea was expressed by another club physiotherapist who said: 'I think if a player is injured they have to work harder and longer and be inconvenienced.' He explained that injured players were made to 'work their nuts off . . . so they'd rather train than be injured'. Describing how injured players were 'inconvenienced', he said that 'you have to make it naughty' and added, 'I will keep him [the injured player] here until the traffic builds up on the motorway.' Shortly after taking over at Tottenham Hotspur in 1998, George Graham was similarly reported to have introduced a system which involved keeping injured players at the ground until the build-up of traffic at the start of the rush-hour on the M25 (*Daily Mirror*, 10 November 1998).

PLAYING WHEN INJURED

The commonly held view that injured players should be inconvenienced expresses a fear that players might feign injury in order to avoid the rigours of training or playing. Our research suggests that such a fear is for the most part unfounded, for the central value of continuing to play, whenever possible, through pain and injury is also recognised and internalised by the players themselves. Indeed, players learn from a relatively young age to 'normalise' pain and to accept playing with pain and injury as part and parcel of the life of a professional footballer. One player described the situation as follows: 'Players are so desperately keen to get back that 90 per cent of them come back to play long before they have made a full recovery. I am no different . . . there is desperation to show that you are keen.'

One indication of players' willingness to play when injured came in response to a question in which we asked players how many matches, in a full season, they played without any kind of pain or injury. Many players – and, in particular, senior players, who had often accumulated many injuries over the years – indicated that they played no more than five or six games in a season entirely free from injury, and one senior player said: 'There's not one player goes out to play who's 100 per cent fit.'

This, then, constitutes the essential backcloth to understanding the role of the club doctor and club physiotherapist in professional football. One club physiotherapist characterised the culture of football, as it related to medical practice, in the following terms:

> Everything has to be done yesterday. The players have to be fit yester-day. If they miss a week, it's like a month to anyone else. The players will play when they're injured. You tend not to get the player injury-free. You . . . manage the level of injury irritation to play ninety minutes of football.

This physiotherapist, who also worked in a private sports medicine clinic in the evenings, described the key difference between his private practice and his practice in the football club as follows:

> In private practice, the client isn't desperate to be fit by Saturday. The client wants to be cured of the injury so it doesn't come back. . . . In private practice, my *modus operandi* is to cure the injury. In profes-sional football, my *modus operandi* is to get the player on the pitch as quickly as possible . . . you get people who are playing on injuries that need constant care. And you just end up performing maintenance on top of treatments in between games.

Being a physiotherapist in a football club was, he said, 'a different job' from being a physiotherapist in private practice, or in the National Health Service. The different constraints under which he worked in private practice and in football meant that, in his view, he was able to provide better-quality care to his private patients than to the players, notwithstanding the array of high-tech equipment, such as ultra-sound scans and MRI scans, which was available to treat the players. Asked about the quality of care he provided in the two contexts, he answered: 'Unequivocally, non-negotiable fact . . . my private clients will get better quality treatment than the players. . . . Don't doubt this. Yes, a fact.'

The need, as this physiotherapist to put it, to 'get players fit yesterday' is a strong and ever-present constraint within football, and every club doctor and physiotherapist whom we interviewed was, without exception, acutely aware of this constraint. Part of the pressure on club medical staff comes, as we noted above, from the players themselves, almost all of whom are keen to continue playing when injured, whenever it is possible to do so. Occasionally, injured players might be encouraged by the nature of their contracts to continue playing for financial reasons, as in the case described below. The physiotherapist involved explained that a player who had broken his toe asked for pain-killing injections in order that he could continue playing:

> He said to me: 'When I have played thirty-five games this season, I get a lump sum. I'm going to have these injections until I've played the thirty-five games. . . . Can you sort me out?' . . . I had a word with the GP [and] the GP said 'Yes, that's quite reasonable . . . he can at any time turn round and say "Look this isn't doing me any good having these injections."' It was a fracture of the toe which was being numbed. Whilst he continued to play with the numbing, obviously that was delaying the union of the fracture so . . . really he was retarding the healing of the bone. The bone would heal anyway, no question about that, so after he played the thirty-five games, he stopped playing . . . [later] the manager bumped into me in the corridor and said 'I can't believe that. Did [the player] say anything to you? Do you know, he's played exactly the number of games that he needed to play to get his lump sum appearance money this season, but he's so daft I can't believe he's twigged it,' and I just sort of smiled to myself and said, 'Oh. That's the way it is.'

More usually, players will try to continue to play through injury for any one of a number of reasons. Foremost among these is the fear of losing their place in the team, which is a very real fear for all but a handful of very well-established players. Players will also try to continue playing if the team has a series of particularly important games coming up. In addition, most players have a strong self-image as professional footballers and a strong sense of professional pride; for many players, playing football is the only job they have ever done and the only job they know how to do. Many players described the frustration which they experience when they are unable to play, while some players expressed a sense of guilt about being injured. One player, who during his second game for his new club received a serious knee injury which prevented him from playing for almost a year, clearly felt that, in some ill-defined but very real sense, he had let his new club down. In describing his injury and subsequent lengthy rehabilitation, he continually emphasised – as if to excuse his inability to make any playing contribution to the club – that the injury 'wasn't my fault'.

Many of the players to whom we spoke described in some detail their own experiences of playing when injured. One senior player described how, over several months, he had played with pain from a knee injury and, in attempting to compensate for the knee injury by changing his running style, had suffered one injury after another. The following is an extract from the transcript of the interview with this player:

PLAYER: Because you've got something that hurts, you are aware of it and you compensate naturally, probably unconsciously, and I was running in a different way. Changing my running style developed new injuries, so on top of one, when you are playing with an injury, then all of a sudden, you are playing with two injuries and then, you know, you get one right and then you've got another one . . . you never give yourself enough time, I never give myself enough time.

INTERVIEWER: Can you describe what it was like playing through these injuries?

PLAYER: You get familiar with it, any pain . . . if you don't step back and . . . get out of the scenario, you kind of get used to the s**t, I'm afraid, and that's what I was doing. I was compensating in other areas. I twisted my ankle in February last year, and that went on top of my knee and I'm compensating and then all of a sudden I'm getting bad toes. I'm getting bad toes 'cos I'm changing my running style . . . and then all of a sudden my back's playing me up.

INTERVIEWER: How did you feel during this period?

PLAYER: It was pretty depressing . . . when you are getting up in the morning and you can't walk and all of a sudden you think to yourself 'Jesus, I've got to go to work today.' You know, it's like any job, if you can't do your job . . . so it was kind of one thing on top of another and it's not a good feeling. . . . It's frustrating, but you get used to the pain and . . . you keep on playing with the pain. That's the thing, you never say 'No, I'm not doing it'.

Later in the interview, he emphasised the continual pressure to return to play as quickly as possible:

We never gave it enough time. We were always chasing our tail with every injury that I've ever had. You know, there's always been a cup semi-final, or there's been a quarter-final in the cup or there's another [international] game . . . you never give yourself time.

It should be noted that, while the player cited above was describing his own experience, his comment that 'you never give yourself enough time' has much more general applicability. We found nothing in our research which would lead us to disagree with the comment of Pat Nevin, the former Chelsea, Everton and Tranmere Rovers player, now at Kilmarnock, who has written that it is 'one of the things about "the English game" that players *almost always* come back too early' (Nevin and Sik, 1998: 84, italics in original). It should also be noted that, throughout the whole of the period to which the above interview relates, the player continued playing, often with the help of pain-killing injections.

Another player described how he had been given two pain-killing injections before every game from late December until the end of the season in

May in order to enable him to continue playing with a broken toe. A senior player told us that in the course of his career he had had no fewer than sixteen operations, but that, as is common in professional football, he had continued playing with most of these injuries and had postponed the surgery until after the end of the season. He explained that, during the latter parts of several seasons, he had been 'getting through' games with injuries to his knees, shoulder or groin. There was, he said, always an incentive to keep playing as the club was usually competing for a place in European competition for the following season, or was doing well in one of the cup competitions. One former player, now retired and suffering with severe arthritis, described how he frequently played while injured and, recalling one particular game in which he played with a pre-existing injury, proudly claimed to be the only captain who had limped to the centre circle to toss up with the opposing captain before the start of the game!

That doctors may be subject to pressure from players for the latter to return to play before they have fully recovered from injury does not, of itself, present any special ethical problems. Numerous studies of doctor–patient relationships have indicated that a normal characteristic of such relationships is the bargaining between doctor and patient over such things as the nature of the treatment which is prescribed, and the time period during which the patient may be excused from work or other social responsibilities. In this respect, the pressure which players are able to exert on club doctors may differ in degree, but probably not in kind, from the pressures which patients more generally are able to exert on their doctors, particularly in general (primary care) practice.[1] In this context we might note that, while players may return to play earlier than the doctor may feel is advisable, if the club doctor has provided the player with full information about any possible side effects of, for example, playing with pain-killing injections, as well as the possible long-term effects of playing with injury, then the doctor may legitimately feel that he (or, very rarely, she – almost all club doctors in English football are male) has properly discharged his responsibilities to the player-as-patient.

Some players indicated that their decision to continue playing through injury had been taken under just such conditions. For example, the player described above, who had tried to compensate for his knee injury and had suffered several other related injuries as a consequence, said of his decision to continue playing following the initial knee injury and the associated surgery: 'It was a calculated risk . . . they [the doctors and physios] left it to me. I knew the implications. [I had] many, many, second opinions, third opinions. . . . I was willing to take the risk.' In the above situation, the player concerned appears to have been given the information required to make a relatively informed decision about whether or not to try to play through his injuries. In some situations, however, relevant information about their medical condition may not be conveyed to players, or may even be deliberately withheld as a matter of policy. A particularly striking example of the latter was provided by a doctor who worked in a club which has only a small squad of players and in which, as a consequence, the pressures on players not to declare themselves unfit are particularly acute. The following is part of the interview with that doctor:

DOCTOR: I x-rayed somebody's tibia last season, as he had an injury there which could have been a stress fracture. I looked at the x-ray and saw an enormous smash on his ankle, a very old injury, but it was a very badly distorted, deranged ankle. He'd suffered a major fracture to his ankle, lower tibia at some stage, the whole thing had fallen half an inch. How can the guy play? So [the physiotherapist] said: 'Don't tell him. Don't tell the player that he's gone and broken his ankle otherwise he'll start being off.'

INTERVIEWER: The player didn't know he'd done it?

DOCTOR: No, and I haven't told the player that the x-ray showed a hell of a fracture from some stage in the past. I said to him: 'Tell me, have you ever somehow damaged your ankle, have you been having any pains in the last few seasons at all, just out of interest?' So I haven't told him.

INTERVIEWER: But [the physiotherapist] didn't want you to tell the player – why?

DOCTOR: Well, because he'll be off and will start asking what's wrong with it, and asking if he should retire now. And it decreases his value when you're sold. So it's a bit like a slave market.

INTERVIEWER: How did you feel about not giving the patient information about his own body?

DOCTOR: I was asking my friends what I should do. What happens when that player actually finds out in 10 years' time that that x-ray was taken by me 10 years before and I never told him, and he played on another 10 years, and has buggered his ankle so badly he can hardly stand on the bloody thing, with arthritis, which he will get?

Nevin and Sik (1998: 83) have recently suggested that managers may seek to withhold information from players about the extent of their injuries and may encourage their physiotherapists to do the same. This is, of course, not a problem which is specific to football; in the United States, there has been a good deal of litigation concerning informed consent in the field of sports medicine, with a central claim in many cases being that information was withheld – either negligently or intentionally – from athletes about the true nature of their condition, thereby preventing the athlete from making a properly informed choice about his/her fitness to return to play (Herbert and Herbert, 1991: 121). Such situations clearly raise serious ethical issues in terms of the relationship between the doctor/physiotherapist and the player-as-patient.

RELATIONSHIPS WITH MANAGERS

Ethical problems also arise in situations where club doctors and physio-therapists, in making clinical decisions about players' fitness to play, may be subject to pressure not only from players but also from managers. Such situations raise problems for two reasons. In the first place, it may be more difficult for the doctor or physiotherapist to resist pressure from the man-ager, for the manager is normally the most powerful person in the club, at least as far as the playing side of the club is concerned. In some respects, the situation of the manager is unusual in that, while the position of club manager is notoriously insecure – the average length of tenure of managers is only about two to three years – it is nevertheless the case that, while he is in post, the manager is very powerful. It is he who has the responsibility of selecting the team and, if he chooses, he can simply ignore the advice of the club medical staff concerning the fitness of players. If he does so, however, there may be adverse longer-term consequences for the health of the players though – and this is the second cause for concern – it is not the manager but the players who have to pay these health costs. Of course, in such situations the manager has to persuade the player to play but, as we noted above, players are normally keen to play whenever possible and they may also be subject to a variety of pressures from the manager to continue playing through injury. Younger players in particular, as well as less established players, may find it particularly difficult to resist such pressures.

The precise nature of the relationship between club medical staff and the club manager varies considerably from one club to another, and it may also change radically within a club when there is a change of manager, as happens quite frequently. The 'best practice' model – 'best' in the sense that medical staff are allowed a substantial degree of clinical autonomy in their treatment of players – is one in which managers are only minimally involved in the direct management of injuries, and where they accept the medical judgement of doctors and physiotherapists concerning the fitness of players. An example of such a 'good practice' model was described by one physiotherapist, who said that one of his former managers was 'brilliant' in relation to injured players. He said this manager had the following attitude toward injured players: 'If a player is not fit, fine, tell me and I will look at what else I have got to work with and we will work with them.'

The doctor at another club said: 'I've been very privileged to work with [the manager]. He does listen to what you say and he will actually support the decisions that you've made. . . . He's always been very supportive.' However, even where medical staff were not placed under any direct pres-sure from managers, they were all very conscious of the need to get players off the injured list as quickly as possible. For example, the doctor quoted immediately above added:

However, obviously he [the manager] wants players to play as soon as they can. . . . It's a very, very grey area really whether a player is fit because we have to push things to the limit in respect that if an injury normally takes four weeks to get better, we want them back in three. But if they break down and are out for another four, then we're in trouble. So we've got to not push things too hard so they break down but, on the other hand, a week out of playing is a very expensive thing for the club . . . so we're always on a tightrope really.

The physiotherapist at another club described his relationship with the manager as follows:

The manager . . . lets us get on with it. He's never once questioned our decision regarding injuries. If I went to [the manager] and said 'This player's not ready yet', he'll say 'When will he be ready?' . . . [The manager] says 'Look, my job's to manage the club, my coaches are there to coach. . . . You're here to rehab the players and treat the players. And he says: 'If I come into the medical room, I don't know what I'm talking about so I don't bother. I let you get on with the job and report to me how the players are.'

The doctor at this same club described his present and previous managers as 'very reasonable': 'If you say that a player is unfit, they will reluctantly accept that and allow them to remain on the list of injured players. They don't like it, and you can see they don't like it, but they accept it.' Nevertheless, and notwithstanding the fact that this doctor had worked with managers whom he described as 'reasonable', he was, like all the club doctors and physiotherapists, acutely aware of the strong and ever-present constraint to get players fit – or, at least, able to play – as quickly as possible, and it was in this context that he talked about what he called the 'unfortunate' need to make medical compromises:

As you know, in this game, there's always compromise, unfortunately. If a player says, 'Well, I want to get on', we say to the manager: 'He's not quite ready, he could do with another week or two weeks' rest and the manager is under pressure because he hasn't got a depth of staff to play or he's got other injuries and he needs this particular player, then sometimes we're overruled. . . . I mean, in those situations it would be very nice for us to keep them out of playing but they're more or less three-quarters of the way there, maybe almost there and they're needed. Sometimes we get away with it and they play and they're all right, sometimes we don't and it puts them back again.

A good example of the kind of compromise referred to by this doctor was provided by the management of an injury to one player at this club. The player concerned, who was described by the doctor as 'a very important player for the club', had had a continuing problem with a groin injury for much of the season. Though he had been unable to do anything other than light training, he had continued to play when injured for several games, but the injury limited his effectiveness as a player and eventually it was decided he required surgery. The doctor explained that:

> [the operation] should have put him out for something like six weeks. . . . He recovered very quickly and after about four weeks he said he felt quite good. The manager was short of a striker and brought him in one to two weeks before we wanted to bring him in . . . the manager was aware that although he seemed all right, [he] still wasn't training with the team or training very lightly with the team. The player said: 'Yeah, I feel OK, it feels a lot better, I feel I can cope.' . . . We said: Well, we'd like to give him another week to two weeks, but if the player is that keen . . . so he went and played and unfortunately within a week or two weeks it had broken down.

The player continued to play while injured, at the same time being given a course of weekly steroid injections, with a local anaesthetic injection before matches. This again proved unsuccessful, however, and the player required a second operation. Asked whether he was happy for the player to continue playing while having the course of steroid injections and the local anaesthetic injections, the doctor replied:

> Not entirely happy, but one was hopeful that they would settle it down . for him but knowing in the back of one's head that it probably wouldn't, and that what the player needed was a long rest. Asking for a long rest in football is asking a lot. But in all honesty . . . he needs a long rest. Now a long rest means, I don't know, maybe two or three months, by which time the season's over.

Thus even in those situations which would, at least within the context of football, probably be regarded as 'good practice' models – in the sense that doctors are working with managers whom they regard as 'reasonable', and where they do not feel under strong or direct pressure from managers – there is nevertheless a clearly felt need to make medical compromises which, ideally, they would prefer not to make. In other situations, however, managers may seek to have a much more direct involvement in the management of injuries and, in such situations, the clinical autonomy of doctors and physiotherapists may be much more directly threatened. In the course of the research, we came across several such cases.

One physiotherapist said that, at his present club, decisions about when injured players are fit to return to play are taken by the player, the doctor and himself. However, he added that the situation varies from club to club: 'if you're working at another club, to my working knowledge, it's not worked like that. You have managers who interfere left, right and centre.' As an example, he cited the following case of an injury to the goalkeeper at a club where he had formerly worked as the physiotherapist. The injury occurred in training on a Friday:

> He's done his lateral ligaments of his ankle, it's swollen, stiff, painful, he's strapped up, he's on crutches and sent home. And of course we've got no goalkeeper at that particular time the day before a game. So the manager's got till 5 o'clock to sign a goalkeeper to play the following day. Now, he's trying to make us bring the player back in to have a fitness test, which we were forced to do – I mean other than actually saying, 'No, I am not doing it', and losing your job possibly. We said we'd bring him in but told him the bloke wasn't fit to play. 'But if you want him to kick a ball, you want him to jump up and do whatever the fitness test involves, we will do it.' So sheepishly I brought the player back in, strapped him up and told him that whatever I did just fall about in agony, basically, so the fitness test would end quickly. And so he did that . . . and the manager accepted that, but there could have been further damage caused to the player . . . I know for a fact, I've done it myself, that you've been involved in those situations, when you know he's not fit and you shouldn't be doing that but you've been told to do it by the manager.

Another physiotherapist described a situation in which he, the club doctor and the player involved combined to resist an attempt by the manager to control the treatment of the player. The club concerned were in a cup semi-final and a key player was injured, but wanted to play. The manager claimed that, at his previous club, the use of a pain-killing injection had proved effective in what he regarded as a similar case, and he wanted the player to have a pain-killing injection. However, the player preferred to play with, rather than to suppress, the pain, and this was also the course of action preferred by the physiotherapist. The latter explained:

> Rather than argue the situation with the manager who, you know, he's great as regards football but not so good when it comes to injuries, rather than argue about it, I said 'Yeah, he can have a pain-killing injection'. And then I go to the doctor and say: 'The manager wants this player to have a pain-killing injection but I'd prefer you not to do it.' And it was easier that way. The player didn't have the pain-killing injection, but the manager thought he had had it, the player played and no one was any the wiser. . . . There sometimes can be a situation where you know you're right, but rather than have a confrontation, you say, 'Yeah, of course he's had the injection' . . . it's easier to do it that way. And everybody's happy then.

In this case, the physiotherapist and club doctor were able to maintain the integrity of their clinical practice, though they had deliberately to deceive the manager in order to do so. In other situations, however, it proved more difficult to resist the involvement of managers in medical decision-making.

One such situation was described by the physiotherapist, cited earlier, who described one of his former managers as 'brilliant', but who subsequently worked under a different manager who sought to intervene in relation to injured players, and to take key aspects of the management of injured players out of the hands of the physiotherapist. This physiotherapist explained:

> We had a player who had sprained his ankle and we were going to do a fitness test on him before he played. So I said to this player: 'Fine, I'll see you at 2.30 and we'll do the fitness test and then the coach is leaving at 3.30.' . . . I told the manager this was what we were doing and he said 'Fine'. He then went and saw the player and said, 'We'll do the fitness test at 1.30', so when I got to the ground at 2.30, he, the manager, had done the fitness test with the player, talked him into playing and decided that was it.

The physiotherapist said that he had been 'very uneasy' about what had happened, and went on to describe another incident with the same manager:

> We signed a player who had an injury at the time he was signed. This was understood, the paperwork went through, he had got a thigh strain. We were playing a game on New Year's Day, so we stayed overnight, New Year's Eve, in a hotel. We had agreed that over the Christmas period he was not going to play. We were going to get him right on this thigh strain. . . . I woke up in the morning and looked out of my bedroom window and there was this player having a fitness test on a piece of waste ground with the manager and the two coaches. I went down and said, 'What's happening? I thought we'd agreed he was not playing.'
>
> [The manager said] 'I'm the manager. If you are not happy, the train station is round the corner, get on the train and go home.'
>
> Well, I sort of said, 'I'm not saying that, but I thought we'd agreed that this player was not fit.' He actually survived forty minutes of the game and had to come off . . . because he had aggravated the thigh strain.

This physiotherapist suggested that, in such situations, club medical staff have two options. The first of these was that 'if you bite your tongue, there will come a . . . time when that manager will then inevitably move on anyway. I reckon they probably have a three-year life-span at a club.' Asked what happened if the club doctor or physiotherapist did not bite their tongue, he replied:

> Then he will either get rid of you or you will be forced to leave. . . . What happened in my case . . . was the very day before pre-season training started. He just called me into the office and said, 'I am not comfortable with the situation we have here. You want to be in charge of the treatment room, to treat the injured players your way, and I am not comfortable with that.' To which I said, 'What you are saying is that you want to be physiotherapist as well as manager . . . and I cannot work that way.' He said, 'I think we are going to have to let you go.' He used the classic phrase, 'We've got to let you go. I don't want you to work here any more.' . . . I then said, 'Have you spoken to the club's doctors about this?' Because I had a very good working relationship with the club's doctors. And he said, 'No. I am the manager of this football club and I make the decisions.' To which I said something in the terms of 'Well, f*** you,' and I got up and walked out. I sued the club through the Chartered Society of Physiotherapists because obviously . . . it was unfair dismissal and I got compensation. They settled out of court. For a sum which . . . although it was quite nice, would be quite miniscule in the overall budget of the football club.

A not dissimilar situation was described by the club doctor who said that he was 'privileged' to work with his current manager but who, like the physiotherapist referred to above, had had a difficult relationship with his previous manager, a relationship which the doctor described as 'tainted'. He explained:

> I think my experience with him was perhaps tainted by my own inexperience when I first joined the club. . . .. I'm older and wiser now . . . when you come into this sort of establishment it's very easy to be over-powered by the environment in which you're working and by the personalities and I found that very difficult . . . in that respect [the current manager] is a very different personality and I have a much closer working relationship with him than I ever did with [the previous manager].

Asked to explain in what respects his relationship with the previous manager was tainted, he said – with a very diplomatic choice of words – that 'perhaps he was a bit more forceful in his thoughts to injured players'. He went on to explain that when he had become team doctor a few years previously, the club had not had a qualified (that is, chartered) physiotherapist on the staff and, as a consequence:

I was a single voice and if I disagreed with what was going on, then there were a lot more people around at that time to perhaps try to persuade me to change my mind . . . that the players were fit. . . . All I could say in those situations [was that] players were not . . . fit and they [the managerial team] would then have to take the consequences of their playing. The majority of them would then break down and they would be out for a lot longer. . . . And then the situation arose where I began to find it difficult to continue in my capacity here. My recommendations were not being considered.

It was at this time that the manager, who had not been successful in terms of results on the field, left the club; the doctor indicated that, had the manager not left the club, then he, the doctor, might well have done so.

Perhaps the most remarkable situation was at one club where the senior player at the club described how the current manager took a particularly 'hard line' towards injured players and frequently made them train, even when injured, and against the advice of the club physiotherapists. This approach eventually resulted in the physiotherapists and the club doctor combining against the club manager to demand a change in the system of medical care which removed the manager entirely from all decisions about the injury status and the fitness of players to train or play. The player concerned said that training sessions began with a 20-minute run, and the manager's view was that 'if players could stand . . . he wanted them out running'. He cited an example of a player who had cracked a rib in a first team game the previous day, who was in considerable pain and was unable to breathe properly, but who was nevertheless required to train. The player also described an incident involving himself, the physiotherapist and the manager. Although the player had a painful toe injury, he had continued to train and play. Following the player's rest day (Monday), the toe had improved considerably as a result of the rest:

By Monday night, the toe was a heck of a lot better. . . . On Tuesday, I said to the physio: 'The toe's a lot better. I think another day today without kicking a ball around or having physical contact [and] I'll be able to train for the rest of the week, fully fit, without pain. . . . At that stage, the manager walked in and the physio said, 'I don't think [the player] should train today' and the manager went mad. He turned round and had a right go at the physio and a right go at me and said, 'You're training.' And that's to me, the most senior player here.

Incidents of this kind eventually led the physiotherapists and the club doctor to demand a radical change in the system of dealing with injured players. The following is part of the transcript of the interview with this player, who described the new system, and how it had come about:

PLAYER: That came about because of all the problems we had with the manager. . . . He was overriding [the physiotherapists] and saying, 'He's training. He's training. He's training.' . . . The physios here and the doctor together talked a lot about it because they were very unhappy. . . . He didn't treat them with respect.
INTERVIEWER: The doctor and physios?
PLAYER: The physios especially. He would overrule them.
INTERVIEWER: So the physios and the club doctor got together?
PLAYER: Yes. They had discussions, and I was fuming with the physios and the doctor after I was made to train with my toes that day.

The medical staff made their grievances known – presumably to the club chairman, though this was not entirely clear from the interview – and as a consequence, a number of radical changes were made. The doctor was asked to come into the club on a full-time basis (he had previously been part-time), and decisions about players' fitness were left exclusively in the hands of the club doctor:

> The whole thing has changed here. . . . The club doctor is totally in control as far as players' injuries [are concerned]. On the Monday after a game on Saturday, if a player's got an injury and the doctor feels he cannot train, he gives a list to the manager. So the manager doesn't go to him and discuss which players will train – he [the doctor] will give him a list and say, 'That's it. Those players definitely are not training,' so the manager cannot overrule the club doctor.

The player emphasised, in relation to the role of the club doctor in the new structure, that 'Whatever he says goes, and he is totally concerned with the players' welfare, and the best for the players, and no one on the footballing side of the club can come across and tell him any different.' Significantly, the player indicated that the players at the club were much happier with the new structure, and he added that 'We're going the way the game should be going.'

It is clear from the research reported here that an ever-present constraint on club doctors and physiotherapists is the perceived need to get players playing again as quickly as possible after injury and that all club medical staff are, without exception, aware of and feel the need to respond to this constraint. However, it is important to emphasise that the precise nature, as well as the strength, of this constraint varies considerably from one club to another. In some situations – for example, where managers take a relatively 'hands-off' approach towards the management of injuries – club doctors and physiotherapists may be allowed a significant degree of professional autonomy in their relationship with the player-as-patient. However, in other situations – and particularly where the manager insists on being involved in the management of injuries – their professional autonomy may be severely restricted, and club doctors and physiotherapists may find themselves involved in situations in which players are regularly returned to play before they are medically fit to do so. Under these conditions, club doctors and physiotherapists may simply adapt to and accept the situation, or they may come to feel that their professional autonomy has been so circumscribed that they are unable to do their job in what they consider a properly professional manner. In the latter situation, doctors and physiotherapists are likely to find themselves in recurring conflict with the manager, and this may result in any one of several outcomes. The doctor or physiotherapist may be dismissed from the club. They may become disillusioned and leave football either for another sport or to return to general practice. More rarely, as in the situation described above, the club doctor and physiotherapists may demand a change in the structure which limits the manager's involvement and increases their own professional autonomy in the management of injuries.

CONFIDENTIALITY IN THE DOCTOR–PATIENT RELATIONSHIP

Another area which was probed in the interviews with club doctors and physiotherapists related to the way in which they dealt with information about a player which, in other medical contexts, would normally be treated confidentially. Do the normal rules governing confidentiality within the doctor–patient relationship apply within the football club? What information about players is communicated to the team manager? Does it include information which the manager might want, but which would normally be considered confidential to the doctor–patient relationship, such as information relating to a player's life-style? And what do club medical staff do if they discover that a player has a problem in relation to excessive alcohol consumption or that a player is illegally using drugs? Are such problems handled within the confidentiality of the professional–patient relationship, or do doctors and physiotherapists feel that, since they are employed by the club, they are under an obligation to inform the manager about aspects of a player's life-style which may affect their performance?

Given the variation in relationships between doctors, physiotherapists and managers from one club to another, it is perhaps not surprising that there are considerable variations in terms of both the amount and the kind of information about players which doctors and physiotherapists pass on to managers. Most club doctors are general practitioners – of the fifty-eight who completed the questionnaire, forty-two indicated that general practice is their primary employment – and many seek, in so far as it is possible to do so, to apply the rules governing confidentiality in general practice to their practice within the football club. Asked about how issues involving patient confidentiality were best dealt with, one doctor replied:

I find this one very difficult because coming from a background in general practice obviously anything between a patient and myself is confidential, unless it's an absolutely extreme case. . . . Whereas inside a football club, it seems like everybody else thinks they have the right to know what's going on before the player does and when I have had disagreements with managers it's usually been around this issue. There's also the question of the press, and I think that the right of confidentiality still holds. I don't see why it should be different because you're in a football club.

Asked about the appropriate way to handle a situation in which a player was drinking heavily, this doctor said:

I certainly wouldn't tell the physio or the manager or the board unless he said that it was all right for me to do so. I don't think he would. [I would] see whether he would let me get the PFA [Professional Footballers Association] involved, or where he would accept help, just like in general practice . . . it's the same with drugs . . . I wouldn't tell the manager unless he told me to. I would consider that as a breach of my confidentiality if I told. I mean, that has happened to me [a player using drugs] and I have dealt with it like I would any patient.

This doctor summed up the problem of dual loyalties – to the club as employer and to the player-as-patient – in the following way:

I've always considered myself the players' doctor. You know, it is more difficult because I am employed by the club – fortunately I haven't had the situation where the club would be at risk, but it would make it more difficult. But I would always try to get the player's consent before I involved anybody else.

Another doctor took a broadly similar line in relation to patient confidentiality. Asked about the best way to deal with a situation in which a player confided that he was drinking heavily, this doctor replied:

We would sit down and have a talk about it. I have a very strong feeling about confidentiality with the players. If I tell somebody that they're telling me something in confidence then it doesn't go any further, and I'm sure there are things that I'll probably carry to my grave that people have told me as players that I wouldn't say to anybody unless they said, 'Yes, OK, I'm happy to talk about it.' So I would try to sort out with them what to do, between the two of us.

This doctor indicated that he would encourage the player to talk to the manager, but that if the player did not wish the manager to know, then he could not pass on that information:

> I can't tell the manager. . . . I think players, in order to come to you with confidences, have to be very sure that they can really trust you because clubs are places where that kind of thing goes around in a flash and sometimes physios aren't as discreet as they should be about that kind of thing, and I see my role as being somebody who people can trust, things will go no further.

Whereas most doctors sought to apply within the club the same rules governing confidentiality that they applied in general practice, one doctor differentiated very clearly between his role as an occupational physician for the club and his role as personal physician to the players. He said that, in the former role,

> in respect of what I do with [the players], I share the information with their employer. I also have a personal physician role which means that things that are said between the two of us are entirely confidential and I will not discuss them at all with anyone else unless I have their per-mission . . . if there is information that's coming to me that I feel com-promises the position of the club, compromises the position of the team, that compromises the well-being of the club, I will say to them: 'Right. You've told me this now. This is something that I feel should be shared with the manager . . . and if you don't want me to share it, don't go into this any further. You're going to have to discuss this with somebody different.' It's always been agreed between us that there are two roles that I have. It's not like a normal doctor–patient relationship.

One of the doctors cited above suggested that 'sometimes physios aren't as discreet as they should be', and it is certainly the case that there was con-siderable variation between physiotherapists in terms of how they dealt with issues involving confidentiality. It might be argued that, in relation to such issues, physiotherapists have a particular ethical responsibility, because, as one experienced physiotherapist pointed out, physiotherapists – perhaps more so than doctors, most of whom work only part-time at the club – often get to know a great deal about a player's private life:

> I could tell you more about any player in the football club than the manager, chairman, coach together, because you work one-to-one with them. You get to know, not just the problems themselves, but the families that they have, the children . . . everything about them because

you spend time with them and, you know, you're not prying, you're just asking questions all the time.

This particular physiotherapist was clearly aware of his responsibilities to the club – he said that, if a player had a problem which was affecting the team, then 'it's better that the manager knew' – but he emphasised, in particular, his responsibilities to the players and, in this context, he adopted a position in relation to confidentiality which was not very far removed from that expressed by several doctors. He said, for example, that normally he would not tell the manager if a player was drinking excessively ('a manager's got enough to do without worrying about people who drink') or if a player was using 'social' drugs such as marijuana:

> I know an awful lot of things about players that needn't go any further. It's important it doesn't go any further . . . if you find something out, or the player tells you something in confidence and they ask you not to tell anyone, then you keep that confidence . . . they tell you an awful lot in confidence and if you went running to the manager with everything then you wouldn't probably find these things out.

A player at another club described how the physiotherapist not only did not tell the manager that a particular player was drinking heavily, but actually sought – as this player put it – to 'protect' the player from the manager:

> I used to get changed next to [the player] and . . . at times when he was a bit worse for wear he'd come into the treatment room and [the physio] would protect him and maybe say he'd got a sore so-and-so and he couldn't train that day. Or sometimes, if [the player] had to go out training he would call him back over and say that there's a telephone call or whatever to get him out early. He would protect him that way.

Other physiotherapists, however, appeared to see their primary responsibility as being towards the club and to the manager, and some of these expressed a greater readiness to pass on information. Thus one physiotherapist, asked what information he passed on to the manager, explained, without any further prompting: 'Most physios know more about their staff than anybody in the club, and if it was beneficial that the manager should know [something] – or essential that the manager should know – then I would tell him.'

Asked whether he would inform the manager if a player was drinking heavily, he replied:

> The problem is that I'm employed by the football club. I'm employed by the manager and I'm supposed to be working with him and if I

withhold information which he thinks he should have, then he would say that I wasn't working for the club or for him, so it puts me in a difficult position. . . . If I didn't divulge what I knew and then it came out afterwords, we're in hot water. . . . If I thought it was beneficial to the club . . . that he should know, then I would say.

Another physiotherapist who placed particular emphasis on his responsibility to the club said:

I think if [a player's] breaking the law, ie taking drugs, whether performance-enhancing or whether they were just recreational, I think it's my duty to tell the football club. I work for the football club. And the players know where I sit. I'm not a player. I don't know who they've shagged, I don't know what they've drunk and I don't want to know what substances they're taking. They can do what the f*** they want. If they tell me, it will go back. And the players know that.

If they come to me confidentially and they're breaking the law, it will go back. If they're not breaking the law – I don't mind if they're out night-clubbing twice a week, I'm not judge and jury – but if the performance on the pitch . . . [if] they're not performing well or they're getting muscular irritations, and I know their life-style's all over the place . . . I would go to the manager and say, 'Look, his life-style is in a right mess.'

Given the considerable variation in terms of the way in which physiotherapists – and also, to some extent, doctors – deal with issues involving confidentiality, it is perhaps not surprising that some players expressed considerable reservations about revealing confidential information to club medical staff. One player, asked whether he would be happy to discuss a confidential matter with the club doctor or physiotherapist, answered with an emphatic 'No'. He explained:

Things get back. Things get back all the time. You can't say anything at a football club to anyone because basically they get back. There is no such thing as confidentiality at a football club. I found that out . . . something got back to a manager that I had said to a doctor. . . . Well, it should be confidential . . . it was something [non-medical] I commented on . . . and it came straight back which I thought was a bit out of order. . . . No, I wouldn't have confidence in anyone.

One ex-player, asked if confidential information about players was ever passed on by the physiotherapist, said:

I think maybe that happened at [the club] sometimes, where you'd say So-and-so is the gaffer's eyes and ears . . . in the treatment room. I think the manager does have certain members of his staff to keep a listen out to what players are saying in the treatment room . . . word quickly gets round who you should be careful of saying things to . . . players do tend to open their hearts out in there when they are on a bed for half an hour or more, or under a machine, and they just talk and things come out and, you know, really if the physio is hearing that type of stuff it should be for his ears only and really shouldn't go any further.

I mean . . . if he was a normal physio [and] he'd got a private practice, of course he wouldn't mention things his patients had said. It is a slightly different situation in a football club . . . because the manager's his boss and if the manager asks him something he might feel duty bound to tell him. . . . So, with somebody in that position, it's not just a question of treating [the players] and whatever they say stays there.

Another senior player indicated that a particular cause for concern was where a new manager came to the club and brought with him his own 'backroom staff', including the physiotherapist, from a previous club: 'When a manager brings in his own people, that is where there is concern because this person is relying on the manager for his job and he's not going to go against the manager.' He indicated that, under a previous manager: 'Anything that was said in the physio's room went straight back to the manager. The manager had a huge input, even in the physio's room.' Players, he said, joked about this situation, but were very careful about what they said in the physiotherapist's room.

It was not, however, just in relation to physiotherapists that players expressed reservations about the degree to which information which they provided would be held in confidence, for some players also expressed reservations in this regard about club doctors, and one player provided a striking example of unprofessional conduct on the part of the club doctor.

In this incident the club doctor was clearly acting as an agent on behalf of the club, and used confidential medical information about a player to advance the interests of the club over and against those of the player. The player described what happened as follows:

The club doctor, in my opinion, totally compromised his situation. I'd had [an operation] and my contract was up at the end of the season. . . . I was approached by [three leading English clubs], Atlético Madrid and Lyon. Three or four weeks later, when I was talking to these clubs, I got summoned to the club doctor's . . . the club doctor called me and said would I go round to his house. . . . I arrived there and he was there with the surgeon who did my operation . . . the surgeon wasn't particularly happy about being there. He [the club doctor] said, 'You're thinking about leaving the club this summer?' I said 'Yes'. He said, 'Well, the surgeon has told us that you've only got another year at the most to play football. If we make that common knowledge, no club in the world would pay millions of pounds for you.' I said, 'Well, what are you telling me?' He said, 'Well, if you're thinking of leaving the club and we made that common knowledge, then . . . no one would buy you.' So . . . I ended up agreeing a new deal to stay.

The incident described by the player had taken place several years previously and, at the time of the interview, the player was still playing for the same club. The player said that he thought the club doctor was probably acting under great pressure, not in this case from the manager but from the club chairman, but he added that this did not excuse the doctor's behaviour: 'He was probably under great pressure to do that, but he's done wrong.'

CONCLUSION

As we have seen, there is very considerable variation in the roles of the club doctor and the club physiotherapist from one club to another, and these roles may also change radically within a club when there is a change of manager. Underlying these variations is the fact that, in relation to clinical decision-making, there appears to be no standardised framework within professional football in terms of which the respective rights and responsibilities of club doctor, physiotherapist and manager are defined. Rather, these relationships are negotiated individually between the participants involved on a club-by-club basis.

The absence of a clearly defined role for club doctors and physiotherapists is, in terms of the quality of medical care available to players, a matter of some concern. In some situations, doctors and physiotherapists may be allowed a substantial degree of clinical autonomy in relation to the management of players' injuries, and in terms of decision-making about players' fitness to play. However, in other situations the manager may – despite his lack of any qualifications in medicine or physiotherapy – insist on being involved in clinical decisions and, given the relatively powerful position of the manager within the club, it may be difficult for doctors and physiotherapists to resist what some of them certainly see as 'interference' by managers. In extreme situations, as we have seen, the manager may ignore the advice of, or simply overrule, his club doctor or physiotherapist. It is difficult to see how such conditions can be conducive to good clinical decision-making, and it is unlikely that they are in the best long-term interests of the players' health.

Similarly, there is considerable variation from club to club in terms of the amount, and kind, of information about players which is communicated to the manager by doctors and physiotherapists. In some clubs medical staff try to operate more or less on the basis of the rules governing confidentiality which apply in general practice, whereas in other clubs medical staff may be rather more ready to pass on personal information about players and, in some cases, there are grounds for concern about the ethicality of such behaviour.

The absence of any clear framework for defining and regulating the role of club doctors is strikingly pointed up by the fact that, of the fifty-eight doctors who completed the questionnaire in this study, only six had a written job description. An additional problem which inhibits the development of a common framework of practice is that there is relatively little contact between club doctors. Most club doctors work full-time in general practice, and do not normally travel with the team to away matches, the convention being that the doctor of the home club deals with any serious medical emergencies which may arise. However, the fact that most club doctors have relatively little contact with their colleagues in other clubs means that they have relatively few opportunities to discuss common problems in the management of injuries and that they also have little knowledge about the precise conditions under which their colleagues in other clubs work. As a consequence there has been within professional football no attempt either to identify, or to disseminate, a 'good practice' model in relation to the role of either the club doctor or the club physiotherapist. It is hoped that the research reported in this chapter will, by highlighting the need for a 'good practice' model, make some contribution towards improving the quality of medical care available to professional footballers and, by implication, for other professional and elite sportspeople.

Part II
Sport and drugs

5 Doping in sport
Problems of involvement and detachment

In some respects, public attitudes towards drug use appear curiously
ambivalent for, though most people would strongly deprecate both the use
of performance-enhancing drugs in sport and 'drug abuse' within the wider
society, it is almost certainly the case that, in modern western societies, we
have come to be more dependent on the use of prescribed drugs than at
any previous time in history. As we shall see in Chapter 7, the increasingly
widespread acceptance of drugs in everyday life provides an essential part
of the backcloth for understanding the use of drugs in sport.

Some aspects of the ambivalence surrounding public attitudes towards
drug use – and in particular towards drug use in sport – are occasionally
brought into very sharp focus. In sport, the use of drugs to improve performance is not only prohibited under the rules of the International Olympic
Committee (IOC) and of most sports governing bodies, but it is also a practice which normally calls forth the strongest public condemnation, often
coupled with a strong sense of moral outrage and with calls for severe
punishments for those found guilty of a doping offence. However, such
public condemnation and the associated moral outrage can, on occasions,
be strangely muted. Consider, for example, the case of Mark McGwire
who, in September 1998, set a new record for the number of home runs
scored in baseball in a single season. It is difficult to overemphasise the
significance of McGwire's achievement within the context of sport in the
United States. The home run record is arguably the most significant record
in American sport and, as McGwire approached the record, news of his
latest home run frequently displaced the unfolding story of the relationship
between President Clinton and Monica Lewinsky as the top story on TV
newscasts across the United States. Writing in the *San Francisco Chronicle*
(13 September 1998), Joan Ryan described how she watched on television
as McGwire hit his record-setting home run as two children from next
door played in her house. Ryan's evocation of the excited atmosphere of
triumphal record-breaking and hero worship is worth quoting at length:

> With one gorgeous swing in the fourth inning, McGwire sent the
> ball over the left-field fence. I punched the volume way up. 'Look!

He did it!' I said in a voice that must have alarmed the two children. I sounded as if I either might cry or start tossing furniture.

'What?' the girl said.

'McGwire broke the home run record!'

The roar of the crowd 1,700 miles away in St Louis thundered through my living room. . . .

McGwire skipped to the first base like a Little Leaguer, leaping and punching the air, so swept away he had to double back to touch the bag. The Cub's first baseman slapped him gently on the backside as he passed.

At home plate, McGwire scooped up his 10-year-old son and kissed him on the lips. Teammates poured from the dugout to envelop him.

But soon McGwire broke away to climb into the stands and embrace the children of the man whose record he had just eclipsed. Then he took a microphone and thanked his fans, his team, his family and his God.

I had known McGwire during his days with the Oakland A's, and I never thought of him as particularly charming or humble, eloquent or joyful. But now he was all those. He was Paul Bunyon and George Bailey.

I understood that it was not just the historic record that held me to the television set. It was the uncommon joy of watching a man rise so magnificently to the occasion.

In a year when our most powerful men have been diminished by their lack of courage and class, McGwire played his role as if scripted by Steven Spielberg. . . .

McGwire's dignity and humility lifted everyone around him. Fans who caught his home run balls returned them to McGwire rather than cash in with collectors. McGwire's rivals repaid his respect in kind. . . . The strength of McGwire's character got people to deliver the best in themselves.

I looked at the two children from next door. . . . They'll know baseball only in the era of musical-chair rosters and autograph auctions. They'll hear the old-timers, even as we did growing up, talk wistfully about the good old days, when heroes were heroes and the game was pure.

'These', I said out loud, 'are those days.'

A few weeks before he broke the record, McGwire publicly admitted that he had been taking regular doses of androstenedione, an anabolic steroid which is on the list of drugs banned by the International Olympic Committee.[1] There is, however, nothing in Ryan's writing to suggest, or even to hint, that McGwire might have behaved in an unsporting or unethical manner, or that his record might have been tarnished in even the slightest way by his use of steroids. Rather, McGwire is held up as a model of 'dignity and humility', as a man who loves his family and his God, who is noteworthy for his 'strength of character' and for his ability 'to rise so magnificently to the occasion'. We are even told that McGwire – the anabolic steroid-using McGwire – symbolises 'the good old days, when heroes were heroes and the game was pure'. One might ask how different the reaction of journalists such as Ryan might – no, certainly would – have been had the drug-using athlete in question been not a national American sporting hero like McGwire but, for example, a Soviet Olympic gold medallist at the height of the Cold War.

We should not, however, be surprised that public attitudes towards the use of drugs are not entirely consistent, for such inconsistencies are frequently expressed in attitudes relating to issues, such as the use of drugs, which arouse strong emotions and which, as a consequence, frequently generate rather more heat than light. Indeed, this is one of the reasons why, when studying such phenomena, we should seek strenuously to study them in as detached a manner as possible.

The highly emotive and heavily value-laden character of much of the debate about the use of drugs in sport has been noted by Coakley (1998a), who has made a useful contribution to our understanding of deviance, including drug use, in sport (though, for some criticisms of Coakley's work, see Chapter 7). Coakley has pointed out that journalists, policymakers and others connected with sports and sport organisations frequently 'express extreme disappointment about what they see as the erosion of values in contemporary sports'. Coakley describes what he calls the 'loss of values' analysis as follows:

> In the eyes of these men [*sic*], today's sports lack the moral purity that characterized sports in times past, and today's athletes lack the moral character possessed by athletes in times past. These men recount memories of a time when, they believe, sports were governed by a commitment to sportsmanship, and athletes played purely because they loved the game. And as they recount these memories, they grieve what they see as the loss of this purity and commitment.
>
> As they grieve, these men often use their power and influence to call for more rules and regulations in sports, for tougher policing of athletes, for more agents of social control, more testing, more surveillance, stricter sanctions – anything that will rid sports of the 'bad apples' who are spoiling things for everyone.
>
> (Coakley, 1998a: 111)

As Coakley points out, the values of those who argue this way are evident not only in that such views are premised on the idea that sport has an 'essential' nature but also in that they reflect a highly romanticised notion of the past. They ignore, for example, the fact that sports in the past have frequently been characterised by systematic racism and sexism as well as a form of class-based discrimination which excluded those from the lower social classes from full participation in sport.

Coakley notes that value-laden analyses of this kind are not confined to journalists, policy-makers and others who are involved practically in sport, but may also be found in segments of the academic literature where what is offered as scientific analysis is sometimes heavily imbued with the author's own non-scientific values. This is particularly notable, for example, in what Coakley elsewhere (1998b) has called the 'absolutist' or the 'it's either right or wrong' approach. He writes:

> Despite the confusion created by this absolutist approach, most people use it to discuss deviance in sports. When the behaviors of athletes, coaches, management, or spectators do not contribute to what an individual considers to be the ideals of sports, that individual identifies those behaviors as deviant. In other words, 'it's either right or wrong'. And when it's wrong, the behavior and the person who engages in it are seen as problems.
>
> This is the traditional structural-functionalist approach to deviance, and it is not very effective in producing an understanding of deviant behavior or in formulating programs to control deviance. It assumes that existing value systems and rules are absolutely right and should be accepted the way they are, so that the social order is not threatened. This leads to a 'law-and-order' orientation emphasizing that the only way to establish social control is through four strategies: establishing more rules, making rules more strict and inflexible, developing a more comprehensive system of detecting and punishing rule violators, and making everyone more aware of the rules and what happens to those who don't follow them.
>
> This approach also leads to the idea that people violate rules only because they lack moral character, intelligence, or sanity, and that good, normal, healthy people wouldn't be so foolish as to violate rules.
>
> (Coakley, 1998b: 148–9)

Coakley reiterates that such an approach 'does little to help us understand much of the deviance in sport, and it provides a poor basis for developing programs to control deviance in sport' (1998b: 149). This is not altogether surprising, for such an approach tells us as much about those who adopt it – and in particular their own values and prejudices about sport – as it does about the sporting phenomena which they claim to be investigating.

In general, it is reasonable to suggest that, in so far as we are able to put our own values – at least temporarily – to one side, to stand back and to analyse social phenomena in a relatively detached way, then we are more likely to generate explanations which have a high degree of what Elias (1987) called 'reality congruence' or 'reality adequacy'. By contrast, in so far as our orientation to our studies is characterised by a relative lack of detachment, by a high degree of commitment to non-scientific values and by a high level of emotional involvement, then we are more likely to end up by allocating praise or blame rather than enhancing our level of understanding. This is why Elias suggested that we should seek to resolve practical problems, such as the use of drugs in sport, not directly, but by means of a detour, which he described as a 'detour *via* detachment'. What this means is not that we should cease to be concerned about solving practical problems which concern us but that, at least for the duration of the research, we try, as sociologists, to put these practical and personal concerns to one side, in order that we can study the relevant processes in as detached a manner as possible. As was noted in the Introduction to this book, a relatively detached analysis is more likely to result in a relatively realistic analysis of the situation. This in turn will provide a more adequate basis for the formulation of relevant policy. In contrast, policies formulated in a highly emotionally charged situation, and where the policy-makers feel under political or other pressure to 'do something' – for example, where sporting bodies are under pressure to 'take strong action' following a major doping scandal – are rather less likely to be based on a cool, calm and reflective (in short, a relatively detached) examination of the situation.

It is important to note that while a relatively detached analysis of this kind is likely to generate findings which offer a more realistic basis for the formulation of policy, such an analysis might also generate findings which may be uncomfortable for some of the governing bodies in sport; for example by casting doubt on the wisdom of existing policies, or by suggesting that existing policies – such as the 'law and order approach' to doping, which tends to be most generally adopted – may have unintended, and what may be held to be undesirable, consequences. Thus it would be quite wrong to assume that a relatively detached analysis would necessarily validate the actions and policies of those who would claim to be the upholders of 'morality', even in situations such as the use of drugs, where the moral issues might, at least at first sight, seem to be relatively clear cut.

This point may be illustrated by reference to the following example. When athletes take the decision to use performance-enhancing drugs, they, together with their advisers, will bear in mind a number of considerations, including the effectiveness of different kinds of drugs in boosting performance, the relative health dangers associated with different drugs and the ease with which different drugs can be detected. Inevitably, the severe penalties which normally follow detection mean that athletes and their advisers, when considering which drug to use, are constrained to place greater importance on the detectability rather than on the relative safety of different drugs. This has given rise to what Dr Robert Voy, a former Chief Medical Officer for the US Olympic Committee, has described as a 'sad paradox'.

Writing in 1991, Voy noted that the oil-based esters of nandrolone, or 19-nortesterone, because of their slow release process, probably had the fewest dangerous side effects of the three forms of anabolic-androgenic steroids (AAS). He also noted that, because these drugs do not have to be cleared first through the liver, they do not create the risks of liver disease run by taking oral anabolic-androgenic steroids. He went on to point out:

> A sad paradox is that after drug testers and sport federations world-wide have worked so hard to eliminate the AAS problem because of the potential health risks to athletes, we have in a sense steered the athletes toward more dangerous drugs. The types of drug testing programs used by doping control authorities today have unintentionally created a greater health danger in that athletes are now using the shorter acting, more toxic forms of drugs to avoid detection. Athletes have stopped using nandrolone, which in relative terms is a safe AAS, and are now using the more dangerous orally active forms of AAS, the C-17 alkyl derivatives. In addition, many have gone to using the third, and most dangerous, type of anabolic-androgenic steroids: the esters of testosterone.
>
> (1991: 19)

In other words, the implementation of a policy which, as we will see in Chapter 6, is justified partly in terms of a desire to protect the health of athletes has, paradoxically, had the effect of constraining athletes to place more importance on the detectability of drugs and less importance on their safety. As a consequence, it has constrained athletes to use drugs which are likely to be more, rather than less, damaging to their health. It is reasonable to suppose that this outcome was not intended by those responsible for developing anti-doping policies in sports and that this is not a consequence which they welcome.[2] However, as has been argued elsewhere (Dopson and Waddington, 1996), the process of formulating and implementing policy is a complex one which, almost inevitably, has consequences that are not only unplanned but that, in many cases, may be held to be undesirable.

To make this point, and to draw attention to the fact that anti-doping policies may have some consequences which are the very reverse of those which were intended by the policy-makers, is not to argue that existing anti-doping policies are wrong. It does, however, indicate that we should not simply assume, ostrich-like, that policies necessarily have only those consequences which they were intended to have and no others, and that we should be sufficiently open-minded to recognise that some of the consequences may actually be the opposite of what was intended. Armed with a relatively detached analysis of the kind proposed here, we will then be in a better position to judge whether we should continue with existing policies, or whether those policies need modifying. In this connection, it is worth

reminding ourselves that, as Elias pointed out, there is an important difference between sociological detachment and ideological involvement and
that the proper task of sociologists is not to establish the validity of a pre-
conceived idea about how societies – or, one might add, a particular seg-
ment of society such as sport – *ought* to be ordered. Rather, the proper
task of sociologists is 'to find connections between particular social events,
how their sequence can actually be explained, and what help sociological
theories can offer in explaining and determining the trend of social
problems – and, last but not least, in providing practical solutions to them'
(Elias, 1978a: 153). Elias noted that to adopt this approach in our work
requires a special effort of detachment. Such an effort may not be easy to
make, especially in relation to such an emotive issue as drugs, but it is an
effort which, both in terms of improved understanding and of responding
more effectively to the policy issues involved, is one well worth making.

6 The emergence of doping as a problem in modern sport

Writing in the *Guardian* about the doping revelations in the 1998 Tour de France, Richard Williams correctly pointed out that doping is 'generally felt to be the worst of sporting crimes' (*Guardian*, 1 August 1998). This view of the seriousness of doping as an offence is widely shared by many people, both inside and outside sport. For example, the former Olympic gold medallist Sebastian Coe stated that: 'We consider this [doping] to be the most shameful abuse of the Olympic ideal: we call for the life ban of offending athletes; we call for the life ban of coaches and the so-called doctors who administer this evil' (see Donohoe and Johnson, 1986: 1).

Calls for such swingeing punishments are by no means unusual in the context of discussions about drug use in sport. In a survey of public attitudes towards doping in sport, carried out for the Sports Council in 1994, over half of those questioned felt that sportspeople who used steroids should be given life bans (Sports Council, 1996a: 3–4). In November 1998, the International Olympic Committee (IOC), meeting in London, put forward proposals for consideration at a later meeting in Lausanne for life bans and fines of up to $1 million (£650,000) for athletes testing positive for steroid use (*Independent*, 26 November 1998). The demand for such heavy punishments, together with the emotive language which is often used – note Coe's reference to the use of drugs an an 'evil' – is indicative of the strength of feeling which the issue of doping in sport often arouses. But why does the use of drugs in sport evoke such strong feelings? Why does it call forth from many people within the world of sport such strong condemnation? And why does it give rise to demands for such swingeing punishments for those found to be using drugs? The central objective of this chapter is to try to answer these questions, not from a moralistic but from a sociological perspective.

DRUGS IN SPORT: THE EMERGENCE OF A 'CAUSE FOR CONCERN'

As Black (1996) noted, the two major justifications for the ban on the use of performance-enhancing drugs in sport relate to the protection of the health of athletes and to the maintenance of fair competition. These arguments were clearly set out in the 1996 policy statement on doping by the Great Britain Sports Council:

> The Sports Council condemns the use of doping substances or doping methods to enhance artificially performance in sport. *Doping can be dangerous*; it puts the health of the competitor at risk. *Doping is cheating* and contrary to the spirit of fair competition.
>
> (Sports Council, 1996b: 7; emphasis added)

The position could hardly be stated more clearly. The Sports Council is opposed to the use of drugs, first, because it may be damaging to the health of athletes, and second, because doping is a form of cheating. The first objection – that the use of drugs may be harmful to health – was considerably elaborated in an earlier, undated leaflet produced by the Sports Council, entitled *Dying to Win*. The leaflet contained on the front cover a health warning reminiscent of the Government health warning on cigarette packets: 'Warning by the Sports Council: taking drugs can seriously damage your health.' The leaflet detailed some of the side effects which, it claimed, are associated with the use of stimulants, narcotic analgesics and anabolic steroids, and referred on several occasions to the possibility of death as a result of drug abuse. The leaflet concluded by advising coaches, teachers and parents to 'warn athletes of the great dangers of these drugs. . . . Tell them that by taking drugs, what they would be doing would literally be DYING TO WIN.'

These two arguments – that doping may damage the health of athletes and that it is a form of cheating – have, ever since the introduction of anti-doping regulations in the 1960s, been consistently cited as the major justifications for the ban on the use of performance-enhancing drugs, though it is interesting to note that, more recently, an additional rationale for the ban has been added. In its Annual Report for 1997–98, the Ethics and Anti-Doping Directorate of the United Kingdom Sports Council (which took over responsibility for the doping control programme in the United Kingdom from the Great Britain Sports Council in 1997) referred in its policy statement both to the health-based arguments and to those relating to cheating, but it added a third argument: that doping 'is harmful to the image of sport' (UK Sports Council, 1998a: 3). We will return to this justification later in this chapter but, for the moment, let us concentrate on the other two more usual, and certainly more longstanding, arguments. Before we turn to these arguments, however, it may be helpful to clarify the precise nature of the problem a little further.

DOPING IN SPORT: A MODERN PROBLEM

The use by athletes of substances believed to have performance-enhancing qualities is certainly not a new phenomenon. The Greek physician Galen, writing in the third century BC, reported that athletes in Ancient Greece used stimulants to enhance their performance. In Ancient Egypt athletes similarly had special diets and ingested various substances which, it was believed, improved their physical capabilities, while Roman gladiators and knights in medieval jousts used stimulants after sustaining injury in order to enable them to continue in combat. In the modern period, swimmers in the Amsterdam canal races in the nineteenth century were suspected of taking some form of dope, but the most widespread use of drugs in the late nineteenth century was probably associated with cycling, and most particularly with long-distance or endurance events such as the six-day cycle races (Verroken, 1996: 18; Donohoe and Johnson, 1986: 2–3; Houlihan, 1999: 33).

The use of performance-enhancing substances within the sporting context is, then, a very longstanding phenomenon. Attention is drawn to this fact not simply out of antiquarian interest – in the way in which many authors seem routinely to make this point – but in order to clarify the following aspect of the problem surrounding the ban on the use of performance-enhancing drugs in sport. Performance-enhancing drugs have been used by people involved in sport and sport-like activities for some 2,000 years, but it is only very recently (specifically, since the introduction of anti-doping regulations and doping controls from the 1960s) that this practice has been regarded as unacceptable. In other words, for all but the last three or four decades, those involved in sports have used performance-enhancing drugs without infringing any rules and without the practice giving rise to highly emotive condemnation and stigmatisation. Consider, for example, the following series of events, relating to two soccer matches in the English FA Cup between Arsenal and West Ham United in the 1924–25 season, and described by Bernard Joy in *Forward, Arsenal* (1952):

> There was little compensation in the Cup and apart from 1921–2, when they reached the last eight, Arsenal were dismissed in the First or Second Rounds. They even resorted to pep-pills to provide extra punch and stamina in the First Round against West Ham United in 1924–5. Although fog was about, the prescription was followed of taking them an hour before the start of the game at Upton Park. The fog thickened and the refereee abandoned the game, just when the pills

were beginning to take effect. The pills left a bitter taste, a raging thirst and pent-up energy for which there was no outlet.

It was the same again on the Monday. The pills were taken and once more fog intervened. On Wednesday the match was staged at last and the stimulant enabled Arsenal to have all the play in the second-half after being overrun in the first. Aided by luck, West Ham held on and it was a goalless draw. The hard match accentuated the thirst and bitter taste so much that the players had a most uncomfortable night and refused the pills for the replay at Highbury.

(Joy, 1952: 32–3)

What is perhaps most striking about this passage is the fact that Joy is perfectly open about Arsenal's use of stimulants, while his matter-of-fact style of reporting is completely devoid of any suggestion that Arsenal might have been cheating or doing anything which might have been considered improper. Moreover, this absence of any suggestion of cheating is particularly significant given Joy's personal career in football, for Joy cannot be tainted with any of the negative connotations of 'gamesmanship' which sometimes surround the concept of professionalism. Joy was one of the last great amateurs to play at the highest level of English football – he played as an amateur for the Corinthians, the Casuals and Arsenal, and was the last amateur player to win a full international cap for England, in 1936 – and one of those who typified what is sometimes regarded as the 'true amateur spirit' of the game. It is therefore particularly significant that this 'true amateur' apparently saw nothing reprehensible in Arsenal's use of stimulants.

The above example – and more generally, the acceptance of the use of performance-enhancing drugs for the greater part of sporting history – throws into sharp relief an oft-forgotten fact about our current approach towards the use of drugs to enhance sporting performance; namely, how very recent that approach is. It is important to emphasise that it is not the use of performance-enhancing drugs which is new, for that is a very ancient practice; what is relatively new is the perspective which regards the use of such substances as illegitimate and which seeks to prohibit their use. How, then, can we explain the development of this specifically modern approach to drug use in sport? In this context we need to ask not just 'Why are performance-enhancing drugs banned?' but, no less importantly, 'Why was their use *not* banned until relatively recently?' In other words, what is it about the structure of specifically modern sport, and the structure of the wider society of which sport is a part, that has been associated with the development of anti-doping policies in sport? Armed with these questions, we are now in a position to examine the arguments in relation to health and cheating which are most commonly used to justify current anti-doping policies in sport.

Before we examine these arguments, however, it is necessary to make one final preliminary point. The object of the following discussion is not to suggest that the use of performance-enhancing drugs either should or should not be permitted. My concerns – and given the highly emotive subject matter, it may be necessary to reiterate the point occasionally – are sociological and, as such, I am not concerned to argue about what *should* or *should not* be, or about what we *ought* or *ought not* to do, for such issues are philosophical or moral issues rather than properly sociological ones. Rather, my object is to examine the arguments which are conventionally used to justify the ban on performance-enhancing drugs, and to locate those arguments within the context of broader social processes, including changing practices and ideas within the structure both of modern sport and of the wider society.

DOPING AS A DANGER TO HEALTH

That at least part of the objection to the use of drugs should rest upon grounds of health is, perhaps, not altogether surprising, for there is little doubt that one aspect of the development of modern societies has involved a growing concern with health and health-related issues. Writing about Victorian England, for example, Holloway (1964: 320) suggested that the emphasis on individual achievement which was such a marked feature of Victorian middle-class belief systems necessarily placed a high premium on the maintenance of health, for good health came increasingly to be seen 'both as a prerequisite for success and as a necessary condition for the enjoyment and exploitation of success'. It might be noted in passing that this growing concern for health, and the associated increase in the demand for medical care, were important processes in the development of the modern medical profession in the nineteenth century (Waddington, 1984).

Goudsblom has similarly drawn attention to our growing sensitivity to and awareness of health issues; indeed, he suggests that 'in the twentieth century, concern with physical health has apparently become so overriding that considerations of hygiene have gained pride of place among the reasons given for a variety of rules of conduct' (1986: 181). Moreover, this is so even where – as is by no means uncommon – those rules had, at least in the first instance, little or nothing to do with considerations of health. Since this point is of some relevance for understanding the broader social context of the medical arguments in relation to doping in sport, it is worth examining in a little more detail. The point may, perhaps, be most clearly illustrated by reference to the work of Norbert Elias, on which Goudsblom drew.

In *The Civilizing Process* Elias analyses the development and elaboration over several centuries of a variety of rules of conduct relating to bodily functions such as eating, drinking, nose-blowing and spitting. In relation to the way in which such bodily functions are managed, Mennell noted that, because the way in which these functions are performed clearly has important implications for health, there is a tendency among people today to assume that these functions must have been regulated largely in the interests of health and hygiene. As Mennell puts it, to the modern mind

> it seems . . . obvious that considerations of hygiene must have played an important part in bringing about higher standards. Surely the fear of the spread of infection must have been decisive, particularly in regard to changing attitudes towards the natural functions, nose blowing and spitting, but also in aspects of table manners such as putting a licked spoon back into the common bowl?
>
> (1992: 46)

In fact, however, as Elias (1978b: 115–16) demonstrates, a major part of the controls which people have come to impose upon themselves in relation to bodily functions has not the slightest connection with 'hygiene', but is concerned primarily with what Elias calls 'delicacy of feeling'. Elias's argument is that over a long period and in association with specific social changes, the structure of our emotions, our sensitivity – our sense of shame and delicacy – also change, and these changes are associated with the elaboration of controls over the way in which bodily functions are carried out. It is only at a later date that these new codes of conduct are recognised as 'hygienically correct', though this recognition may then provide an additional justification for the further elaboration or consolidation of these rules of conduct.

In many respects Elias's analysis provides a good starting point for a re-examination of the debate about sport, drugs and health. Could it be that what Elias argues in relation to codes of conduct relating to such things as nose-blowing or spitting or washing one's hands is, at least in some respects, also applicable to a rather different set of rules of conduct: namely, those relating to the use of drugs in sport? In other words, is the ban on the use of certain drugs in sport based primarily on a concern for the long-term health of athletes? Or are the arguments about health essentially secondary or supporting arguments which, because of the cultural status of medicine and the value generally placed upon health, lend particularly useful support to a code of conduct which is based primarily on considerations having little, if anything, to do with health? It is not claimed that what is offered here is in any sense a definitive answer to this problem. However, a preliminary exploration of this question is worthwhile, not least because it raises a number of other interesting problems concerning the relationship between sport and health.

THE SPORT–HEALTH IDEOLOGY

At the outset we might note that, in so far as the ban on performance-enhancing drugs is based on an expressed desire to prevent athletes from damaging their own health, then it reflects what might be described as a paternalistic approach to protecting the welfare of sporting participants. Writing from a legal perspective, O'Leary (1998: 165) argues that in terms of traditional jurisprudence, such an approach 'is only valid if the effect of the prohibition is to protect those unable to make an informed and rational judgement for themselves or to prevent harm to others'. The obvious example of the former, he suggests, would be a ban on the taking of performance-enhancing drugs by children and junior athletes, but he adds that 'extending the ban beyond this point is difficult to justify on this basis', and he concludes that 'it is difficult to sustain an argument for the prohibition of performance enhancing drugs taken by adults' (1998: 166). It is also rather curious that action resulting in the most extreme damage to one's health – that is, suicide, or death resulting from action deliberately intended to cause one's own death – was legalised in Britain in 1961, and it might strike the independent observer as somewhat curious (I put it no more strongly than that) that during the decade in which the legislature took a more liberal position in relation to the most extreme form of self-harm, the sporting authorities in Britain and elsewhere were taking a less liberal and more punitive position in relation to athletes who chose to take rather less extreme risks with their health. However, since my concerns here are exclusively sociological, I do not wish to become embroiled in the niceties of arguments concerned with issues in philosophy or jurisprudence, though it is perhaps appropriate to bear in mind that the philosophical grounds for preventing adults from harming themselves, as opposed to harming others, are by no means secure. However, let us turn to more properly sociological issues.

If the concern for health constitutes one of the principal objections to the use of drugs in sport, then we might reasonably expect a similar concern for health to inform other aspects of the organisation of sport. Is this in fact what we find? As we noted in Chapter 1, it is undoubtedly the case that, at least at an ideological level, there is a strong link between sport and health, and the idea that sport is health promoting is one which is frequently stressed by those involved in sport. Though the ideology linking sport and health is a very powerful one – and one which is certainly widely accepted – an examination of certain aspects of the organisation of sport casts some doubt on the assumed closeness of the relationship between sport and the promotion of healthy life-styles. One such feature of modern sport, and to which attention has already been drawn in Chapter 1, involves the large-scale sponsorship of sport by the manufacturers of two of the most widely used drugs in the western world: alcohol and tobacco. Without exaggeration, it might be suggested that it is more than a little anomalous that sports organisations which ban the use of drugs on the grounds that they may damage athletes' health have so readily accepted sponsorship from the manufacturers of tobacco, in particular, for the medical case against tobacco use would appear to be much stronger, and much more clearly established, than is the medical case against many of the drugs which are on the IOC banned list.

However, the question of whether the banning of certain drugs in sport reflects a primary concern with health issues may be approached rather more directly. In this regard a brief examination of the use of several drugs which are not banned and which are widely used in the treatment or management of sports-related conditions is very revealing.

Since, as we have seen, part of the case against the use of drugs such as anabolic steroids rests on the possible health risks associated with those drugs, it is of some interest to note that several drugs which are very widely – though perfectly legally – used within sport also have a variety of potentially serious side effects. Prominent among these drugs are several pain-killers. Injections of local anaesthetic drugs, for example, can produce cardiac disorders and should not be used 'on the field'. In very large doses they cause stimulation of the central nervous system, convulsions and death. The Medical Commission of the International Olympic Committee (Sports Council, 1998a: 39) permits the use of local anaesthetics 'only when medically justified' – by which is presumably meant only where there is an injury which would otherwise prevent a competitor from taking part – and 'only with the aim of enabling the athlete to continue competing' (Donohoe and Johnson, 1986: 95). One might reasonably ask whether these regulations express a primary concern for the health of the athlete or whether considerations relating to the value of competition are ranked more highly.

Several anti-inflammatory drugs which are widely used for the treatment of sports injuries are known to have a variety of harmful side effects. The most common side effects associated with the use of non-steroidal anti-inflammatory drugs (otherwise known as NSAIDS) are gastro-intestinal pain, nausea and diarrhoea, while prolonged use can lead to ulceration or perforation of the stomach or intestines. More rarely, use of NSAIDS may give rise to skin rashes, bronchospasm, dizziness, vertigo and photo-sensitivity, while renal failure can occur if NSAIDS are used by those with pre-existing renal (kidney) impairment (Simbler, 1999). The former England soccer captain Gary Lineker, who retired in 1994 after a long struggle with a chronic foot injury, indicated that he had been concerned about continually using these drugs. He was reported as saying of his retirement: 'It is as if a huge weight has been lifted from me. I no longer have to worry whether I'll be fit enough to get through a match and I will no longer have to suffer the dizzy spells and stomach complaints that come with a dependency on anti-inflammatory drugs' (*Daily Mirror*, 21 November 1994).

The former England cricket captain Ian Botham has also been very critical of the widespread use of non-steroidal anti-inflammatory drugs. Botham writes that, in professional cricket in England, 'players have become accustomed to treating these drugs as though they were sweets', and he says that, for most of the last ten years of his own career as a player, he 'dropped pain-killing and anti-inflammatory drugs like they were Polo mints' (Botham, 1997: 236–7). Botham highlights the potentially damaging side effects of the long-term use of anti-inflammatories, notably on the stomach and liver, and says of his own use of these drugs that, to deal with the stomach irritation which they produced, he 'turned to Gaviscon in larger and larger doses. In the end I was drinking it like milk just to enable me to take the anti-inflammatory pills in the first place. And I didn't break out of that vicious circle until the day I packed it all in' (p. 238).

Of the many anti-inflammatory drugs which are used within sport, most concern has, perhaps, been expressed about the use of phenylbutazone, or 'bute' as it is commonly known. Introduced in 1949 for the treatment of arthritis, phenylbutazone is a powerful anti-inflammatory drug which has a large number of toxic side effects, some of which have had fatal outcomes. The most serious side effects are the retention of fluid, which in predisposed individuals may precipitate cardiac failure, and interference with normal blood cell production most commonly resulting in aplastic anaemia and agranulocytosis which can occur within the first few days of treatment. A Washington consumer group has called for bans on phenylbutazone and another anti-inflammatory drug, oxyphenbutazone, claiming that their side effects may have led to 10,000 deaths world-wide. Many physicians argue that phenylbutazone is too dangerous to use for the treatment of self-limiting musculoskeletal disorders, and in Britain it is now indicated only for the treatment of ankylosing spondylitis in hospital situations. However, in the United States it has been widely used – Elliott (1996: 136) prefers to say 'abused' – for many years in the sports context to reduce pain and swelling in joints and ligaments, most notably in the National Football League (Donohoe and Johnson, 1986: 97; Elliott, 1996: 135–6). Phenylbutazone, it might be noted, is not on the list of drugs banned by the IOC.

From what has been said it is clear that, while there may indeed be potentially dangerous side effects associated with the use of certain banned drugs, much the same may also be said about many drugs which are not banned and which are widely used within the sporting context. It might also be noted that, as Black (1996: 377) pointed out, there are several drugs which are either banned or whose use is restricted under IOC regulations, but which are readily available to the general public, are widely used in daily life and appear to present no major health threat. Obvious examples include caffeine and ephedrine, the latter being readily available to the public in over-the-counter cold remedies. These inconsistencies – and in particular the fact that several potentially dangerous drugs are used perfectly legally within sport – suggest that, whatever the ideological rhetoric linking sport and health, considerations of health may not constitute the primary basis underlying the decision to ban certain drugs but not others. To return to the question raised earlier, could it be that health considerations – though they may not be entirely irrelevant – provide a convenient and useful but essentially secondary justification for a ban which rests primarily on other values having little or nothing to do with health? If this is the case, then what might these other values be?

'FAIR PLAY' VERSUS 'CHEATING'

The Sports Council policy statement cited earlier gave a second reason for the Council's opposition to the use of performance-enhancing drugs: namely, that 'doping is cheating and is contrary to the spirit of fair competition'. Could it be that it is this concern with cheating and fair competition, rather than a concern for health, which constitutes the primary objection to the use of drugs in sport? That this might be the case is suggested by the relatively tolerant attitude taken, at least until fairly recently, by many sporting bodies towards the 'social' use of drugs such as marijuana and cocaine, the latter of which may have potentially dangerous side effects and both of which (unlike many of the drugs banned by the IOC) are illegal in many countries. (It should be noted that during the 1990s, many sporting bodies began to take a less tolerant attitude towards the use of 'social' drugs. This recent policy shift is examined in more detail later in this chapter; for the moment, I wish to examine the debate around the use of 'social' drugs in sport in the 1980s, for this debate was in some respects very revealing about the underlying rationale for banning the use of some drugs but not others.)

Let us first consider the case of marijuana. There was no testing for marijuana at any Olympic Games before 1988. However, prior to the Seoul Olympics of that year, the IOC was asked by several countries to test for marijuana 'to see whether there was a problem among top-class competitors'. A small number of competitors at those Games were found to have smoked marijuana recently. The possession of marijuana is a criminal offence in Korea, but the names of the athletes involved were not released because the use of cannabis was at that time neither banned nor restricted by the IOC. The rationale for this was perfectly clear; in the words of the president of the IOC's Medical Commission, 'Marijuana does not affect sporting performance.' A similar position was expressed by Professor Arnold Beckett, another leading member of the IOC Medical Commission, who argued that 'If we started looking at the social aspect of drug-taking then we would not be doing our job' (*The Times*, 14 September 1988).

Some sporting bodies at the time took a similarly tolerant position in relation to the use of cocaine, which, although technically a stimulant and therefore on the list of drugs banned by the IOC, is also very widely used for 'recreational' purposes. It was presumably this latter consideration which, during the 1980s, led the tennis authorities at the Wimbledon Championships to adopt a similarly tolerant attitude towards tennis players found to be using cocaine. Thus when tests for cocaine were introduced for male tennis players at Wimbledon in 1986, it was revealed that no action would be taken against those who tested positive; instead, psychiatric help would be offered (*The Times*, 14 September 1986).

These examples would seem to suggest that the major basis of differentiation between those drugs which are banned and those which are permitted may be found not in the fact that the former pose a threat to health while the latter do not – such an argument would be exceedingly difficult to sustain – but in the fact that the former are perceived as being taken in order artificially to boost performance, thereby giving competitors who use drugs an unfair advantage over those who do not. Perhaps, then, the more fundamental objection to the use of drugs lies in the fact that, in the words of the Sports Council, 'doping is cheating'.

But why should the practice of cheating be regarded as so objectionable? At first glance the answer may seem self-evident, for such is the strength of feeling against cheating that we might be tempted to think that the idea of cheating 'naturally' arouses strong hostility. The matter is, however, considerably more complex than this, for an analysis of the development of the concept of cheating and of the associated notion of 'fair play' raises some interesting questions about the development of modern sport.

There is a taken-for-granted or 'common-sense' view that the values associated with what we now call 'fair play' and which are institutionalised in the rules of modern sports are universal values that have always been shared by those involved in sport and sport-like contests. Such a view is, however, quite wrong. Elias, for example, has pointed out that central to the ethos of the 'sports' of Ancient Greece were values such as honour and glory rather than the values of fair play. Indeed, he points out that the Greek games – despite the way in which they are sometimes misleadingly depicted as representing the 'true spirit' of sport – 'were not ruled by a great sense of fairness' (Elias, 1986a: 138), at least in the sense in which we understand it today. For example, one aspect of 'fairness' in the modern sports of boxing and wrestling is that each fighter is matched against an opponent of roughly similar weight, but neither the 'boxers' nor the 'wrestlers' of Olympia were classified according to weight.

It is therefore essential to see concepts such as 'cheating' and 'fair play' not as cultural universals, but as relatively modern concepts which have emerged as an integral part of the development of a broader pattern of social relationships. More specifically, the development of these concepts – at least in the sense in which they are used within modern sport – can be seen as part of that process which Elias termed 'sportization'. Though the concept of 'sportization' may jar upon the ear, it does, as Elias noted, fit the observable facts relating to the development of modern sports quite well. Elias's argument (1986b: 151) is that, in the course of the nineteenth century – and in some cases as early as the mid-eighteenth century – with England as the model-setting country, some leisure activities involving bodily exertion assumed the structural characteristics which we identify with modern sports. A central part of this 'sportization' process involved the development of a stricter framework of rules governing sporting competition. Thus the rules became more precise, more explicit and more differentiated while, at the same time, supervision of the observance of those rules became more efficient; hence, penalties for offences against the rules became less escapable. One of the central objectives – perhaps *the* central objective – of this tightening up of the rules was to ensure that sporting competitions were carried on with proper regard for what we now call 'fairness', the most important element of which is probably the idea that all competitors must have an equal chance of winning.

It is worth noting that this developing concern for fairness related as much to the interests of spectators – and specifically to the interests of those who placed wagers on the outcomes of sporting contests – as it did to the interests of the players. Thus, describing the development of what he calls the 'English ethos of fairness', Elias writes:

> Gentlemen watching a game-contest played by their sons, their retainers or by well-known professionals, liked to put money on one side or the other as a condiment of the excitement provided by the contest itself. . . . But the prospect of winning one's bet could add to the excitement of watching the struggle only if the initial odds of winning were more or less evenly divided between the two sides and offered a minimum of calculability.
>
> (1986a: 139)

Betting was thus an important part of the context within which a concern for fairness – defined as an equality of chances for both sides in a sporting contest – came to be institutionalised. The importance of betting in this context is clearly indicated by the fact that while anti-doping regulations in human sport were not introduced until the 1960s, the doping of horses – often undertaken with a view to 'nobbling' a particular horse rather than improving its performance – was banned in Britain as early as 1903 (Verroken, 1996: 19).

As part of the 'sportization' process, the idea of 'fairness' – and the associated abhorrence of cheating – have come to be widely regarded as perhaps the most fundamental values underpinning modern sporting competitions. In this context one might, for example, compare the relatively highly rule-governed character of modern sports with the relative absence of rules governing many traditional folk-games in pre-industrial Europe, many of which had few, if any, rules governing such matters as physical contact or even the number of players permitted on each side (Dunning and Sheard, 1979: 21–45). The importance of the 'sportization' process and its relationship to the concept of cheating may be brought out very simply: where there are no rules one cannot cheat. The development of the concept of cheating, therefore, is closely associated with the development of a body of relatively clearly defined rules. In this sense, it is important to note that the concepts of 'cheating' and of 'fair play' are specifically modern concepts which had no precise counterparts in the 'sports' of the ancient world or of medieval or early modern Europe.

To return to the question raised earlier: could it be a concern with what might be regarded as the fundamental values of modern sport – values concerned with fair play and the avoidance of cheating – rather than a concern for the health of athletes that provides the primary rationale for the prohibition on the use of performance-enhancing drugs? Such an argument is, at least superficially, attractive. There is no doubt that many people within the world of sport do continue to express a real commitment to the value of fair play, notwithstanding the increasing importance which has come to be attached to winning, and which will be examined in the next chapter. Moreover, since the use of performance-enhancing drugs does constitute a clear breach of the rules of modern sport, it does unambiguously constitute a form of cheating. To this degree, an understanding of the centrality of the concept of fair play helps us to understand, at least partially, the ban on the use of performance-enhancing drugs. However, any explanation of the ban that is based on the concept of fair play can be at best, only very partial. A problem in this regard is that the concept of fairness, or what is sometimes called the concept of the 'level playing field', is, in practice, implemented in sport only very imperfectly and in a very limited way, for the reality of high-level sporting competition is that it often involves individuals or teams which are highly differentiated in terms of their access to resources and support systems.

Consider, for example, the way in which the concept of fairness is implemented within sporting competition. All participants are formally subject to the same set of rules, so that, in a soccer match, for example, each team may have only eleven players on the field at any one time, no team may use more than the permitted number of substitutes, and no players, other than the goalkeepers, are permitted deliberately to touch the ball with their hands. Similarly, in a 400-metre race on the track, each runner is required to run the same distance, no one is permitted to take a short cut and no runner is allowed to impede any other runner. However, the implementation of rules of this kind ensures that the contest is fair only in a very formal and limited sense, for whereas the rules of most sports govern what takes place in the sporting contest itself, they usually have little or nothing to say about equalising the resources available to the competitors outside of the specific context of the competition itself.

These inequalities in resources may arise from a number of sources. Thus O'Leary (1998: 167) pointed out that a skier who is raised in Austria or Switzerland may be considered to have an advantage over a skier raised in Belgium, while the runner living at high altitude may have an advantage over one living nearer sea level. In addition to such climatic advantages which may be associated with particular geographical locations, however, there are many other advantages associated with the degree of financial and other support which may be available to athletes living in different countries. For example, elite athletes living in Britain or the United States may enjoy financial sponsorship which enables them to train full-time on a year-round basis, and they are also likely to have access to the very highest-quality support systems in terms of medical support and expertise from specialists in disciplines such as biomechanics, exercise physiology, nutrition and sports psychology, as well as advice from leading coaches. A similar range of supporting facilities and personnel will be much less readily available to athletes from many of the poorer countries of the developing world.[1]

There are, however, three other considerations which also limit the explanatory power of the argument which suggests that the ban on the use of performance-enhancing drugs can be explained in terms of a concern with fair play. In particular, the following questions need to be addressed:

1 How does one explain the more recently imposed restrictions on drugs which are not performance-enhancing but which are used for 'recreational' purposes, such as marijuana?
2 There are many forms of cheating, but how does one account for the fact that the use of drugs usually calls forth not only far stronger, but – and this is very important – much more highly emotive forms of condemnation than do other forms of cheating?
3 And how, if at all, do these questions relate to the third objection to doping, recently added by the UK Sports Council: namely, that doping 'is harmful to the image of sport'?

Let us turn to examine these issues.

'RECREATIONAL' DRUGS IN SPORT

As we noted earlier, throughout the 1980s, many sporting bodies, including the IOC, took a relatively tolerant attitude towards the use of 'social' or 'recreational' drugs. However, in 1990, the IOC signalled a change in its position in relation to one of the most widely used recreational drugs, marijuana. The IOC was reported to have changed its policy not because it considered that marijuana boosted athletic performance but on the grounds that it was held to be 'damaging to youth and a threat to world peace' (*European*, 8–10 June 1990). Marijuana, it should be noted, is not on the list of drugs whose use is banned by the IOC, but it is now listed as one of a number of drugs which are 'subject to certain restrictions', and different governing bodies in sport have different regulations in relation to marijuana.

In Britain, since the early 1990s athletes have been tested for marijuana under the system of doping controls which is operated by the Sports Council, and in 1996 the Council expressed concern at the growing number of athletes testing positive for marijuana. In 1992–93 and in 1993–94 there were just two positive tests each year in Britain for marijuana use, but in 1994–95 the figure increased to ten and there were a further ten positive tests in 1995–96. In the Annual Report of its Doping Control Service in 1996, the Council held that the 'increasing number of findings of social drugs is of concern and will require further efforts in drug prevention partnerships to address the problem' (Sports Council, 1996b: 26). The Sports Council's statement provides a striking contrast with the statement made by Professor Beckett in 1988, and noted earlier in this chapter, in which he said that if the IOC and governing bodies became involved in 'the social aspect of drug-taking then we would not be doing our job'.

It is important to note that the use of recreational drugs such as marijuana raises different issues from those raised by the use of drugs such as anabolic steroids or stimulants, for, unlike the latter, marijuana is not a performance-enhancing drug. Moreover, this fact is, as we noted earlier, recognised by the IOC. However, since marijuana is not a performance-enhancing drug, it follows that one of the arguments most frequently used to justify doping controls – that those involved in doping derive an unfair advantage over other competitors and are therefore cheating – cannot be used to justify controls on the use of marijuana. Given that this is so, it might be suggested that the attempt to control the use of marijuana within a sporting context is best understood, not in terms of considerations which are specific to sport but, rather, in terms of the growing concern about drug 'abuse' within the wider society. This point leads us into a consideration of some of the broader issues associated with doping and doping control in sport. We can approach these issues by re-examining the argument that doping is a form of cheating.

That doping is conventionally regarded as a form of cheating might, for many people, constitute an adequate explanation of why the practice is generally regarded as so objectionable and why it arouses such strong emotions. However, such simplistic answers often obscure rather more than they reveal. If the generally highly emotive reaction to the use of drugs in sport arises primarily from the view that drug use constitutes a form of cheating, then one might reasonably expect an equally strong and emotive reaction to the many other forms of cheating in sport. Is this, however, what we find? In all sports there are actions which involve breaches of the rules and which constitute clear forms of cheating, but which do not arouse the same emotional response nor the same demands for swingeing punishments. One could cite in this connection forms of cheating such as handling the ball or pushing an opponent in soccer; playing the ball on the ground with the hands after a ruck has formed in rugby union; 'holding' or 'pass interference' in American football; and holding an opponent or deliberate blocking fouls in basketball.

All of these actions constitute attempts to gain an unfair advantage over one's opponents – that is, they are all forms of cheating – but they do not, save in quite exceptional circumstances, evoke the same kind of emotional response associated with the specific form of cheating which involves the use of drugs. In the average soccer or rugby match, for example, there may be several dozen incidents of foul play, but the usual response to each incident is that the appropriate penalty is awarded against the offending player who may be gently or more severely admonished by the referee. However, that player is not normally publicly accused of undermining the very foundation of the sport and there are no demands for lifelong bans for soccer players who control the ball with their hands, or for the rugby player who tackles a player who does not have the ball.

The use of drugs, then, is *not* treated just like any other form of cheating, for the public response to the use of drugs in sport is both more forceful and more emotive than the public response to most other forms of cheating. How, then, do we account for these very different responses to the different forms of cheating?

It is clear that the strong emotions aroused by drug use in sport cannot be adequately understood without reference to processes within the wider society which have little to do directly with sport. In this connection, it is suggested that public attitudes towards the use of drugs in sport have been 'contaminated', as it were, by the widespread public concern about the possession, sale and 'abuse' of controlled drugs in society more generally. These activities, it should be noted, are not only illegal in their own right in most western societies but are also widely held to be associated with other forms of criminal activity and with a wide variety of other social problems, with physical and psychological addiction, with dangers to the 'moral health' particularly of young people, and with severe risks to health including the risk, in the case of injecting drug users, of hepatitis and, more recently and even more anxiety-arousing, AIDS. It is suggested that the generally emotive response to the use of performance-enhancing drugs in sport is to be explained, at least in part, by reference to the widespread public concern – 'moral panic' would not perhaps be too strong a term – relating to other patterns of 'drug abuse' within society more generally.

It is therefore important to locate the concern about drugs in sport within the context of this wider concern about the use of controlled drugs in society more generally. More specifically, it is important to recognise how public attitudes and anxieties towards the use of controlled drugs in society generally have 'spilled over' into the sports arena and have influenced anti-doping policies in sport.

This 'spillage' of public anxieties about drugs in general into the sporting arena can be illustrated by reference to recent policy statements by the UK Sports Council. As we noted earlier, the Council has recently added a third anti-doping argument to the more conventional arguments based on considerations concerned with the health of athletes and with cheating. This third argument states that 'drug misuse . . . severely damages the image of sport, even *when the motivation to use drugs is not to improve sporting performance*' (UK Sports Council, 1998b: 1; italics added). This new rationale for anti-doping policies is clearly designed to provide a justification for controls on marijuana and other recreational drugs. However, what is particularly striking about this rationale is that it has little, if anything, to do with values which are specific to the sports context – people who use marijuana cannot, for example, be accused of seeking an unfair advantage – while it draws heavily upon the negative images associated with drug use in society more generally.

This is made explicit when the Sports Council spells out the two main ways in which, it suggests, the use of 'recreational' drugs might 'damage the image of sport'. The Sports Council points out, first, that possessing or supplying drugs such as marijuana is illegal, and the argument here thus relates not to sporting values, but – and this is a significant departure from previous rationales – to the criminal law. The second argument relates to the influence of sportspeople as role models. In this context, the Sports Council argues that the 'behaviour of elite competitors can have a significant impact on young people as they admire and aspire to emulate their sporting heroes, especially their actions and attitudes'. Again, the argument is one which represents a shift away from sport-specific values, for the argument is not that sportspeople who use recreational drugs are contravening the ethics of sport, but that this particular aspect of their *non-sporting lifestyle* is considered to offend against widely held public sentiments relating to the use of controlled drugs within the society more generally.

This 'spillage' of public attitudes towards drugs in general into the sporting arena is, however, problematic. One of the problems in this respect is that, as we noted earlier, drug use within the wider society has come to be associated with a large number of what are held to be 'anti-social' activities such as a variety of forms of crime and delinquency. As a consequence, the word 'drug', as Black (1996) pointed out, has come to have a whole variety of negative connotations which have little to do directly with sport but which have undoubtedly 'contaminated' public attitudes and sporting policy towards doping in sport. This 'contamination' of the issue of doping in sport by wider anxieties about the use of controlled drugs more generally, and of course the associated emotive connotations of the word 'drug', have always been present since the development of modern anti-doping policies in the 1960s, but they have been made particularly explicit by more recently imposed controls on the use of recreational drugs in sport. It is important to recognise this broader context within which anti-doping policy in sport has been made; it is even more important to recognise that this emotively charged context is not one which is conducive to thinking about doping in sport in a relatively detached way, and not one which is conducive to effective or consistent policy-making in this area. Some key aspects of policy-making in relation to doping in sport are examined in Chapter 10.

7 Doping in sport
Towards a sociological understanding

Although we cannot be sure of the precise level of drug use in modern sport (the relevant data are reviewed in some detail in Chapter 10) there are nevertheless grounds for suggesting that the illicit use of drugs by athletes has increased very markedly in the post-war period and more particularly in the last three decades. This is certainly the view of Michele Verroken, who heads the Ethics and Anti-Doping Directorate of the UK Sports Council. Verroken writes:

> Around the time of the Second World War, the development of amphetamine-like substances reached a peak. . . . Not surprisingly, in the 1940s and 1950s, amphetamines became the drugs of choice for athletes, particularly in sports such as cycling, where the stimulant effects were perceived to be beneficial to enhancing sporting performance.
>
> (1996: 19)

She suggests that the use of drugs in sport had become widespread by the 1960s. In almost identical fashion, Donohoe and Johnson (1986: 2–4) have suggested that the 'production of amphetamine-like stimulants in the thirties heralded a whole new era of doping in sport', and they go on to suggest that in recent times 'a massive acceleration in the incidence of doping in sport has occurred'.

However, if there has been a significant increase in the use of performance-enhancing drugs in the last few decades – and, as we shall see later, the available evidence does support such an interpretation – then we need to ask why and how this process has taken place. The most common explanation for this increase in the use of performance-enhancing drugs by athletes in the last few decades is probably that which is couched in terms of technological developments. Verroken, for example, while pointing to 'a more liberal approach to experimentation in drug taking in society in general' in the 1960s, adds that 'of far greater significance' was the 'pharmacological revolution' of this period, which resulted in the development of more potent, more selective and less toxic drugs (Verroken, 1996:

19). Like Verroken, Donohoe and Johnson similarly argue that the increase in the use of drugs in sport can be explained largely in terms of improvements in chemical technology.

It is perhaps not surprising that authors such as those cited above should couch their explanations largely in terms of pharmacological developments. Donohoe and Johnson are pharmacists and their training will have made them keenly aware of such developments. Verroken, in her analysis, relies very heavily on the earlier writing of Mottram (1988), who is also a pharmacist. It is, perhaps, rather more surprising to find that what is, in effect, a technological determinist argument has also been adopted by some sociologists. Particularly striking in this respect is the work of the American sports sociologists Jay Coakley and Robert Hughes. To their credit, Coakley and Hughes offer a considerably more detailed analysis of the increase in the use of performance-enhancing drugs than do Verroken, Mottram or Donohoe and Johnson, but their work – perhaps because of the greater detail which their analysis contains – illustrates very clearly the problems associated with this approach. Coakley and Hughes, it might be noted, describe their approach as involving what they call a 'substance availability hypothesis' though this is, in effect, a variant of the technological determinist approach of writers like Verroken and Mottram. Let us examine what Coakley and Hughes have to say.

Coakley and Hughes (1998) have correctly noted that there is evidence to indicate that athletes have for many centuries used a variety of substances in an attempt to improve their performances, and they suggest that

> Historical evidence also shows an increase in the use of performance-enhancing drugs in the 1950s. This was due to two factors: (1) the development and official use of amphetamines in the military during World War II, and (2) advances in biology and medicine that led to the laboratory isolation of human hormones and the development of synthetic hormones, especially hormones fostering physical growth and development.
>
> Experiences with amphetamines during the war alerted many physically active young men to the possible use of these drugs in other settings, including sports. Athletes in the 1950s and 1960s fondly referred to amphetamines as 'bennies' (slang for benzedrine, a potent 'upper'). Research on the use of synthetic hormones in sport had been done as early as the 1920s, but it wasn't until the 1950s that testosterone, steroids, and growth hormones from both humans and animals became more widely available. They didn't become very widely used, however, until weight training and strength conditioning programs were emphasized in certain sports. . . . As might be expected, the growth of bodybuilding also has been closely connected with substance use, especially the use of hormones and hormone derivatives.
>
> (Coakley and Hughes, 1998: 167)

They note that when Harold Connelly, the 1956 Olympic hammer-throw champion, testified before a US Senate committee in 1973, he said that the majority of athletes 'would do anything, and take anything, short of killing themselves to improve athletic performance'. They suggest that, in making this statement, Connelly

> was probably describing what many athletes through history would have done. The reason drug use has increased so much since the 1950s is not that sports or athletes have changed but that drugs believed to enhance physical performance have become so widely available.
> (Coakley and Hughes, 1998: 167–8)

Coakley and Hughes elaborated on this point in an earlier (1994) version of this argument. Referring again to Connelly's statement that most athletes would 'do anything and take anything' to enhance their performance, they argued that

> Other evidence suggests that this willingness to do anything and take anything exists among both men and women in capitalist and socialist, industrial and pre-industrial societies. . . . If today's drugs had been available in the year 300, 1600, or 1800, they would have probably been used to the same extent they are used by athletes in the 1990s.
> (Coakley and Hughes, 1994: 151)

In considering explanations of this kind, it is of course important to recognise that in recent years more, and more effective, performance-enhancing drugs have been produced. It is also the case that any properly sociological analysis of drug use among athletes would certainly have to take these pharmacological developments into account. However, to say that we should take such developments into account is very different from suggesting that the development of pharmacology should be given privileged status, and even further from the idea that it be given sole status, as an explanatory variable.

Explanations which are couched simply in terms of technological developments, like other forms of monocausal explanation, have a simplicity which is in some respects attractive. However, those who are attracted to the seductive simplicity of what is in effect a form of technological determinism – that is, the view that social processes (in this case, drug use) can be explained simply by reference to technological developments (in this case, pharmacological developments) – pay a heavy price in terms of understanding the complexities of social reality, whether in the area of sport and drugs, or in any other area of social life.[1] Let us consider some of the problems associated with the type of explanation offered by writers such as Donohoe and Johnson, Verroken, and Coakley and Hughes.

Technologically based explanations rest not only on the assumption that social processes can be explained simply in terms of technological developments, but also on the closely related assumption that technological developments *are themselves autonomous or self-contained processes with their own internal dynamics, and that the development of technology itself therefore requires no further explanation in terms of broader social processes.* However, such an assumption is simply not tenable, for science and technology do not develop in a social vacuum. The development of science and technology – including the science and technology of doping in sport – are *social* processes, and we cannot adequately understand these processes without locating the activities of scientists and technologists within the broader network of social relationships of which they are a part. This point may be illustrated by reference to what is, in many respects, a particularly telling example relating to the development of a drug which has subsequently been widely used in sport. The drug concerned in this example is the anabolic steroid Dianabol or, in generic terms, methandrostenolone. The development of Dianabol is examined in considerably greater detail in the next chapter but, within the present context, the following brief description will suffice.

In the early 1950s, it was rumoured that Soviet scientists had been carrying out hormonal experimentation in order to help their athletes enhance their performances. According to Voy (1991), positive confirmation of these rumours came at the 1956 World Games in Moscow, when Dr John B. Ziegler, an American physician who was a member of the medical staff for the Games, witnessed urinary catheters being used by Soviet athletes. Ziegler was not surprised by this, for he knew that the use of testosterone would enlarge the prostate gland, possibly to the point where the urinary tract would be obstructed, thus making it difficult for the athletes to urinate. Because of this, athletes sometimes used urinary catheters in order to facilitate urination (Voy, 1991: 8–9).

After the 1956 World Games, Ziegler returned to the United States and began informing the medical and sports communities about the use of steroids by Soviet athletes. Voy (1991: 9) notes that in 'an attempt to help Western athletes compete more effectively against the Soviets who used testosterone, and in an effort to reduce the bad side effects of testosterone', Dr Ziegler helped the CIBA Pharmaceutical Company to develop Dianabol. Dianabol was, according to Voy, among the first 'big-time' anabolic-androgenic steroids and quickly became widely used by American athletes.

How, then, can we best understand the development and use of Dianabol? Can we understand it simply in terms of the availability of the drug as a result of the development of pharmacology? Or, for a fuller understanding, do we need to locate this – and indeed, all such developments – within the broader social context?

Consider once again some of the basic information provided in Voy's description of the development of Dianabol and its rapid adoption by athletes. Should we not ask whether it is purely coincidental that the two countries which figure centrally in this story – the United States and the Soviet Union – were at the time the world's two superpowers? In this context, it is worth reminding ourselves that the period to which the story relates (namely, the 1950s) was the period of the Cold War, in which superpower rivalry was particularly intense, and in which sport was used by each of the superpowers as a means of demonstrating the claimed superiority of its own political and economic system. In relation to the Soviet Union, Riordan pointed out that following the Second World War, the Soviet leadership set a new national target – namely, to catch up and overtake the most advanced industrial powers – and he adds, 'and that included catching up and overtaking in sport' (Riordan, 1977: 161–2). There is no need to examine here all aspects of the significance of superpower rivalry in sport, but enough has been said to indicate that our understanding of these early Soviet experiments in the use of testosterone to boost athletic performance is enhanced if we locate these developments within the context of the Soviet attempt to catch up and overtake the West in sport. Equally, however, it is clear from Voy's description that the American response to these Soviet experiments – that is, the development and use of Dianabol – can also be more adequately understood if we locate it within the context of the structure of international competition and conflict, and particularly competition and conflict between the superpowers. If we broaden the framework of our analysis in this way, we can begin to understand some of the socio-political processes associated with the development and use of anabolic steroids in those countries and at that time. By comparison, the argument of technological determinists – which amounts to the claim that Soviet and American athletes took drugs because technological developments made them available – really tells us very little.

While Donohoe and Johnson, like Verroken, simply suggest that the increased use of illicit drugs by athletes can be understood in terms of the so-called 'pharmacological revolution', Coakley and Hughes go further by explicitly denying the relevance of broader social processes such as those relating, for example, to the changing structure of sport and of sporting competition. In this context, let us remind ourselves of the key aspects of their position. They argue that athletes throughout history and in a wide variety of societies – as they put it, 'both men and women in capitalist and socialist, industrial and pre-industrial societies' – have shown a similar willingness 'to do anything and take anything' in order to win. Historical evidence, they claim, suggests that the increased use of drugs in sport is primarily due to the increased availability of substances 'rather than to changes in the values or character of athletes or changes in sports', and they conclude by suggesting that if athletes in the past had had access to the drugs available today, 'they would probably have been used to the same extent they are used by athletes in the 1990s'.

Perhaps the first point to make about this argument is that it rests on the remarkable assumption that all athletes at all times have placed equal importance on winning, and have been equally prepared to do anything in order to win. Despite their claim that their argument is supported by historical evidence, Coakley and Hughes do not cite any supporting historical evidence. What is clear, however, is that there is a good deal of historical data which run directly counter to their assertion.

Even a cursory glance at the history of sport indicates that the structure of sport and sporting competition has changed radically through time, and that it has varied very considerably from one society to another. As we saw in the last chapter, it is important to remember that sport, in the form in which we know it today, is a relatively recent phenomenon, having developed in the course of what Elias called the 'sportization' of pastimes in England from the late eighteenth and early nineteenth centuries (Elias, 1986a: 128–9; 1986b: 151). Elias and Dunning have drawn attention to major differences between the structure of modern sports on the one hand, and what are commonly and very loosely called the 'sports' of classical antiquity and the medieval period on the other. Indeed, it is precisely because of these major differences that Elias preferred to restrict the use of the term 'sport' to describe certain kinds of activities which have developed only since the late eighteenth and nineteenth centuries, and to describe earlier kinds of 'sports' as game-contests, folk-games or pastimes.

Given the importance of these changes – changes such as the formal elaboration and standardisation of written rules, the development of formal organisations on the local, national and international levels and the growing competitiveness of sport, particularly but not exclusively at the elite level – it would be little short of astonishing if, as Coakley and Hughes suggest, the attitudes of athletes towards winning really had remained constant throughout history. It is surely stretching our credulity too far to ask us to accept that athletes' attitudes towards winning, and their motivation to win, have been unaffected by the changing social significance of, and the rewards attached to, winning in different societies and at different times. We will return to the changing significance which has come to be attached to winning in modern sport, and the implications of this change for an understanding of doping in sport, later in this chapter.

However, if the increased use of illicit drugs in sport cannot be adequately explained simply in terms of pharmaceutical developments, then how can it be best explained? It is suggested that, if we wish to understand why sportsmen and sportswomen have, in recent years, increasingly used performance-enhancing drugs, then it is necessary to examine some of the major changes which have taken place in the structure of sport and sporting competition. However, the increased use of drugs in sport cannot adequately be understood if we limit our analysis merely to changes within the structure of sport itself, for sport – like any other any social activity – is linked to wider social processes in a variety of ways. More specifically, the argument in this chapter is that the increasing use of drugs in sport has been associated with two largely autonomous sets of social processes, one within the world of sport and the other within the world of medicine. The central focus of the analysis is therefore on developments in, and changes in the interrelationships between, sport and medicine. This focus also provides the central theme for the next chapter. These two chapters taken together, it is suggested, provide an understanding of the broader social context within which new and more effective performance-enhancing drugs have been developed. Let us begin with an analysis of some recent and relevant changes in the structure of medical practice.

THE MEDICALISATION OF LIFE

In a very influential essay which G. Williams (1996) has properly described as a classic of medical sociology, Irving Zola (1972) argued that in modern industrial societies medicine is becoming a major institution of social control. This process, he argued, was a largely insidious and often undramatic one which was associated with the 'medicalising' of much of daily living, a process which involves 'making medicine and the labels "healthy" and "ill" *relevant* to an ever increasing part of human existence' (Zola, 1972: 487). The medicalisation process has involved an expansion of the number and range of human conditions which are held to constitute 'medical problems', a label which, once attached, is sufficient to justify medical intervention. Zola cites four such problems – ageing, drug addiction, alcoholism and pregnancy – the first and last of which were once regarded as normal processes and the middle two as human foibles and weaknesses. This has now changed and medical specialities have emerged to deal with these conditions, one consequence of which has been to expand very considerably the number of people deemed to be in need of medical services. A similar process has occurred as a result of the development of 'comprehensive' and psychosomatic medicine, both of which have considerably expanded the areas of life which are held to be relevant to the understanding, treatment and prevention of disease. The development of preventive medicine, in particular, has justified increasing medical intervention in an attempt to change people's life-styles, whether in the areas of diet, sleep, work, marital relationships, exercise, tobacco and alcohol consumption, or in those of safer driving or the fluoridation of water supplies.

The theme of the medicalisation of life was subsequently taken up by a number of other writers. Waitzkin and Waterman (1974: 86–9), for example, analysed this process in terms of what they called 'medical imperialism'. However, perhaps the most famous thesis of this kind is that associated with Ivan Illich. Illich argued that the medicalisation of life involves a number of processes, including growing dependence on professionally provided care and on drugs, medicalisation of the life-span, of prevention and of the expectations of lay people. One of the consequences has been the creation of 'patient majorities', for, argued Illich (1975: 56), people 'who are free of therapy-oriented labels have become the exception'. Large numbers of people are now regarded as requiring routine medical attention, not because they have any definable pathology, but 'for the simple fact that they are unborn, newborn, infants, in their climacteric, or old' (1975: 44). In other words, the expansion of that which is deemed to fall within the province of medicine has expanded to the point where, as de Swaan (1988: 243) put it, 'there remain only patients and those not yet patients'.

THE MEDICALISATION OF SPORT

It is an important part of the argument in this chapter that, particularly in the last three decades or so (that is, very roughly, the period coinciding with the most rapid growth in the illicit use of drugs), the medicalisation process has encompassed sport. This process has been most evident in the rapid development, particularly since the early 1960s, of what is now called sports medicine, an area of practice which has been described by two of the earliest and most prominent of British exponents (J. G. P. Williams and P. Sperryn, 1976: ix) as 'an integrated multi-disciplinary field embracing the relevant areas of clinical medicine (sports traumatology, the medicine of sport and sports psychiatry) and the appropriate allied scientific disciplines (including physiology, psychology and biomechanics)'.

Some of the processes involved in the medicalisation of sport – and in particular the development of an ideology justifying increasing medical intervention – can be illustrated by reference to some of the early textbooks in the area of sports medicine. This ideology is clearly expressed in one of the very first British texts in the field – J. G. P. Williams' *Sports Medicine*, which was published in 1962 – in which the author argues that the intensity and diversity of modern competitive sport have 'resulted in the emergence from the general mass of the population of a new type of person – the trained athlete'. Williams goes on to argue – some may feel that the case is overstated – that the trained athlete 'is as different physiologically and psychologically from "the man in the street" as is the chronic invalid'. This argument is, however, important in establishing a justification for medical intervention, for he goes on to suggest: 'Just as extreme youth and senility produce peculiar medical problems, so too does extreme physical fitness' (1962: vii). One can see here the early development of the idea, now very widespread, that athletes require routine medical supervision not because they necessarily have any clearly defined pathology but, in this case, simply because they are athletes. This position was, in fact, spelt out quite unambiguously in the foreword to Williams' book by Sir Arthur (later Lord) Porritt, who was at that time the President of the Royal College of Surgeons of England and the Chairman of the British Association of Sport and Medicine. Porritt's position (in Williams, 1962: v) could hardly have constituted a clearer statement of what is involved in the medical-isation process, for he argued quite baldly that 'those who take part in sport and play games are essentially patients'. Athletes thus became yet one more group to add to Illich's list of those – the unborn, newborn, infants and so on – who are held *by definition* to require routine medical super-vision, irrespective of the presence or absence of any specific pathology.

One consequence of the development of the discipline of sports medicine, and of closely associated disciplines such as exercise physiology, bio-mechanics and sports psychology, has been to make traditional methods of training for sporting events increasingly inadequate as a means of prepara-tion for high-level competition. At least at the higher levels of sport the image of the dedicated athlete training alone or with one or two chosen friends has become increasingly outmoded. Instead, the modern successful athlete is likely to be surrounded by – or at least to have access to – and to be increasingly dependent upon, a whole group of specialist advisers, including specialists in sports medicine. Moreover, this dependence of athletes on practitioners of sports medicine quickly went beyond the treat-ment of sports injuries; as another early British text pointed out, as 'practice for the competitive event takes place . . . the sportsman [*sic*] seeks systematic methods of preparation. He examines such technical and scientific infor-mation as is available about the way his body performs its athletic function and turns to the doctor as physiologist' (J. G. P. Williams and P. Sperryn, 1976: 1). One consequence of these developments has been to make top-class athletes more and more dependent on increasingly sophisticated systems of medical support in their efforts to run faster, to jump further or to compete more effectively in their chosen sport. As the former Amateur Athletics Association national coach, the late Ron Pickering noted in his foreword to Sperryn's *Sport and Medicine* (1983: vi), few would deny that 'nowadays medical support is essential for the realization of the athlete's natural capacity for optimum performance'. Indeed, at the highest levels of competition the quality of the medical support may make the difference between success and failure. Just how sophisticated modern systems of medical back-up have become is illustrated by Pickering's admittedly tongue-in-cheek comparison between the limited amount of scientific knowledge which was available to coaches at the start of his career and the vast amount of knowledge which has subsequently been gained from experiments on athletes 'who have given blood, sweat, urine, muscle biopsies and personality inventories, have often been immersed in tanks, and photographed naked in three dimensions at altitude'.

It would, however, be quite wrong to suggest that athletes are simply unwilling 'victims' of medical imperialism, for, as de Swaan (1988: 246) noted, professionals – in this instance, doctors – 'do not simply force them-selves upon innocent and unknowing clients'. In the case of sport, a number of developments, particularly in the post-Second World War period, have led sportsmen and women increasingly to turn for help to anyone who can hold out the promise of improving their level of performance. The most important of these developments are probably those which have been associated with the politicisation of sport, particularly at the international level, and those which have been associated with massive increases in the rewards – particularly, but not exclusively, the material rewards – associated with sporting success. Both these processes, it is suggested, have had the consequence of increasing the competitiveness of sport, and one aspect of this increasing competitiveness has been the downgrading, in relative terms, of the traditional value associated with taking part while greatly increasing the value attached to winning.

Although the trend towards the increasing competitiveness of sport has been particularly marked in the post-1945 period, the trend itself is a very much longer trend which can be traced back over two or more centuries and which has been associated with the processes of industrialisation and state development. Before we examine the relatively recent developments associated with the politicisation and commercialisation of sport, it may be useful to outline briefly the social roots of this longer-term trend towards the increasing competitiveness of sport or, what is the same thing, towards the 'de-amateurisation' of sport.

THE 'DE-AMATEURISATION' OF SPORT

The emphasis which has come to be placed on the importance of winning and which has come to be such a striking feature of modern sports, particularly but not exclusively at the elite level, is a relatively modern phenomenon. Dunning and Sheard (1979: 155), for example, have noted that the amateur ethos which was articulated in late-nineteenth-century England emphasised the importance of sporting activity as 'an "end in itself", i.e. simply for the pleasure afforded, with a corresponding downgrading of achievement striving, training and specialization'. The competitive element was important but the achievement of victory was supposed not to be central; indeed, the English public-school elite who articulated the amateur ethos were opposed to cups and leagues because such competitions were, it was held, conducive to an overemphasis on victory and to an 'overly serious' attitude to sport which, ideally, should be played for the intrinsic pleasure which it provided, rather than for the extrinsic pleasure associated with winning cups or medals or the satisfaction obtained from the kudos enjoyed by the winners (Dunning and Sheard, 1979: 154–5). The situation described by Dunning and Sheard offers a striking contrast with the highly competitive character of modern sport, and with the much greater emphasis which has in more recent times come to be placed on the importance of winning.

In his analysis of this long-term trend towards the increasing competitiveness of modern sport, Dunning (1986a: 205–23) argues that the pattern of social relationships in pre-industrial Britain was not conducive to the generation of intense competitive pressure in sporting relations. The relatively low degree of state centralisation and national unification, for example, meant that 'folk-games', the games of the ordinary people, were played in regional isolation, with competition traditionally occurring between adjacent villages and towns or between sections of towns. There was no national competitive framework. The aristocracy and gentry formed a partial exception in this respect for they were, and perceived themselves as, national classes and did compete nationally among themselves. However, their high degree of status security – that is, their power and relative autonomy – meant that the aristocracy and gentry were not subject, in a general or a sporting sense, to effective competitive pressure either from above or below. As a result, the aristocracy and gentry, whether playing by themselves or with their hirelings, were able to develop what were to a high degree self-directed or egocentric forms of sports participation. Put more simply, they were able to participate in sport primarily for fun and, in this sense, came close to being amateurs in the 'ideal-typical' sense of that term.

Dunning argues that the growing competitiveness of sporting relations since the eighteenth century has been associated with the development of the pattern of inter-group relationships characteristic of an urban-industrial nation-state. Inherent in the modern structure of social interdependencies, he suggests, is the demand for inter-regional and representative sport. Clearly no such demand could arise in pre-industrial societies because the lack of effective national unification and poor means of transport meant that there were no common rules and no means by which sportsmen from different areas could be brought together. In addition, the 'localism' inherent in such societies meant that those who played the 'sport-like' games of the period perceived as potential rivals only those groups with which they were contiguous in a geographical sense. However, modern industrial societies are different in all these respects. They are relatively unified nationally, have superior means of transport and communication, sports with common rules, and a degree of 'cosmopolitanism' which means that local groups are anxious to compete against groups that are not geographically contiguous. Hence such societies come to be characterised by high rates of inter-area sporting interaction, a process which leads to a hierarchical grading of sportsmen, sportswomen and sports teams, with those that represent the largest social units standing at the top.

Dunning suggests that one consequence of these processes is that top-level sportsmen and women are less and less able to be independent and to play for fun, and are increasingly required to be other-directed and serious in their approach to sport. That is, they are less able to play for themselves and are increasingly constrained to represent wider social units such as cities, counties and countries. As such, they are provided with material and other rewards and facilities and time for training. In return, they are expected to produce high-quality sports performances which, particularly through the achievement of sporting victories, reflect favourably on the social units which they represent. The development of the local, national and international competitive framework of modern sport works in the same direction, and means that constant practice and training are increasingly necessary in order to reach and to stay at the top. In all these ways, then, the network of relationships characteristic of an urban-industrial nation-state increasingly undermines the amateur ethos, with its stress on sport 'for fun', and leads to its replacement by more serious and more competitive forms of sporting participation.

THE POLITICISATION OF SPORT

Although the relationship between politics and sport is by no means exclusively a post-Second World War phenomenon – witness the 'Nazi Olympics' of 1936 (Mandell, 1987) – there can be little doubt that sport has become increasingly politicised in the period since 1945. To some extent, this process has perhaps been associated with the development of independent nation-states in Black Africa and elsewhere, and with the emergence in many of those states of several outstanding athletes whose international successes have been a major source of pride in new nations whose governments have been struggling to establish a national identity and a sense of national unity.

Of rather greater importance, however, was the development of communist regimes in many parts of Eastern Europe and, associated with this, the emergence of the Cold War and of superpower rivalry. Within this context, international sporting competition took on a significance going far beyond the bounds of sport itself, for sport – at least within the context of East–West relations – became to some extent an extension of the political, military and economic competition which characterised relationships between the superpowers and their associated blocs.

The Helsinki Olympics of 1952 were the first Olympics at which western athletes competed against athletes from the Soviet Union. With this development, the Olympics, as Guttmann noted, 'took on a new political dimension . . . one that was destined to grow increasingly important in the decades to follow' (Guttmann, 1992: 97). The athletes were clearly aware of this new dimension. Guttmann suggests that the American winner of the decathlon in those Olympics, Bob Mathias, spoke for many when he wrote: 'There were many more pressures on American athletes because of the Russians. . . . They were in a sense the real enemy. You just loved to beat 'em. You just had to beat 'em. . . . This feeling was strong down through the entire team.' The Soviet athletes, for their part, were housed not in the Olympic Village, where they might have interacted with fellow athletes from the rest of the world, but in their own isolated quarters near the Soviet naval base at Porkkala, while the Soviet officials 'seemed to care only for the gold medals needed to certify the superiority of "new socialist man"' (ibid.). Meanwhile, newspapers 'concentrated on the "battle of the giants" and published daily statistics on the number of unofficial points earned by the United States and the Soviet Union' (1992: 98).

Comparisons of the number of Olympic medals won by the United States and the Soviet Union – or, following the admission of separate teams from West Germany and East Germany from the 1968 Olympics (Hill, 1992: 39), the medals won by the two Germanies – thus came to be very important, for the winning of medals came to be seen as a symbol not only of national pride but also of the superiority of one political system over another. As many governments came to see international sporting success as an important propaganda weapon in the East–West struggle, so those athletes who emerged as winners came increasingly to be treated as national heroes with rewards – sometimes provided by national governments – to match.

SPORT AND COMMERCIALISATION

If the politicisation of sport has been associated with an increase in the competitiveness of international sport, this latter development has also been facilitated by the growing commercialisation of sport, particularly in the West. While the winning of an Olympic medal has undoubtedly been considered an honour ever since the modern Olympics were founded in 1896, it is indisputably the case that in recent years the non-honorific rewards – and in particular the financial rewards – associated with Olympic success have increased massively. Although this development appears to be a fairly general one within western societies, the financial rewards associated with Olympic success are probably greatest in the United States. Voy pointed to the huge financial rewards which are available in the United States to Olympic gold medal winners, who are able not only to demand very high appearance fees for competing in major meetings but, much more importantly, can also earn huge incomes from sponsorship, from television commercials and from product endorsement. However, Voy went on to point out that such fabulous rewards are available only to those who come first, for, as he put it, 'second place doesn't count' ('On the Line', 1990).

As the rewards to be gained from sporting success have increased, so the emphasis placed on winning has also increased. This process has, according to the US athletics coach Brooks Johnson ('On the Line', 1990), resulted in a situation in which many top-class international athletes 'wake up with the desire and the need and the compulsion and the obsession to win, and they go to sleep with it. . . . Make no mistake about it, an Olympic champion is clinically sick.' A not-dissimilar point was made by Angella

Issajenko, a former world record-holder over 50 metres indoors who, like Ben Johnson, was coached by Charlie Francis and who, also like Johnson, admitted taking steroids. Issajenko took the decision to use steroids after being beaten by East German sprinters and, in explaining her decision ('On the Line', 1990), she said that most people 'had no idea of what goes on in the mind of an elite athlete. Nobody wants to be mediocre. Nobody wants to be second best.'

In their history of sports in America since 1945 – significantly entitled *Winning is the Only Thing* – R. Roberts and J. Olsen summarise the impact of the political and economic processes outlined above on the growing competitiveness and seriousness of sport. They write:

> There was a time in United States history, back in the pre-World War II era, when sports knew its place in American culture. It was a pastime, diversion, leisure, recreation, play – fun. In sports people found relief from the real things of the world and their own lives – wars, unemployment, social conflict, politics, religion, work, prices, and family. But after World War II, sports assumed an extraordinary significance in people's lives; games became not only a reflection of the changes occurring in the United States but a lens through which tens of millions Americans interpreted the significance of their country, their communities, their families, and themselves. Americans came to take sports very seriously, and they watched and played for the highest economic, politic, and personal stakes.
>
> (Roberts and Olsen, 1989: xi–xii)

Leaving aside a hint of romanticism – and the rather strange implied suggestion that somehow sport before 1945 was not one of the 'real things' of the world – Roberts and Olsen do nevertheless highlight a very important change in the structure of sport in the post-1945 period. Sport is now more competitive and more serious than it used to be. A greater stress is laid upon the importance of winning. And sport is played for higher – sometimes much higher – stakes, whether these be economic, political or personal. This is an important part of the context for an understanding of the increased use of drugs within sport.

THE SPORT–MEDICINE AXIS

At this stage it might be useful to summarise briefly the argument thus far. I have suggested that what appears to have been a significant increase in the illicit use of drugs in the last three or four decades has been associated with two major processes. The first of these relates to what has been called the 'medicalisation of life' or 'medical imperialism', while the second relates to the increasing competitiveness of sport and to a growing emphasis on the importance of winning. More specifically, it is suggested that certain developments within the medical profession have meant that medical practitioners have been increasingly prepared to make their professional knowledge and skills available to athletes at the very time when athletes, as a result of other developments within sport, have been increasingly eager to seek the help of anyone who could improve the level of their performance.

The conjuncture of these two processes, it is suggested, has been associated with two closely related developments. One of these developments – and one which is generally viewed as wholly legitimate – involves the emergence of sports medicine; the other – which is normally regarded as illegitimate – involves the increasing use by athletes of banned substances to improve their performance. The close association between these two developments was clearly noted by Brown and Benner who pointed out that, as increased importance has been placed on winning, so athletes

> have turned to mechanical (exercise, massage), nutritional (vitamins, minerals), psychological (discipline, transcendental meditation), and pharmacological (medicines, drugs) methods to increase their advantage over opponents in competition. A major emphasis has been placed on the nonmedical use of drugs, particularly anabolic steroids, central nervous system stimulants, depressants and analgesics.
>
> (1984: 32)

In other words, the very processes which have been associated with the development of sports medicine have also been associated with a rapid growth in the illicit use of drugs. The relation between illicit drug use and processes of medicalisation has also been noted by Donohoe and Johnson, who point out that

> we live in a drug-oriented society. Drugs are used to soothe pain, relieve anxiety, help us to sleep, keep us awake, lose or gain weight. For many problems, people rely on drugs rather than seeking alternative coping strategies. It is not surprising that athletes should adopt similar attitudes.
>
> (1986: 126–7)

Houlihan has also recently made a similar point, stressing that the use of performance-enhancing drugs

> needs to be seen in the context of an increasingly pill-dependent society. It is unrealistic to expect athletes to insulate themselves from a culture which expects pharmacists and doctors to be able to supply medicines for all their ills whether physical or psychological.
>
> (1999: 31–2)

Houlihan adds that 'it is also unrealistic to ignore the importance of legitimate drugs in the intensely scientific training regimes of most, if not all, elite athletes in the 1990s'.

It should be noted that since the analysis offered here stresses the conjuncture of two processes, one within the world of medicine and the other within the world of sport, it follows that the increasing use of drugs in sport *cannot be explained simply by reference to the changing patterns of behaviour among athletes.* Rather, it is argued that the increasing use of illicit drugs has been associated with the emergence, in both the world of sport and the world of medicine, of those who may be described as innovators or entrepreneurs. Referring first to the world of sport, it is hardly surprising that, given the increased emphasis which has come to be placed on winning, some athletes – and almost certainly a growing number – have been prepared to innovate by making illicit use of the fruits of medical and pharmacological research. Equally, however, it is a clear implication of the above analysis that there are doctors – and again the probability is that their number is growing – who may be regarded as medical 'entrepreneurs' in the sense that they are prepared to stretch the boundaries of 'sports medicine' to include the prescribing of drugs with the specific intention of improving athletic performance.

This point is of some importance for it suggests that the increasing use of drugs in sport has been associated with the development of a network of co-operative relationships between innovators or entrepreneurs from the two increasingly closely related fields of sport and medicine. In this respect, the analysis is rather different from that of some other writers. For example, John Goodbody, a much respected sportswriter on the London *Times* who has long campaigned against doping in sport, has argued: 'Each generation of competitors uses the experience of its predecessors to find new illegal methods of improving performances. Each generation of administrators and doctors tries to stop every loophole, extend the number of banned drugs and become more sophisticated in its testing and trapping of offenders' (*The Times*, 27 May 1987).

However, Goodbody's argument is too simplistic, primarily because it posits an unrealistic dichotomy or opposition between two groups – competitors and doctors – one of whom, it is suggested, seeks to use, and the other to prevent the use of, illicit drugs. As indicated above, and in marked contradistinction to Goodbody's argument, it appears to be the case that the illicit use of drugs is often premised upon a significant degree of co-operation between 'innovating' athletes and 'entrepreneurial' doctors. Donohoe and Johnson (1986: 62), in a phrase which echoes Goodbody's argument, have similarly suggested that 'Athletes are enterprising people; as soon as detection methods are developed for one anabolic agent they move on to another.' However, their argument, like that of Goodbody, and for similar reasons, is misleading. No doubt there are many athletes who are indeed enterprising people, though one might reasonably doubt

whether many of them are sufficiently well informed about recent developments in medicine and pharmacology to devise their own drug programmes
– and more particularly, to avoid detection, as many undoubtedly do –
without professional advice. In this context, it is worth noting that many
drug regimens, such as those involving 'stacking', a technique which is
particularly used by weightlifters and which involves the use of several
different types of anabolic steroid concurrently, are very complex. Without
overstating the argument, one might reasonably doubt whether complex
drug programmes such as those involved in stacking have been worked out
by the athletes themselves, without access to specialised advice, while it
seems even more improbable that athletes have the specialised technical
knowledge required to avoid detection, for this necessarily involves keeping
one step ahead of what are becoming increasingly sophisticated testing
procedures.

However, perhaps most tellingly, there is much direct evidence relating to
the involvement of doctors in the use of drugs in sport. In this regard, the
Dubin Commission of Inquiry, established by the Canadian Government
following Ben Johnson's infamous positive test at the Seoul Olympics,
proved something of a watershed, for it provided detailed evidence of the
networks of relationships of those, including medical practitioners, involved
in doping in Canada and the United States. Even before the Dubin Commission, however, there was already growing evidence of the involvement
of physicians in doping. The early work of Dr John Ziegler in developing
anabolic steroids has already been noted in this chapter. We also know
that physicians were involved in blood-doping the US cycling team at the
1984 Los Angeles Olympics, while evidence of the systematic involvement
of doctors in doping in Eastern Europe was already beginning to emerge,
often as a result of the defection of sportspeople to the West, in the 1980s.
These three instances shed a good deal of light on the changing relationship
between elite-level sportsmen and sportswomen and practitioners of sports
medicine, and they provide the basis for three detailed case studies in the
next chapter.

There are many other well documented examples of the involvement
of physicians in doping. For example, there is evidence that at the 1984
Olympics at least some team doctors were involved in blatantly exploiting
a loophole in the doping regulations. Although beta-blockers were not at
that time banned by the IOC, team doctors had to fill in declarations for
all athletes using them and state the doses used. If competitors produced a
doctor's certificate stating that they needed the drugs for health reasons,
they would not be disqualified if drug checks proved positive. However,
when urine specimens were screened there were several positives in the
modern pentathlon contest. To the amazement of officials, team managers
came forward with doctors' certificates covering *whole teams*. In October
1984 Colonel Willy Grut, the secretary-general of the world body governing

the modern pentathlon, challenged the IOC to reveal the names of those athletes who 'clearly took dope, not for medical reasons, but to improve performance' (Donohoe and Johnson, 1986: 85–6). What is of importance in the context of the present argument is not that these athletes took drugs but that the drugs appear to have been taken with the knowledge of team doctors who then protected the athletes against disciplinary action.

The Dubin Commission provided perhaps the clearest picture of the network of relationships between doctors, athletes and coaches in relation to doping. Angella Issajenko, who was the first of the athletes coached by Charlie Francis to use anabolic steroids, testified to the Commission that she obtained her first prescription for Dianabol from Dr Gunther Koch, a physician practising in Toronto, in 1979. In 1983, she went on a different drug programme following a visit to Dr Robert Kerr in San Gabriel, California, while from the autumn of 1983 until 1988, her drug programme was supervised by Dr Jamie Astaphan, who also supervised the drug progamme of Ben Johnson (Dubin, 1990: 244–6).

In his evidence to the Dubin Commission, Dr Astaphan indicated that a number of Canada's leading track and field athletes, in addition to those trained by Charlie Francis, had consulted him, and that he had provided them with advice and assistance in regard to anabolic steroids and other performance-enhancing drugs. Astaphan testified that he had also been consulted by athletes from many other countries, including the United States, Italy, Holland, Australia, Sweden, Finland, West Germany, Bulgaria, Jamaica, East Germany, the United Kingdom and several African nations. They included athletes in a number of sports. In addition to advising athletes in track and field, Astaphan also supervised drug programmes for football players, weightlifters, powerlifters and body builders (Dubin, 1990: 251).

Elsewhere in its report, the Dubin Commission noted that the 'names of physicians willing to prescribe anabolic steroids and other performance-enhancing drugs circulate widely in gyms' and that such physicians 'may develop practices with a focus on athletes and performance-enhancing drugs'. One such practitioner named in the report was Dr Ara Artinian, a Toronto general practitioner who had been prescribing and administering anabolic steroids to athletes regularly for several years. Between 1981 and 1988, he purchased anabolic steroids worth $215,101 from various pharmaceutical companies. He administered injections and provided pills to athletes in return for cash payments rather than providing a prescription to fill at a pharmacy. Artinian worked mainly with football players and bodybuilders rather than elite athletes in Olympic sports (Dubin, 1990: 356).

The Commission also took evidence from Bruce Pinnie, a former shot putter who at the time of the Inquiry was a throwing coach, and who testified that he had obtained anabolic steroids for performance-enhancement purposes from his doctor as early as 1972. Pinnie also indicated that there were, even at that early date, several doctors in Winnipeg who were well known for their willingness to supply steroids (Dubin, 1990: 356–7). In relation to the situation in Canada the Dubin report noted that

> The Commission also heard evidence from many other athletes that they received anabolic steroids directly from physicians. Clearly, there are physicians in most major centres across the country who have at one time or another been involved in prescribing anabolic steroids and other performance-enhancing drugs to athletes.
>
> (1990: 357)

Dubin also pointed out that the situation in the United States appeared to be similar. The shot putter and discus thrower Peter Dajia described visiting a doctor's office in Fort Worth, Texas, and obtaining a prescription for anabolic steroids simply by indicating what he wanted. Particularly revealing was the evidence of Dr Robert Kerr, a California sports physician, who estimated that there were at least seventy physicians in the Los Angeles area alone who prescribed anabolic steroids to athletes. Kerr, who is the author of *The Practical Use of Anabolic Steroids with Athletes* and who was often referred to as the 'steroid guru', had an extensive practice principally involving US athletes, though he indicated that he had also prescribed anabolic steroids for athletes from Canada, South America, Australia and the Far East (Dubin, 1990: 357). In his evidence, Kerr also testified that he had prescribed anabolic steroids to approximately twenty medallists at the 1984 Olympic Games (Armstrong, 1991: 61).

The Commission also noted that in Australia, a Senate Committee investigating the use of drugs in sport had estimated that 15,000 users obtained anabolic steroids through physicians. Forty-one per cent of a group of Australian bodybuilders who were surveyed indicated that physicians were their source of supply. One medical witness who gave evidence to Dubin stated that in Sydney there were between ten and twenty doctors who prescribed anabolic steroids, and that he himself would see up to 200 'patients' a year for this purpose. Another medical witness testifed that he was prescribing anabolic steroids for fifty male bodybuilders, one female weight-lifter and three other athletes (Dubin, 1990: 357).

We also now know – though this was not revealed until a *Sunday Times* investigation was published in 1995 – that at about the same time that Charlie Francis and Dr Astaphan were supervising the drug programme of Ben Johnson, Dr Jimmy Ledingham, who was the doctor to the British Olympic men's team between 1979 and 1987, was prescribing steroids to British athletes and also offering advice on how to avoid detection. The same report also revealed that Britain's national director of coaching from 1979 to 1994 had 'turned a blind eye' to athletes who had told him they were taking steroids (*Sunday Times*, 29 October 1995).

Ben Johnson's positive doping test at the Seoul Olympics was, in a number of respects, a watershed in the history of doping in sport. The event generated huge media coverage – Johnson was, after all, the then reigning world champion, world record holder and 'winner' of the Olympic final and, as such, he had an undisputed claim to be 'the fastest man on earth' – and it raised public awareness of doping in sport to a level which was almost certainly unprecedented. The ramifications of Johnson's positive test, and in particular the establishment of the Commission of Inquiry under Mr Justice Dubin, also marked a watershed in some respects, for it provided more systematic, more reliable and more detailed information about the network of relationships among those involved in doping than had ever been available before.

If Johnson's positive test marked one watershed in the history of doping in sport, then it may well be that the major doping scandal in the 1998 Tour de France cycle race will come to be regarded as a second watershed, both in terms of the amount of media coverage which it generated and in terms of the amount of information about the organisation of doping in professional cycling which was made publicly available during and after the Tour. Moreover, this information made it unambiguously clear that, once again, physicians – this time in the form of team doctors – were heavily implicated in the organisation of doping. The revelations about doping in the 1998 Tour are examined in some detail in Chapter 9.

As a preface to the examination of the 1998 Tour, however, we might note that in 1996, when two French professional cyclists, Philippe Gaumont and Laurent Desbiens, tested positive for the steroid nandrolone, it was revealed that the drug had been supplied by their team doctor, Patrick Nedelec, who had previously worked for both the French national cycling federation and the international governing body of cycling, the Union Cycliste Internationale (*Cycling Weekly*, 29 June 1996). The 1998 Tour de France indicated very clearly that this practice was not unique to the team for which Gaumont and Desbiens raced, but that it was a common practice among professional teams on the European continent.

Without anticipating too much of the detailed examination in Chapter 9 of the 1998 Tour de France, we might note that almost all of the media coverage of the doping scandal in that Tour was, perhaps unsurprisingly, heavily emotive and highly censorious, and did little to enhance our understanding of the processes involved. One of the few exceptions, and one which brought out particularly clearly the involvement of team doctors, was a piece written for *The Times* by James Waddington, a novelist who is also a cycling fan. Waddington pointed to the enormous physical demands which the Tour makes upon riders; he described the Tour as 'not just healthy exercise' but 'close to punishment and abuse', and suggested that, in the attempt to keep their team members in the race, the team doctors will draw upon an exhaustive knowledge of a range of substances – nutritional, hormonal and anabolic. He continued:

It is a complex regime, with maybe 20 different components. . . . Only the team doctor has this exhaustive knowledge, and thus the average professional cyclist with no scientific background becomes not a partner but a patient. He opens his mouth, holds out his arm, and trusts. That trust, not the reflex shriek of 'drugs, the excrement of Satan', should be the crucial point in the whole discussion.

(*The Times*, 25 July 1998)

One might perhaps take issue with Waddington's characterisation of professional cyclists as passive participants in the doping process. There is a considerable literature within medical sociology which indicates that patients are often involved, to a greater or lesser degree, in managing their own health problems in partnership with their doctors (S. J. Williams and M. Calnan, 1996; Anderson and Bury, 1988; Elston, 1991), and there is no reason to suppose that professional cyclists are any different from patients in general in this respect; indeed, there is direct evidence in the form of statements from some of the cyclists themselves to suggest that they were not passive participants. However, in two other respects, Waddington draws our attention to points which are of fundamental importance. The first of these is that, as he correctly notes, the 'reflex shriek of "drugs, the excrement of Satan"' is singularly unhelpful. His comments in this regard are very much in line with the arguments about involvement and detachment which were made earlier in this book.

The second point, which Waddington makes very forcefully, is that if we wish to understand doping in sport then it is crucial that we understand the centrality of the relationship between elite-level athletes and practitioners of sports medicine. Some further aspects of the development of sports medicine, and of the changing relationships between sports physicians and elite-level athletes, are explored in the next chapter.

8 The other side of sports medicine
Sports medicine and the development of performance-enhancing drugs

In the last chapter it was argued that, in order to understand the development of sports medicine, it is necessary to examine not only the changing structure of sport and sporting competition, but also to locate these changes within the context of changes in the structure of the wider society and, more particularly, within the context of changes in the structure of modern medical practice. In this regard, it was argued that the process of 'medicalisation' has been of particular significance, and that the development of sports medicine can be seen as an aspect of the medicalisation of sport. Attention was also drawn to the importance of changes in the structure of modern sport and, in this context, attention was focused, in particular, on the increased competitiveness of modern sport, and on the increased emphasis which has come to be placed on winning. It was argued that developments within the structure of medical practice have meant that medical practitioners have been increasingly prepared to make their professional knowledge and skills available to athletes at the very time that athletes, as a result of developments within sport, have been increasingly eager to seek help from anyone who can hold out the prospect of improving their level of performance. The conjuncture of these two relatively autonomous processes, it was argued, has been central to the development of sports medicine.

Given the undoubted significance of the development of sports medicine for modern sporting competition – one writer has suggested that 'the entire enterprise of elite sport is best understood as a recent chapter in the history of applied medical research into human biological development' (Hoberman, 1992: 4) – it is perhaps surprising that the development of sports medicine has received scant attention from both sports sociologists and medical sociologists. The central object of this chapter is build on the analysis in the last chapter and to examine further the changing relationship between sport and medicine. More specifically, this chapter focuses on two interrelated problems. The first part of the chapter traces in broad terms the development of sports medicine in the twentieth century. The second part focuses on some aspects of the relationship between the development of sports medicine and the development and use of performance-enhancing drugs and techniques.

SPORTS MEDICINE: A BRIEF HISTORY

Although some writers have suggested that the origins of sports medicine can be traced back to the Ancient Greeks and Romans (McIntosh, 1976; Percy, 1983; American Academy of Orthopaedic Surgeons, 1984; A. J. Ryan, 1989), the development of sports medicine in the form in which we know it today – that is, the more or less systematic application of the principles of medicine and science to the study of sporting performance, and the institutionalisation of this practice in the form of professional associations, research establishments, scientific conferences and journals – is more properly seen as a development of the late nineteenth and twentieth centuries. According to Ryan (1989: 3), the first use of the term 'sports medicine' to describe an area of research and clinical practice centred on the performances of athletes appears to have been in February 1928, when two doctors attending the Second Winter Olympic Games at St Moritz in Switzerland convened a meeting of physicians who were attending the Games with the teams of competing nations. It was at this meeting that the Association Internationale Médico-Sportive (AIMS) was founded. In 1934, the Association changed its name to the Fédération Internationale de Médecine Sportive (FIMS), which it has retained ever since (Tittel and Knuttgen, 1988: 7–8).

Germany has, perhaps, a longer tradition of sports medicine than any other European country. The world's first sports college, which included a sports medical curriculum, was founded in Berlin in 1920, while the world's first sports medical journal was founded in 1924 by the German Association of Physicians for the Promotion of Physical Culture (Hoberman, 1992: 219). It is, therefore, perhaps not surprising that the first book to use the term 'sports medicine' in its title was German – Dr F. Herxheimer's *Grundriss der Sportsmedizin*, published in 1933. The first book in English to use this title was J. G. P. Williams' *Sports Medicine*, published in 1962 (Ryan, 1989: 4).

Within Great Britain, a significant development was the establishment of the British Association of Sport and Medicine, which was founded in 1953 by Sir Adolphe Abrahams and Sir Arthur (later Lord) Porritt. The BASM now works closely with the National Sports Medicine Institute of the United Kingdom, which was formed in 1992 out of the former London Sports Medicine Institute. In the United States, the American College of Sports Medicine was established in 1954. In the same year, the American Medical Association appointed an *ad hoc* committee on injuries in sports, which, in 1959, became a standing committee, the Committee on the

Medical Aspects of Sports. Other significant developments within the United States included the establishment of a Committee on Sports Medicine by the American Academy of Orthopaedic Surgeons in 1962 and the founding of the American Orthopaedic Society for Sports Medicine in 1975 (Ryan, 1989: 17–18). The American Academy of Pediatrics and the American Academy of Family Physicians have also established committees on sports medicine.

During the last thirty years or so, most countries have established national organisations concerned with sports medicine, and many of these have affiliated to FIMS which, in 1989, had eighty-three member states (Hollmann, 1989: 5). FIMS has also encouraged the formation of sports medicine groupings based on regional and linguistic criteria. These currently include the Confederación Panamérica de Medicina del Deporte, the Northwest European Chapter of Sports Medicine, le Groupement Latin de Médecine du Sport, l'Union Balkanique de FIMS, the Asian Confederation of Sports Medicine, the Arab Federation of Sports Medicine, l'Union Africaine de Médecine du Sport and la Société Méditerranéenne de Médecine du Sport (Tittel and Knuttgen, 1988: 11). Further evidence of the growing significance of sports medicine as an area of practice is provided by the drafting in 1981 by the World Medical Association of a code of practice for doctors involved in sport (McLatchie, 1986: 22–4).

The development of sports medicine has been particularly rapid since the Second World War. What was, before 1945, a relatively small and marginal area within both sport and medicine has now become a well-established part of the sporting scene, and of modern medicine. However, the growing involvement of medical practitioners in a sporting world which has become very much more competitive and success-orientated in the post-1945 period has been associated not only with a rapid expansion of the discipline of sports medicine, but also with an important change in the orientation of practitioners of sports medicine, particularly on the part of senior practitioners involved in research, who have had the ability largely to define the agenda – and therefore the major lines of development – of sports medicine. This development has been associated with a radical change in the nature of sports medicine in the post-1945 period. In order to understand this point more fully, it is necessary to retrace our steps and re-examine in a little more detail some of the key aspects of the development of sports medicine.

THE EARLY DEVELOPMENT OF SPORTS MEDICINE

The development of modern sports medicine can be traced back to the end of the nineteenth century and the first decades of the twentieth century. However, in tracing its development back to this period, there is a danger of overemphasising the continuities while failing to recognise the discontinuities in this developmental process. In this regard, it is important to note that the difference between contemporary sports medicine and the sports medicine of the turn of the century lies not simply in the greater quantity of information which is now available, important though this undoubtedly is, but also in that, in the earlier period, the orientations of the researchers and the problems they sought to resolve were also rather different from what they are now. This aspect of the changing structure of sports medicine has, perhaps, been brought out most clearly by Hoberman.

In describing the work of the early pioneers of sports medicine in the late nineteenth and early twentieth centuries, Hoberman pointed out that the investigation of human athletic potential was not a primary goal of those who studied the human organism at that time. In those days, the high-performance athlete was 'still a curiosity and not a charismatic figure at the centre of huge commercial enterprises like the Olympic Games' (Hoberman, 1992: 6). Sport was considered as just one among a number of activities which were of interest to the physiologist and, as a source of interesting physiological data, sport occupied a relatively humble position within a much broader range of physical performances such as manual labour and military service. In commenting on this early period in the development of sports medicine, Hoberman (1992: 6) pointed out that the 'scientific marginality of sport during this period, and the general lack of interest in boosting (as opposed to investigating) athletic performance, has a quaintly premodern quality'.

It is important to emphasise the general absence among the pioneers of sports medicine of any interest in boosting athletic performance, for this is one of the most important characteristics which distinguishes the sports medicine of the late nineteenth and early twentieth centuries from the sports medicine of today. In relation to the former, Hoberman (1992: 8) has pointed out that

> the scientists who turned their attention to athletic physiology during the late nineteenth and early twentieth centuries did so not to produce athletic wonders but to measure and otherwise explore the biological wonders presented by the high-performance athlete of this era. It was a time, one scientist of the age wrote, when phenomena once considered mere curiosities or freaks of nature called out for scientific investigation.

Those involved in the experimental approach to athletics showed little interest in boosting performance. The Austrian physiologist Oscar Zoth, for example, studied the pedalling action of cyclists as a problem in muscle physiology without referring to the possibility of improving performance. Similarly, in 1903, an American physiologist offered a scientific rationale for the 'warming-up' procedure for sprinters but said nothing about faster sprinting. To cite Hoberman again:

In short, the primary interest of these scientists was to discover the natural laws that regulated the functioning of the body. If they did not express an interest in applying science to the boosting of athletic performance it was in part because the scientific mysteries they found in the world of high-performance sport were already exciting enough.

(1992: 10)

Not only did these scientists have little interest in boosting athletic performance, but some of the leading sports physicians of the period also expressed concern about what they saw as the physiological dangers of sporting overexertion – for men as well as for women – and, for this reason, actively opposed the search for new records in athletics.[1] Particularly interesting in this respect was the career of Philippe Tissié. Born in 1852, Tissié was a contemporary and fellow countryman of Pierre de Coubertin and probably the most important sports physician of the *fin de siècle*. Although Tissié made some pioneering medical observations on a record-breaking long-distance cyclist, he was by no means an advocate of such record-breaking attempts; indeed, one of the characteristics which sets this early pioneer of sports medicine apart from his modern counterparts is the fact that Tissié actually disapproved of the high-performance sport of his era. Tissié did not share de Coubertin's view that breaking records was a central part of the athlete's task and, indeed, Tissié strongly opposed, because of what he saw as their medical dangers, the competitive sports which de Coubertin promoted. The conflict between the two came to a head in 1894 when, at the conference of the French Association for the Advancement of Science, Tissié successfully opposed de Coubertin's appeal for track and field events (Hoberman, 1992: 80–4).

The orientation which characterised the work of the early exponents of sports medicine – and in particular the emphasis on scientific puzzle-solving rather than on boosting athletic performance – can also be seen in the work of some leading sports physicians in the early inter-war period. A prominent example is provided by the work of A. V. Hill, the British physiologist and Nobel Prize winner who was based at Cornell University and who analysed athletic performance as part of a larger-scale scientific problem. In commenting on Hill's work, Hoberman (1992: 11) pointed out that 'In the last analysis, . . . and despite all its physiological sophistication, Hill's approach to athletic performance was not so different from the turn-of-the-century idea that the high-performance athlete was a wonder of nature – a marvellous phenomenon that did not require improvement.'

In summarising the characteristics of sports medicine at the turn of the century, Hoberman suggested that:

By the standards of our technological and sports-obsessed age, the last decades of the nineteenth and the early decades of the twentieth centuries were a premodern world in terms of physiological investigations

of human performance. Dynamic athleticism was a peripheral pre-
occupation rather than the self-evident ideal it has become for many
people in widely varying cultures across the globe. What we call
'sportive' aptitudes and efforts were viewed in the context of a plethora
of human frailties and performances, all of which could be studied to
yield clues about the nature of the human mind and body.

(Hoberman, 1992: 63)

The early sports physicians, Hoberman suggested, saw 'sportive performances serving physiology as experimental data, rather than the other way
round', with the emphasis being placed on the 'discovery of physiological
laws rather than the application of these discoveries to athletic achievement'. In more recent years, however, the increased emphasis which has
come to be placed on winning and on breaking records has dramatically
changed the relationship between athletic performance and sports medicine.
If, in the early years of this century, 'sport served the ends of science rather
than the other way round', it is now the case that, in contrast to that earlier
period, 'the modern outlook sees symbolic importance in the pursuit of the
record performance, thereby putting physiology in the service of sport'
(Hoberman, 1992: ix, 78).

It might perhaps be argued that, in setting up a dichotomous conceptualisation of the relationship between athletic performance and sports
medicine – that is, *either* sport serves medical science *or* medical science
serves sport – Hoberman overstates his case. It might be suggested, for
example, that the present relationship between sport and medicine is one
from which both medical scientists and sportspeople derive what they consider to be benefits, the former in terms of increased knowledge of human
physiology and the latter in terms of improved athletic performances.
Nevertheless, Hoberman properly draws attention to a process which,
beginning sometime in the inter-war period and accelerating rapidly in the
last three or four decades, has involved a dramatic shift in the research
orientation of many leading sports physicians and, associated with this, an
equally dramatic change in the nature of sports medicine as a discipline.
This process has involved a radical shift away from the situation in which
sports physicians, in the first few decades of this century, saw sport
primarily as a source of data for the study of human physiology and were
more or less uninterested in, and in some cases even hostile to, the attempt
to set new athletic records. Conversely, as sports physicians have become
more and more involved in a sporting world which, particularly in the
post-1945 period, has become increasingly competitive, so have their scientific activities increasingly both underpinned and been given meaning by
the search for winning, and perhaps above all, for record-breaking athletic
performances. If the late-nineteenth- and early-twentieth-century pioneers
of sports medicine were largely unconcerned about improving athletic

performance, this has now become an important part of the *raison d'être* of contemporary sports medicine.

These changes within the structure of sports medicine should not be seen as unproblematic, for an examination of the development and contemporary structure of sports medicine – and in particular, an examination of the growing involvement of practitioners of sports medicine in the search for improved athletic performance – suggests that there are some aspects of the practice of modern sports medicine which raise a number of problems, not just on a sociological level, but also in terms of medical and ethical considerations. One such area concerns the relationship between the development of sports medicine and the development and use of performance-enhancing drugs. Within the context of this chapter, my concern is with the sociological issues raised in this connection; I am happy to leave discussion of the medical and ethical issues to others.

SPORTS MEDICINE AND THE DEVELOPMENT OF PERFORMANCE-ENHANCING DRUGS

A more or less standard feature of all modern textbooks on sports medicine is the inclusion of a chapter on the use of performance-enhancing drugs. Such chapters usually include basic information on the performance-enhancing effects of different drugs, on the side effects and other medical complications which may be associated with their use, and advice to physicians on how to recognise the illicit use of drugs by athletes under their care. Associated with the inclusion of information of this kind in such textbooks is the public perception of the practitioner of sports medicine as an expert who plays a vital role in the fight against what is commonly regarded as the abuse of drugs in sport. However, an analysis of the relationship between the development of sports medicine and the development and use of performance-enhancing drugs suggests that this relationship is rather more complex than at first sight it appears, and certainly a good deal more complex than is usually presented in textbooks of sports medicine. In particular, such an analysis suggests that the growing involvement of practitioners of sports medicine in high-performance sport, especially from the 1950s, has increasingly involved them in the search for championship-winning or record-breaking performances, and that this has led them in the direction not only of developing improved diet or mechanical and psychological techniques but that, on occasions, it has also led them (though it is not suggested that they have always been aware of the longer-term consequences of their actions) to play an active part in the development and use of performance-enhancing drugs.

Thus it is suggested that, far from being one of the key bastions in the fight against the use of performance-enhancing drugs in sport, sports medicine has actually been one of the major contexts within which performance-enhancing drugs have been developed and used. In this sense, it may be said that *the development of performance-enhancing drugs and techniques is not something which is alien to, but something which has been an integral part of, the recent history of sports medicine.* This aspect of the development of sports medicine is worth examining in rather more detail, and will be explored via an examination of three illustrative case studies: the relationship between sports medicine and the use of drugs in some of the former communist countries of Eastern Europe; the early development and use of anabolic steroids in the United States; and the development of the technique which has come to be known as 'blood-doping'.

SPORTS MEDICINE AND DRUG USE IN EASTERN EUROPE

For many years prior to the collapse of the communist regimes in Eastern Europe, there were widespread suspicions among western observers that the outstanding successes of many East European, and particularly East German and Soviet, athletes were associated, at least in part, with the use of performance-enhancing drugs. Since the collapse of those regimes, much more information has become available, and we now know that performance-enhancing drugs were used systematically by those involved in the sports medical establishments of some Soviet-bloc countries in their attempt to produce Olympic medal-winning athletes.

It is important to recognise that there were differences between the former communist countries of Eastern Europe, and it would be wrong to assume that in all of these countries the use of drugs to boost athletic performance was a common phenomenon. In this context, it should be noted that, while states such as the former East Germany and the Soviet Union systematically used sport as a means of seeking international recognition and prestige, other communist countries, of which Albania was perhaps the most striking example, were characterised by a relative lack of involvement in international sporting competition and there is no evidence to suggest, nor any reason to suppose, that athletes in countries such as Albania were involved in the systematic use of performance-enhancing drugs.

It would also be very misleading to suggest that the successes of East German and Soviet athletes can simply be explained in terms of the use of performance-enhancing drugs, for in both countries there was a well-developed system for talent-screening, while all aspects of the training and development of elite athletes were carefully monitored by sports physicians who worked within a highly sophisticated system of sports medicine. Nevertheless, it is clear that the systematic use of drugs was an integral part of the East German and Soviet systems. The leading western expert on sport in the former Soviet Union is probably James Riordan, who pointed out that 'It should come as no surprise that, given the "win at all costs" mentality that came to dominate the sports administrations in some East European countries, there had been long-term *state* production, testing, monitoring and administering of performance-enhancing drugs in regard to athletes as young as 7–8' (1994: 11; italics in original).

Elsewhere, Riordan (1991: 122) suggested that practices such as this have cast 'a shadow over the role of sports medicine, or at least that part of it that has worked on producing ever faster, stronger, more skilful athletes – at any cost'.

There is, perhaps, no need to document in detail the multiplicity of ways in which, we now know, members of the sports medicine establishments in the Soviet Union and East Germany were involved in the use of performance-enhancing drugs. What is important to note is that the use of such drugs was a systematic part of Soviet and East German sports policy, and that it involved a wide variety of people, including the 'coach-pharmacologist', sports physicians and government ministers. In East Germany, for example, the administration of performance-enhancing drugs to athletes involved personnel in a number of organisations, including the German College of Physical Culture (DHfK), the Research Institute for Physical Culture and Sport (FKS), the Central Institute for Microbiology and Experimental Therapy (ZIMET), the pharmaceutical company VEB Jenapharm, the Central Institute for Sports Medical Services, the Central Doping-control Laboratory in Kreischa, the Institute for Aviation Medicine, and the Health Ministry in East Berlin. According to Hoberman (1992: 222), a 'Sports Medical Commission passed doping instructions down the line to sports physicians and trainers who would distribute the drugs and often extract a vow of silence from athletes'. Similarly, it was revealed in 1989 that, seven years earlier, two deputy sports ministers in the Soviet Government had signed a document prescribing anabolic steroids as part of the preparation for Soviet cross-country skiers, and setting out a programme to test the effects of steroids and for research into ways of avoiding detection (Riordan, 1991: 122–3). As Riordan noted:

> drug taking was organised *at the top* and involved parts of the sports medical establishment; no athlete was allowed overseas unless he or she had a clearance test at a sports medicine dispensary before departing. At the Olympics of Montreal (1976) and Seoul (1988), it has now been revealed, the Soviet team had a hospitality ship used as a medical centre to ensure that Soviet competitors were 'clean' at the last moment.
> (Riordan, 1991: 123; italics in original)

It is important to emphasise that the use of drugs by Soviet and East German athletes was not something which was done against the advice, or without the knowledge and consent, of those involved in the sports federations and in the sports medicine establishments of those countries. Rather it is the case that the drugs were provided by the state, and that all aspects of the athletes' development, *including those relating to the administration of drugs, were supervised and monitored by specialists in sports medicine.* Within the context of sport in some of the former communist regimes of Eastern Europe, therefore, it is not possible to separate out the development and use of performance-enhancing drugs from the development of sports medicine, for the one was an integral part of the other. The use of performance-enhancing drugs was viewed simply as one part of the scientific armoury which also included such things as diet, exercise physiology and biomechanics, and which was available to sports physicians in their efforts to produce medal-winning athletes.

THE DEVELOPMENT AND USE OF ANABOLIC STEROIDS IN THE UNITED STATES

As we noted briefly in Chapter 7, in the early 1950s there were persistent rumours to the effect that sports scientists in the Soviet Union had been experimenting with the use of testosterone in an attempt to boost the performances of Soviet athletes. The validity of these rumours was confirmed by evidence obtained by Dr John Ziegler, who was the team physician to the US team at the 1956 World Games in Moscow.[2] On returning to the United States, Ziegler obtained some testosterone and tested it on himself, on the US weightlifting coach, Bob Hoffman, and on several east coast weightlifters. Ziegler was impressed by the anabolic, or muscle-building, effects of testosterone but concerned about some of the side effects. According to Voy:

> In an attempt to help Western athletes compete more effectively against the Soviets who used testosterone, and in an effort to reduce the bad side effects of testosterone – namely, acne, hair loss, prostate enlargement, and shrinkage of the testicles – Dr Ziegler aided the CIBA Pharmaceutical Company in the development of Dianabol, or, in generic terms, methandrostenolone.
>
> (1991: 9)

As developed by CIBA, the drug was not intended for use by athletes, but was developed for use in treating patients suffering from burns and certain post-operative patients. However, as Todd (1987: 94) noted, Dr Ziegler 'had another agenda, and what he did with Dianabol was critical in the spread of anabolic drugs in sport'. With the co-operation of the national weightlifting coach, Ziegler persuaded three weightlifters to begin using Dianabol. Almost immediately, the three lifters began making very rapid gains in strength and muscle size and, as the lifters began to approach the world record level, other lifters clamoured for information about how this rapid improvement had been achieved. It soon became widely known that the success of the three lifters, by this time all national champions, had been associated with their use of Dianabol. Voy (1991: 10) noted: 'With the introduction of Dianabol in the late 1950s, anabolic-androgenic steroids really got their initial use', and he adds that they 'became popular very quickly'; indeed, anabolic steroids were adopted so quickly by American athletes that it was estimated that by 1968, a full third of the US track and field team had used steroids at the pre-Olympic training camp held at Lake Tahoe, prior to the Mexico Olympics (Todd, 1987: 95).

As both Voy and Todd recognise, Ziegler played a central role in helping to produce 'a climate of rising expectations in which strength athletes began a big arms race, fueled by an ever expanding array of pharmaceuticals' (Todd, 1987: 94).[3] In the mid-1980s, the central role of Ziegler in the development and use of anabolic steroids was recognised, with wonderful irony, in the name of a California-based business which supplied athletes with steroids by mail order; the business was called the John Ziegler Fan Club (Todd, 1987: 104).

As noted earlier, it is not suggested that sports physicians who have become involved in the search for performance-enhancing drugs have been fully aware of the longer-term consequences of their actions, for their actions, like all human actions, are constrained by a complex network of relationships of which they are likely to have, at best, only a limited awareness. In the case of Dr Ziegler, Voy (1991: 10) pointed out that, particularly when he became aware of the high doses being taken by some athletes, he 'realized the mistake he had made by helping to introduce these drugs to the athletic community. It was almost a sports world analogy to the story of Dr Frankenstein. Soon after Dianabol hit the market, Dr Ziegler knew he had created a monster, a fact he regretted for the rest of his life.'

It is important to emphasise that it is not possible to dismiss Ziegler simply as a charlatan, as a disreputable practitioner on the fringes or even outside of orthodox sports medicine. Nor is it possible to dismiss him as a cheat whose actions ran counter to the rules of fair play. In this context it must be reiterated that in the 1950s and early 1960s, taking pills to enhance performance was not considered unethical and was not against the rules of any sporting competition, for there were no anti-doping regulations at that time. This was a period, it should be recalled, when more effective drugs – most notably, antibiotics – were becoming available to doctors in their treatment of patients, and when patients were also becoming more aware of the therapeutic possibilities offered by new drugs. America was, as Voy puts it, 'a society that was just developing the pill-popping scene' and, within this context, it is not surprising that both sports physicians and athletes should have looked to the pharmaceutical industry to improve athletic performances, just as it held out the possibility of improving many other aspects of people's lives. In this sense, Ziegler's actions should be seen not as those of an idiosyncratic zealot, nor as those of a disreputable cheat, but simply as those of a sports physician whose involvement in the increasingly competitive world of modern sport led him, just as it led other sports physicians, towards the search for performance-enhancing drugs.

Of course, it might be objected that both case studies cited above are atypical and that, as a consequence, they cannot be regarded as shedding much light on the relationship between the development of sports medicine and the search for, and the use of, performance-enhancing drugs. Thus it might be argued that the example of sports medicine in Eastern Europe related to totalitarian communist regimes that, in one sense or another, were 'abnormal', which can therefore shed little light on the development of sports medicine in the liberal democracies of the West and which, in any case, no longer exist. In similar fashion, it might be objected that the case study of the development of Dianabol, though relating to a liberal democracy, also relates to a period when there were no rules prohibiting the use of performance-enhancing drugs and when the situation was therefore very different from that which exists today, where there are relatively clear rules which prohibit the use of such drugs. On this basis, it might be objected that the situation described in relation to the development of Dianabol was merely an 'unfortunate', one-off incident and not one which would be likely to be repeated today. In the context of possible objections of this kind, the third case study – the development of the technique which has come to be known as 'blood-doping' – is particularly revealing.

BLOOD-DOPING

Blood-doping does not involve the administration of drugs but is a technique involving the removal from an athlete of some blood, which is stored and later reinfused into the athlete. The removal of this blood stimulates the bone marrow to form more red cells, and the athlete's blood returns to normal after ten to twelve weeks. The stored blood is then reinfused into the athlete a couple of days before competition, the extra red cells boosting the oxygen-carrying capacity of the blood, and thus the quantity of oxygen available to the muscles.

Although some early work on blood-doping had been done in the 1940s, the technique did not become associated with sport until many years later. The first systematic research studies to examine the effects of blood-doping on endurance and performance were conducted in Sweden, during the late 1960s and early 1970s, by Professor Bjorn Ekblom and his colleagues at the Institute of Physiology of Performance in Stockholm. They initially reported significant increases in maximum oxygen uptake and went on to claim that blood-doping was associated with significant improvements in performance (Donohoe and Johnson, 1986: 116–17). In the 1970s and early 1980s many similar studies were undertaken by sports physicians and related specialists within sports medicine with a view to discovering whether blood-doping was indeed an effective means of improving performance. Although there were some contradictory findings from the early studies, by the early 1980s a consensus of opinion was emerging to the effect that, carried out in the appropriate way, blood-doping was indeed an effective way of increasing maximum oxygen uptake and endurance capacity (M. H. Williams, 1981; Gledhill, 1982).

A review of the contradictory findings from earlier studies also led to considerable refinements in the technique of blood-doping. Thus, for example, it was suggested that the failure of some of the early studies to find a significant improvement in performance following reinfusion was associated with the use of inadequate reinfusion volumes, or with premature reinfusion of blood following removal, or with inappropriate methods of storing the blood. Sports physicians were thus able to indicate that, for the maximum impact in terms of improving athletic performance, a specified minimal amount of blood should be reinfused, there should be a specified minimal interval between removal of the blood and reinfusion, and that the blood should be stored by freezing rather than by refrigeration in order to avoid the loss of red cells in the blood (Gledhill, 1982).

Outside the world of sports medicine there had been some popular interest in blood-doping in the 1970s, when some commentators suggested that the Finnish runner Lasse Viren, a double gold medallist at both the 1972 and 1976 Olympics, had been blood-doped. Viren vigorously denied the suggestion, saying that he drank only reindeer milk. Media and popular interest in the technique was revived when, following the spectacular success of the US cycling team at the Los Angeles Olympics in 1984 – the United States, which had not won an Olympic cycling medal since 1912, dominated the cycling events at the 1984 Games, winning a total of nine medals, including four golds – it was revealed that several members of the US team had been blood-doped (Cramer, 1985; Pavelka, 1985; Weaver, 1985). Following these revelations, the IOC declared the practice illegal and funded research into the development of methods for detecting blood-doping (Collings, 1988).

In considering the development of the technique of blood-doping from the early 1970s, it should be noted that the research which demonstrated that blood-doping was an effective method of boosting athletic performance and which also led to considerable refinements of that technique – thus improving its effectiveness as a means of boosting performance – was carried out by sports physicians and related specialists within sports medicine. It is important to emphasise that those involved in this research were not those who might be regarded as 'quacks', working on the illegitimate fringes of sports medicine and rejected by their more reputable colleagues, but that they were highly reputable sports physicians working within the mainstream of sports medicine, and their research was published, not in underground publications which circulated illicitly but in the mainstream journals in sports medicine.

Viewed sociologically, what one might call the 'moral career' of blood-doping is very interesting, for, within two decades, what had formerly been regarded as a legitimate research area for sports physicians seeking to improve athletic performance has now come to be regarded as a form of cheating which is banned under the anti-doping rules of the IOC. A brief examination of the shift in the status of blood-doping, from legitimate to illegitimate technique, is particularly revealing in terms of understanding the relationship between sports medicine and the use of performance-enhancing drugs and techniques.

An examination of the early literature on blood-doping suggests that sports physicians initially regarded blood-doping simply as one of many science-based techniques which held out the possibility of boosting athletic performance and that, at least in these early stages, they had little awareness of the possibility that its use might be construed as a form of cheating. For example, in one of the early major British textbooks, *Sports Medicine*, by J. G. P. Williams and P. N. Sperryn (1976), there was just one brief reference to blood-doping, which was as follows:

> Experimental re-transfusion of subjects with their own red cells after an interval of four weeks was thought to give improved performance, but this has subsequently been denied by further studies. In view of the dangers inherent in the whole process of blood transfusion, it is unlikely that further developments can be expected.
>
> (1976: 158)

We need not concern ourselves here with the inaccuracy of their forecast about future developments; what is of interest is the absence of any suggestion that such a technique might be construed as cheating. This is confirmed by the fact that the discussion of blood-doping is located, not in the chapter on doping, but in a chapter entitled 'General medical aspects of sport'. Within this chapter, the brief discussion of blood-doping is located in a section on 'Hazards of exercise', which deals with such things as general medical screening, inoculations, routine clinical examinations, physiological testing, infections, sex and skin disorders. One can only conclude that Williams and Sperryn considered it appropriate to discuss blood-doping under the heading 'General medical aspects of sport' and that they saw no reason to include it in their discussion of doping. This would suggest that they regarded it as a legitimate area for research and development – even if, in their view, it was an unpromising development – for practitioners of sports medicine.

Seven years later, Sperryn's *Sport and Medicine* (1983) included a slightly expanded discussion of blood-doping, but there was still no suggestion that blood-doping might be construed as a form of cheating. After a brief discussion of some of the technical aspects of blood-doping, Sperryn concludes:

'In summary, while this method is theoretically attractive, its practice must be extremely difficult to regulate safely and efficiently under all the stresses of athletic competition and, in view of all the provisos outlined, it is unlikely to become widespread' (1983: 27).

Again we are not concerned with whether or not Sperryn's prediction about the use of blood-doping was correct – this was just one year before the US cycling team used the technique to such good effect – but with the absence of any suggestion that the use of the technique may be considered a form of cheating. In this context, Sperryn rejects the technique not because he considers its use runs counter to the spirit of 'fair play', but because of certain technical difficulties in using it 'under all the stresses of athletic competition'. It is once again significant that this discussion of blood-doping is located not in the chapter on doping in Sperryn's book but, on this occasion, in a chapter on 'Cardiovascular and respiratory systems'. Given the date of publication of *Sport and Medicine*, it is perhaps surprising that he made no reference to any ethical issues in his discussion of blood-doping for, by the late 1970s and early 1980s, sports physicians were increasingly raising the question of whether the technique which they themselves had pioneered might not give rise to ethical concerns relating to concepts of fairness and cheating. However, it should be emphasised that, particularly in the 1970s, most researchers appeared to be as unconcerned with ethical issues as were Williams and Sperryn. It might be noted that two research papers on blood-doping which did explicitly raise ethical issues were those by Videman and Rytömaa (1977) and by Williams *et al.* (1978). However, in both cases, the ethical issues which were discussed related not to fair play and cheating, but to the rather different ethical issues, such as those relating to informed consent, which are raised when using human subjects in experimental programmes.

By the late 1970s and early 1980s, however, it was becoming increasingly common for researchers to discuss not only the technical aspects of blood-doping, but also to raise the question of whether or not blood-doping could be regarded as a form of cheating (Gledhill and Froese, 1979; Gledhill, 1982; M. H. Williams, 1981). Writers at the time seemed to see this as a difficult issue to resolve, not least because a similar effect to that obtained by blood-doping could also be obtained by training at altitude, a practice which was allowed – and still is allowed; indeed, how could it be banned? – by all sports governing bodies (Gledhill and Froese, 1979: 25). Williams concluded his brief discussion of ethical issues by calling on the governing bodies of sport to consider the matter: 'Because it is an effective method of improving distance running performance, its place in the sports world should be determined by the various governing bodies' (M. H. Williams, 1981: 61).

By this time, it is clear, the status of blood-doping was changing. From being a technique which, in the early 1970s, raised technical issues but not, for most researchers, issues of fairness, it had become a technique the ethical status of which was now uncertain. It was not yet, however, unambiguously regarded as a form of cheating.

The most recent stage in the 'moral career' of blood-doping came with the decision by the IOC, following the 1984 Olympic Games, to ban the practice of blood-doping. Once the IOC had taken this decision, the view that blood-doping was a form of cheating quickly became established as the orthodoxy among practitioners of sports medicine. Thus in 1987, the American College of Sports Medicine issued a 'position stand', in which it stated: 'It is the position of the American College of Sports Medicine that the use of blood doping as an ergogenic aid for athletic competition is unethical and unjustifiable' (1987: 540). The following year Dirix, writing in *The Olympic Book of Sports Medicine*, held that the procedures involved in blood-doping 'contravene the ethics of medicine and of sport' (1988: 674). There was, it is true, still the occasional sceptical view, such as that expressed in 1988 by Nuzzo and Waller, who reminded their readers that training at high altitude can lead to an increase in red blood cells (RBC), and suggested that this could place athletes trained at low altitude at a disadvantage. They then went on to ask: 'Should blood-doping be permitted to make all competitors have equal RBC concentrations?' (1988: 148).

By this time, however, such views were rare. Much more common was the view expressed by Eriksson and his colleagues (1990: 383) and by Cowan (1994: 327), who not only echoed the sentiment which had earlier been expressed by Dirix, but also used his precise words: 'These procedures contravene the ethics of medicine and of sport.' Mottram (1988: 23) similarly held that, 'Apart from contravening the ethics of sport and medicine, this procedure carries tremendous risk to the individual recipient'. Macauley (1991: 83), writing in a book published for the Sports Council for Northern Ireland, described the technique of blood-doping and then noted, 'It is of course banned,' as though the technique were so self-evidently a form of cheating that it was difficult to see how this issue could ever have been problematic. Rather more sophisticated was the position of Wadler and Hainline, who argued that blood-doping

is unique in that the inability to detect its use, coupled with its clear-cut ergogenic potential, demands from the individual athlete a more profound ethical and moral decision. As with other drugs and methods of deception which are always available, the athlete is left with a choice – to embrace the meaning of the essence of sport, or to participate in the practice of winning at any cost.

(1989: 176)

The argument may have been a little more sophisticated, but the message was the same: blood-doping is cheating.

By the late 1980s, then, a new moral orthodoxy in relation to blood-doping had been established. By this time, sports physicians, acting not merely as technical experts but also as moral 'policemen' charged with the responsibility of educating athletes about both the ethics and the medical dangers of using banned substances or techniques, were telling athletes in unambiguous terms that the use of blood-doping was cheating and that this technique should not be used. It is a reasonable supposition that, when advising athletes in their care, they did not tell the athletes that it was they – the sports physicians – who had developed and refined this technique. It is not perhaps surprising that, within this context, sports physicians chose to ignore certain aspects of the history of blood-doping. Thus Goldman and Klatz, in their *Death in the Locker Room II*, wrote in relation to blood-doping that 'Some athletes will go to any length to boost their endurance and performance' (1992: 203). The implication of their statement would seem to be that, if anyone is culpable in relation to the use of blood-doping, then it is the athletes. One might easily get the impression that it was the athletes themselves, rather than Goldman's own colleagues within sports medicine, who had developed the technique.

CONCLUSION

Although sports physicians are often seen as experts who play a front-line role in the fight against 'drug abuse' in sport, a closer examination of the development of sports medicine suggests that the relationship between sports medicine and the use of drugs is rather more complex. In this regard, it has been argued that the growing involvement of sports physicians in the search for record-breaking and competition-winning per-formances, especially since 1945, has increasingly involved them not merely in the search for improved diets or training methods, but also in the development and use of performance-enhancing drugs and techniques, some of which have subsequently come to be defined as forms of cheating. One important implication of this analysis is that, if we wish to understand the processes involved in the increase in recent years in the illicit use by athletes of performance-enhancing drugs, then, as Armstrong (1991) has suggested, we need to shift our focus away from what has hitherto been an almost exclusive concentration on the athletes, and to examine more closely the networks of relationships in which athletes are involved. Clearly, one aspect of this must involve a much closer examination of the relationships between athletes and sports physicians.

The close interrelationship between sports medicine, sports science and the development of what have come to be regarded as illicit drugs and tech-niques was nicely brought out by Cramer in his report on the use of blood-doping by the US cycling team at the 1984 Olympics: 'In the national euphoria after the games, no one thought to pry out any secrets. The US team had won nine medals, dominating the cycling events. "Great riders. . . ." "Great coach. . . ." "Great bikes. . . ." said the press, reporting the daisy chain of back pats. No one thought to add, "Great doctors. . . ."' (1985: 25).

In 1988, the British medical journal *The Lancet* published an article with the title 'Sports medicine – is there lack of control?' It suggested that, although 'evidence of direct involvement of medical practitioners in the procurement and administration of hormones is lacking, their connivance with those who do so is obvious and their participation in blood-doping is a matter of record', and it concluded that

> Members of the medical profession have long been concerned with the health and welfare of people in sport, but never have the stakes been so high. Evidence continues to grow that some are showing more interest in finding new ways of enhancing the performance of those in their charge than in their physical wellbeing. Surely steps must soon be taken to curb the activities of those few doctors practising on the fringe by bringing sports medicine beneath the umbrella of a recognised body within an accredited programme of professional training.
>
> (1988: 612)

With this comment, *The Lancet* was beginning to move towards a more adequate understanding of the relationship between sports medicine and the development and use of performance-enhancing drugs. In one major respect, however, *The Lancet* article did not properly come to grips with an important dimension of this relationship. In suggesting that the search for new, and by implication, unethical, means of enhancing performance is confined to a 'few doctors practising on the fringe', *The Lancet* failed to grasp a key aspect of modern sports medicine. A central argument of this chapter has been that the growing involvement of sports physicians in high-performance sport has meant that the search for performance-enhancing substances and techniques – a search which, as we have seen, has resulted in the development of some drugs and techniques whose use has subsequently been considered unethical – is not confined to a few 'fringe' practitioners. Rather, it has become an increasingly important part of the task of practitioners of sports medicine. In this sense, what *The Lancet* saw as a problem concerning the lack of control of sports medicine is not a problem which is confined to the fringes of sports medicine but, on the contrary, one which goes to its very heart.

9 Doping in sport

A case study of cycling and the 1998 Tour de France

In Chapter 7, it was argued that the use of performance-enhancing drugs by athletes could not be adequately understood if – and this is a characteristic of much of the public and policy discussion of the subject – attention is focused exclusively on the drug-using athletes. It was suggested, instead, that the illicit use of drugs by athletes was premised upon a network of co-operative relationships between those who were described as 'innovating' athletes and 'entrepreneurial' doctors. It would, however, be misleading to suggest that doctors are the only people, other than the athletes themselves, who are involved in the doping process, for it is clear that the network of people involved in fostering the use of drugs in sport, and in concealing their use, is considerably more complex and extensive, and that, in particular, it often involves many people in addition to athletes and doctors.

This was, it might be noted, also one of the central findings of the Dubin Commission. Robert Armstrong, the Counsel to the Dubin Commission, wrote that

> until the Dubin Inquiry came along the focus was always on the athlete. When an athlete tested positive he or she received the assigned penalty and that was the end of the matter, both at the domestic level and with a few exceptions at the international level. No effort was made to ascertain if others were involved. The obvious people – coaches, doctors, trainers – were simply ignored.
>
> (1991: 61)

The central object of this chapter is to explore, by means of a detailed case study of cycling, and in particular the events in the 1998 Tour de France, the network of relationships of those – not just the cyclists themselves and the team doctors, but also team managers, masseurs and others – involved in doping in professional cycling. The revelations about doping in the 1998 Tour de France constituted arguably the greatest ever doping scandal in sport, greater perhaps than even the infamous positive drug test of Ben Johnson at the Seoul Olympics ten years previously. As new information about doping became available on an almost daily basis, so the media coverage of the Tour came increasingly to focus around the police investigation into doping, with the cycle race itself becoming a relatively minor, and in the eyes of many commentators a very tainted, sideshow. The riders themselves went on strike in protest at the way they were being treated during the police investigation and the race was very nearly abandoned altogether; eventually fewer than half the riders finished the race, largely because several teams were either suspended from the race or withdrew in connection with the doping allegations.

Although most media coverage presented the unfolding evidence of doping in the Tour as new and startling revelations, there was already in existence an abundance of data which indicated that, long before the 1998 Tour, doping in professional cycling was widespread. Before we examine the events of the 1998 Tour, and what they reveal about the social organisation of doping in cycling, it may be useful to set the 1998 Tour in context by a brief examination of the way in which the current pattern of doping has developed historically.

What Richard Williams, writing in the *Guardian* (1 August 1998) has described as cycling's 'intimate association with drugs' can be traced back a long way, for cycling was one of the sports in which the use of performance-enhancing drugs became common from a relatively early date. As we noted in Chapter 6, in the late nineteenth century riders in the six-day races used a mixture of heroin and cocaine to increase endurance, and Houlihan (1999: 34) suggested that the death of the cyclist Arthur Linton in 1886 may be the first recorded death of an athlete from an overdose of drugs.[1] In 1924, as Williams pointed out in his *Guardian* article, 'Henri Pélissier, winner of the previous year's Tour, and his brother Francis showed a journalist the contents of their medicine bag: cocaine, chloroform, and various pills.'

Writing about the more recent period, Mottram (1996: 92) noted that 'there are numerous examples of fatalities arising from the use of amphetamines by cyclists', two of the most famous amphetamine-related deaths being those of the Dane Knut Jenson in the 1960 Olympic Games and of the British rider Tommy Simpson in the 1967 Tour de France. In 1966 the first five men in the world road-race championship all refused to take a drugs test. The five included Jaques Anquetil, five times winner of the Tour de France, who later admitted to taking stimulants and who said, 'Everyone in cycling dopes himself and those who claim they do not are liars' (*The Times*, 21 July 1988). In his award-winning *A Rough Ride*, Kimmage (1990; 1998) drew upon his own experiences as a professional rider in the late 1980s to describe the widespread practice of doping, and the pressures on riders to use dope, in professional cycling.

While stimulants and anabolic steroids have been widely used in cycling for many years, growing concern has been expressed in recent years about the use by cyclists of erythropoietin, commonly called EPO. EPO is a naturally occurring hormone which stimulates the bone marrow to produce more red blood cells, which in turn boosts the amount of oxygen in the blood, leading to a significant improvement in the performance of endurance athletes. There are good grounds for thinking that EPO has been widely used among professional cyclists in Europe for several years. In 1997, two French former professional riders, Nicolas Aubier and Gilles Delion, said that among professional cyclists EPO use was widespread, and Aubier was quoted as saying: 'To be honest, I don't think it's possible to make the top 100 on the ranking list without taking EPO, growth hormone or some of the other stuff . . . well, no, that's not true, Chris Boardman is there. During my first two years, I roomed with him a lot and never saw him take an injection. I still don't know how he managed to remain competitive' (Kimmage, 1998: 254). Asked to comment on these allegations, Robert Millar, a former winner of the King of the Mountains prize in the Tour de France and now the British national road-racing coach, said: 'Basically it's true – I can agree with what they're saying' (*Cycling Weekly*, 25 January 1997).

The year before Aubier and Delion made these allegations, the Italian sports paper *La Gazetta della Sport* (31 October 1996) published an article which claimed that the use of EPO was already widespread among top cyclists. Professor Alessandri, who in 1993 had been a trainer for a major Italian-based professional cycling team, was quoted as saying that 'at least 50 per cent of the riders used erythropoietin'. He claimed that 'the strongest European teams were using EPO' as well as several riders on the Italian national team. The article also referred to a study undertaken by Sandro Donati, a professor of exercise physiology and the director of youth training at CONI, the Italian National Olympic Committee. Donati was quoted as saying that 'EPO was being used by more than 80 per cent of all pro cyclists', though one ex-professional cyclist, Giacinto Martinelli, was also quoted as saying that 'Some people say that up to 80 per cent of the riders use EPO. What? I'd go as far as to say 100 per cent. If you want to remain in that world, you have to do it' (Mantell, 1997: 38). In January 1997, the French sports paper *L'Equipe* published, over several days and under the title 'Le terrible dossier', a detailed investigation of doping in cycling, which similarly pointed to the widespread use of EPO among professional cyclists (*L'Equipe*, 14–17 January 1997).

Long before the 1998 Tour de France there were, therefore, many indications that performance-enhancing drugs were widely used in professional cycling. Within the world of professional cycling, the fact that many riders used drugs was hardly a secret; indeed, I will argue later that, largely because of the special characteristics of cycling, there has long been what might be described as a 'culture of tolerance' in professional cycling in relation to the use of performance-enhancing drugs. Nevertheless, both for those within the world of professional cycling and for those on the outside, the revelations of the 1998 Tour came as an unwelcome shock; for those within professional cycling because the revelations brought into the public domain information which they would almost certainly have preferred to have kept within the world of cycling and, for those outside the world of cycling, because they revealed for the first time a world which, in the eyes of many people, was badly, perhaps irretrievably, tainted by the use of drugs.

THE 1998 TOUR DE FRANCE

A few days before the start of the 1998 Tour de France, which began in Dublin, Willy Voet was arrested by French police as he entered France from Belgium *en route* to Ireland. Voet, who was driving an official Tour vehicle, was a *soigneur* (masseur) to the world's top-ranked team, Festina, and he was arrested after the police found 250 batches of anabolic steroids and 400 ampoules of EPO in his car. This discovery prompted a further police search of Festina's team headquarters in Lyon, from where eighteen further samples of 'suspect products' were impounded for tests (*The Times*, 13 July 1998). The first reaction from the Tour organisers was to play down the significance of Voet's arrest. The race director, Jean-Marie Leblanc, was reported as saying, 'This man may have been acting on his own without the knowledge of the team, so there's no question of penalising them,' while the president of the Tour, the former Olympic gold medal-winning skier, Jean-Claude Killy, suggested that there was 'nothing to be worried about because the Tour de France is such a sporting institution that I think I can describe this affair as being a mere sideshow' (*Sunday Times*, 12 July 1998). Very quickly, however, the drugs issue moved centre stage, while the race itself took on more and more the status of a sideshow.

Under police questioning, Voet claimed that, in bringing the drugs to the Tour, he was acting on the orders of the team management and that he had been given similar commissions in the past. A few days later, the Festina team director, Bruno Roussel, and the team doctor, Eric Rijkaert, were charged by French police under the 1989 Anti-Drug Act, which prohibits 'the administration, enticement to use or facilitation of employment of substances or doping procedures during competitions or sporting events' (*Guardian*, 18 July 1998). Voet was also charged with importing 'prohibited merchandise'. Shortly before the arrest of Roussel and Rijkaert, a Swiss sports doctor, Gérard Gremion, had given an interview to *France Soir*, in which he had claimed that '99 per cent of professional cyclists take drugs, including those on the Tour de France', and he also said that he had resigned his position as doctor to Post Swiss, a leading professional team, over the systematic use of banned substances to enhance performance (*The Times*, 16 July 1998).

Shortly after being taken into custody, Roussel admitted to the French police that 'a concerted system for supplying cyclists with drugs was organised between management, doctors, the masseur and the riders in the Festina team'. The objective, he said, 'was to improve performances under strict medical control in order to avoid the unauthorised personal supply to cyclists causing grave attacks on their health which could have been the case in the past' (*Sunday Telegraph*, 19 July 1998). The Tour director issued a statement in which he said that this constituted 'a confession that doping was taking place in the Festina team, and that it was even organised', and the whole Festina team was expelled from the race (*Sunday Times*, 19 July 1998). The team leader, Richard Virenque, who had been the runner-up in the Tour in 1997, denied taking drugs himself, but did admit that doping had been organised within the Festina team. However, he claimed that other teams had similar arrangements: 'There was [drug] trafficking within the team, but also in the other teams', he said (*Sunday Telegraph*, 19 July 1998).

Some other members of the Festina team, including Alex Zulle, the runner-up in the 1995 Tour de France, and Laurent Dufaux, who finished fourth in 1996, did, however, confess to police that they had used EPO. Dufaux, in a press interview, stated that the use of EPO was 'a custom practised in the field now', and said, 'I wouldn't be surprised if this started an avalanche'. He added, 'Maybe the Union Cycliste Internationale should suspend more than 100 riders after the Tour' (*Cycling Weekly* – the leading British cycling magazine – 1 August 1998). The lawyer representing the team doctor, Eric Rijkaert, also gave more details of the organisation of doping within the team. The team, it emerged, maintained a £40,000 'war chest' for the purchase of drugs, the money being siphoned off from the cash paid out by the team to its riders to reward good performances. Rijkaert's lawyer explained that 'the riders were made to put part of their bonuses into a secret fund which was intended to finance the purchase of drugs. The substances, as well as legal medicines, were kept at the team's logistic store in Lyon.' The *soigneur* whose arrest originally triggered off the scandal added that the drug fund was also financed with a proportion of start money paid to the riders by the organisers of criteriums (town centre races) while the team director, Bruno Roussel, told police that since 1993, when he took over the management of the team, about 400,000 francs (£40,000) (or 1 per cent of the team's annual budget of £4 million) had gone into the fund. *Cycling Weekly* (1 August 1998) quoted a 'former top professional' as saying that this was 'standard practice in a well organised team'.

Two days after the suspension of the Festina team, Alain Vandenbossche, a former Belgian national champion, stated publicly that when he rode for the Dutch TVM team he used EPO, 'just like other riders in the team and just like other riders in other teams'. At about the same time, it was announced that in March, the contents of one of the TVM team cars, which had included ampoules of EPO, had been impounded by French police in Reims and that the team was being investigated by French customs officials (*The Times*, 21 July 1998). The TVM team hotel was searched on two occasions during the Tour; on the first occasion, banned drugs and masking agents were found, while after one stage of the race four riders from the TVM team were taken by police to a local hospital where they were required to give samples of blood, urine and hair. A lorry belonging to the French-sponsored Big Mat team was also stopped and searched by police and customs officers (*The Times*, 29 July 1998).

The next day, the riders staged two stoppages in the race and threatened to abandon the race altogether in protest at the actions of the French police. Most riders were eventually persuaded to continue, though three leading teams – ONCE, Banesto and Riso Scotto – withdrew from the race and those riders who did continue rode that stage at a funereal pace and, in a gesture of solidarity with the TVM riders who been forced to provide samples at the hospital, allowed the TVM riders to cross the line first. Three days later, the TVM riders withdrew from the Tour and, shortly afterwards, the team masseur, team director and team doctor were all charged with offences under French anti-drugs laws. The team doctor, Andrei Mikhailov, was reported to have admitted supplying more than 100 doses of EPO which had been discovered in the team vehicle in March. Three months after the Tour, a 200-page report sent to the judge handling the TVM case indicated that the samples taken from the TVM riders had all tested positive for a variety of performance-enhancing drugs (*The Times*, 1 August 1998; *Cycling Weekly*, 21 November 1998).

By this time, the Tour was, not surprisingly, in crisis. In Britain, *The Times* in an editorial (31 July 1998) described the race as the Tour de Farce, while more importantly, in France, the daily *Le Monde* demanded, 'The Tour has to stop.' *Libération* carried a front-page story which said that a 'Tour that runs from the police station to the courtroom is too long', while *L'Equipe*, the sports daily, said the scandal highlighted how the doping issue had been swept under the carpet. *Le Figaro* wrote that the Tour was simply rotten (*Guardian*, 25 July 1998).

The Tour did, however, continue, as did the doping revelations. The next team to be implicated was a French team, Casino. Frédéric Pontier, who had ridden for Casino in the previous season, gave a series of press interviews in which he said that he had used EPO while at Casino, and that the use of riders' prize money to finance the purchase of drugs was a common practice. 'This is the usual system,' he said, adding, 'That's why it's unfair to point the finger at Festina. They simply had the bad luck to be stitched up by their *soigneur*' (*The Times*, 24 July 1998). By the end of the Tour, the hotels or vehicles used by several teams had been searched by police, who found banned substances in those used by four teams – Festina,

TVM, ONCE and Casino. Of the twenty-two teams which started the Tour, one was expelled and five others withdrew from the race because of the doping investigation. A third team doctor, Nicolas Torralbos of the ONCE team, which included the world number one, Laurent Jalabert, was charged under the 1989 Act with supplying banned drugs at sporting events (*The Times*, 1 August 1998). Two months after the Tour, the *soigneur* of another leading French team, Jeff D'Hont of La Française des Jeux, was also charged under the 1989 Act (*Cycling Weekly*, 3 October 1998). After the end of the Tour, it was also revealed that one of the leading riders on the expelled Festina team, Alex Zulle, had told police that he had first used EPO about four years previously when he had been riding with the ONCE team, and that while he was at ONCE, 'about 20 riders were taking EPO under the supervision of the doctor' (*Cycling Weekly*, 19 September 1998).

So much, then, for the events of what one British cycling magazine called the Tour du Dopage (*Cycling Plus*, October 1998). What can be learnt from this case study? How can we best understand the widespread use of performance-enhancing drugs in cycling? And what are the appropriate lessons to draw in relation to anti-doping policy?

Perhaps the first point to be made is that this case study brings out in a particularly clear way the figuration of relationships among those involved in what might be called the doping network. It should be noted that, in some respects the situation in cycling may be rather special – this point will be discussed shortly – and, as a consequence, it may also be the case that in cycling these networks are more organised and more systematised – in a word, they are more highly institutionalised – than in most other sports. Nevertheless, when placed alongside other detailed and reliable case studies, such as those provided by the Dubin Commission of Canada's 1988 Olympic weightlifting and sprint teams (Dubin, 1990: 139–76, 234–59), it is clear that at the elite level it is simply unrealistic to see the individual drug-using athlete as working alone, without the assistance and support of others.

It is therefore important not to focus exclusively on the individual athlete and to recognise that it is not only the athletes who may perceive their best interests to be served by the use of performance-enhancing drugs, for doctors, team managers, coaches, officials and others may also, for whatever reasons – career advancement, national prestige or financial gain, for example – perceive their best interests to be served by encouraging or concealing or at least 'turning a blind eye' to the illicit use of drugs. This is, it might be suggested, one of the primary reasons why the use of performance-enhancing drugs has proved so difficult to control. At the very least, it is clear that, if we hope to develop a more effective anti-drugs policy, then that policy will have to be based on considerably more than a narrowly technological approach, concerned simply with developing more sophisticated testing techniques, and that it must take into account, much more than does existing policy, the complexities of the social networks in which athletes are involved.

But how can we best explain the widespread use of performance-enhancing drugs in cycling? It is, of course, very easy to adopt what Coakley has described as the 'it's either right or wrong' approach and simply to condemn as cheats those cyclists who use drugs. Such an approach, however, does nothing to enhance our understanding of why the use of performance-enhancing drugs is so widespread in cycling, largely because it shows little understanding of the constraints, particularly in sports such as cycling, to use drugs. In this context, it should be emphasised – and this is an important point which cannot be stressed too strongly – that there is a difference between trying to *understand* a particular pattern of behaviour, and seeking to *excuse* that pattern of behaviour. My object here, it should be understood, is not to offer an apology for drug use in cycling, any more than those who study violent crime seek to offer an apology for such behaviour. My object is simply to understand the constraints on professional cyclists to use drugs. As we noted in Chapter 5, such an understanding provides, among other things, a more secure basis for the formulation of policy in this area.

Much of the press coverage of the events in the 1998 Tour de France was, not surprisingly, very emotive and did little to enhance our understanding of these events. There were, however, a few writers who showed some appreciation of the broader context, and in particular the enormous physical demands which are made on professional cyclists, that provide an essential backcloth to understanding the widespread use of drugs within cycling. One of these was James Waddington, who wrote:

> The kind of strain being imposed on a cyclist's body during a three-week stage race, where in a single day it might be commanded to ride the distance from Paris to Brussels, climbing the height of the Himalayas in between, is not just healthy exercise. It is close to punishment and abuse.
>
> (*The Times*, 25 July 1998)

Waddington's use of the term 'abuse' should not be seen as mere hyperbole, for it does draw attention to an important characteristic of professional cycling, and one which is often not fully appreciated by those outside the sport. A similar point to that made by Waddington was also made by Richard Williams, writing in the *Guardian* (1 August 1998):

> You do not have to espouse a radical libertarian belief in the complete legalisation of all chemical assistance for athletes to recognise that cycling might just be a bit different from most other sports. In themselves, running the 100 metres or swimming the length of a pool make no special demands on human endurance. But cycling 150 miles a day

at an average of 30 mph, climbing a 9,000 ft mountain in 100°F and going down the other side in a wintry mist is liable to make significant demands, even before the element of competition is introduced.

As Chris Boardman, the British cyclist who dropped out early on after a crash, once said: 'It's painful, it's dangerous, and it goes on a long time.' And in a sense, bicycle racers use drugs not to go faster but merely to take away the pain.

An 'insider's' description of the pain involved was provided by Robert Millar, who came fourth in the 1984 Tour de France. Millar (*Guardian*, 31 July 1998) said:

> The riders reckon that a good Tour takes one year off your life, and when you finish in a bad state, they reckon three years. . . .
>
> You can't describe to a normal person how tired you feel. . . . In 1987, when I finished in a really bad way it took me until the end of November to recover; by that I mean until I could wake up and not feel tired as if I had already done a day's work.
>
> The fatigue starts to kick in on the Tour after 10 days if you're in good shape, and after five days if you're not in your best condition physically. Then it all just gets worse and worse, you don't sleep so much, so you don't recover as well from the day's racing, so you go into your reserves, you get more knackered, so you sleep less. . . . It's simply a vicious circle.
>
> The best way of describing how you feel is that it's as if you were a normal person doing a hard day's work, you've got flu, and you can just about drive home and fall into bed. By the end of the Tour, you need sleeping tablets.
>
> You can't divide the mental and the physical suffering; you tend to let go mentally before you crack physically. . . .
>
> Riding up one of the mountains in the Tour if you're feeling bad is like being sick. Physically, your body has a limit every day, there's only a set speed you can go at and it might not always be good enough.
>
> The pain in your legs is not the kind of pain you get when you cut yourself, it's fatigue, and it's self-imposed. . . .
>
> It takes two weeks to recover from a good Tour, three months to recover from a bad one.

Given these physical demands, one can perhaps empathise with Millar's comment, 'I can understand guys being tempted to use drugs in the Tour.'

The extreme physical demands of professional cycling also give rise to another characteristic of the pattern of doping in cycling which differentiates it from many other sports. In this respect it is important to note that, in a race like the Tour de France, most riders who use drugs – unlike most drug-using athletes in many other sports – do so not with a view to winning, but simply with a view to completing the race. In any given year in the Tour de France, there are likely to be no more than four or five riders with a realistic chance of emerging as the overall winner of the race, and perhaps a similar number who have a realistic chance of winning one of the two other 'races within a race', the King of the Mountains competition or the points competition. This means that, of the 200 or so riders who normally start the Tour, no more than a dozen or so have a realistic chance of winning a major prize; the majority of riders are *domestiques*, team riders who have no hope of winning a major prize and whose essential task is to remain in the race and support their team leader. Very many riders who take drugs – and this will certainly apply to all the *domestiques* – do so not to win, but simply to help them finish each stage and recover for the next one. For the *domestiques*, it is not winning the race, but simply finishing, which is the height of their ambition. For the *domestiques*, however, finishing the race is very important, not only in terms of professional pride, but also in terms of securing a renewal of their (often short-term) contracts. As Jeremy Whittle noted in an article on the 1998 Tour in *The Times* (20 July 1998), 'possible redundancy at the end of this season hovers over approximately 50 per cent of the riders in the field. For many, the race is not about winning or losing but merely about impressing their team managers sufficiently to guarantee a contract for next year.'

This point was brought out very clearly by the Irish former professional cyclist Paul Kimmage, who rode as a *domestique* with the RMO team in the Tour de France in the 1980s. Kimmage describes the importance of finishing his first Tour in 1986:

> it had been much harder than I had imagined. I had felt like abandoning a hundred times in the last week but I didn't give in. I couldn't, for I felt my survival as a professional rider depended on getting to Paris. RMO was a small team, but at the end of the season the weak men would be sacked and new blood brought in. . . . I had a contract for two years so I was assured of my place for 1987, but already I was thinking ahead to 1988. . . . In a year's time, Thevenet [the team director] would remember not that I had finished the Tour on my hands and knees but that I'd finished.
>
> (Kimmage, 1998: 93)

Kimmage's book, *A Rough Ride* – which was chosen for the William Hill Sports Book of the Year award when it was first published in 1990 – provides a revealing portrait of the life of a professional cyclist. In particular, Kimmage graphically portrays both the physical constraints and the social constraints, including not only the need to remain competitive for career reasons, but also the ready availability of drugs, and the encouragement from teammates, *soigneurs*, *directeurs sportifs* and others to use drugs to alleviate tiredness, all of which, despite his initial and strong objections, eventually led to Kimmage himself taking drugs.

The extreme physical demands placed upon cyclists, it may be argued, are also associated with another important aspect of the world of professional cycling; namely, the development of what may be described as a 'culture of tolerance' in relation to the illicit use of drugs. In the world of professional cycling, the use of drugs is, as we have seen, both widespread and organised, and there appears to be an acceptance by many people within that world that, given the great physical demands placed upon riders, the use of drugs is something which has to be accepted, albeit reluctantly. This means that even those who may have strong objections to the use of drugs nevertheless have to come to terms with, and in some sense implicitly accept, their widespread use in the sport. A good example of this is provided in Kimmage's description of a meeting of the RMO team and the team director, Patrick Valke, prior to a race near Paris:

> On the night before the race, Patrick Valke conducted his team meeting around the dinner table. He emphasised that there would be dope control after the race and warned us not to take any chances. On the morning of the event, Patrick attended a meeting for *directeurs sportifs*. After the meeting the race organiser discreetly pulled him to one side. She had a slight problem, no doctor to conduct the test. . . .
>
> Patrick returned from the meeting and told us there would be no control. Perhaps he should have said nothing, but in a way it was his duty. Most of the other teams would know there was no control. Some of the riders would charge up [use drugs] and our lads would be at a disadvantage. It was Patrick's duty to tell us, even though it disgusted him to have to do so. This is what we are up against: we play with the rules we have been given to play with.
>
> (Kimmage, 1998: 233)

This acceptance of doping – or what I have here called a 'culture of tolerance' of doping in cycling – is shown in a number of ways. In the 1998 Tour de France, it was shown when the riders expressed their solidarity with the TVM team, who had been taken to hospital by police and required to give urine, blood and hair samples, by allowing TVM riders to cross the line first at the end of the following day's stage. It was shown in the riders' 'go-slow' during that stage and in their threat to abandon the Tour altogether in protest at the police searches of team hotels and vehicles. It was shown in the absence of any criticism of either the Festina or the TVM teams by other riders and by the arguing by some riders (and not just Festina riders but riders in other teams) against the expulsion of the Festina team on the grounds that, despite the confessions of the team director, team doctor and masseur, no rider had (at that stage) provided a positive test result (*Sunday Times*, 19 July 1998). This tolerance was also expressed in the fact that the Festina team which was expelled from the Tour was racing again in northern Spain even before the Tour de France had finished (*The Times*, 27 July 1998). And it was shown, this time on the part of the fans when, in their first major race after the Tour de France, the Festina team was given 'massive support' by fans in the San Sebastian Classic in Spain in August. The team hotel was mobbed by large crowds who, apart from the usual practice of demanding autographs from the riders, greeted them with chants of 'Long live Festina!', with the biggest welcome being reserved for Laurent Jalabert, who had led the withdrawal of the ONCE team from the Tour in protest against the police action (*Cycling Weekly*, 15 August 1998).

This culture of tolerance was, perhaps, also indicated by the fact that the Festina team was allowed to compete in the remaining national tours of the 1998 season – the Tours of Spain, Portugal and Switzerland – before any disciplinary action was taken against any Festina riders. The three Festina riders who confessed to taking performance-enhancing drugs – Alex Zulle, Armin Meier and Laurent Dufaux – were given eight-month suspensions to run from 1 October 1998. The suspensions were subsequently reduced to seven months, most of which was served during the out-of-season winter months, so that all three riders were available for most of the big races in the following season, including the 1999 Tour de France. Moreover, in November 1998, the president of the Dutch cycling federation publicly expressed his doubts about the findings of a report from the French justice ministry which indicated that TVM riders had tested positive for performance-enhancing drugs, an action which led *Cycling Weekly* (21 November 1998) to declare: 'If Dutch riders from the TVM team are found guilty of using dope and have to be punished, they won't have to fear much from their own federation.' *Cycling Weekly's* prediction proved correct; in spite of the events of the 1998 Tour de France representing one of the biggest ever doping scandals in modern sport, by the start of the next Giro d'Italia in May 1999, only three people, none of whom was a rider – the three were the former Festina team director, Bruno Roussel, the team doctor, Eric Rijkaert, and the team masseur, Willy Voet – were still under suspension.

Aspects of this same official tolerance – or at least a willingness to turn 'a blind eye' to doping – were also expressed by Bruno Roussel, who had been dismissed as Festina team director after being charged by French police. In December 1998 in his first public statement about the events of the Tour, Roussel said: 'The cases now being investigated by French law courts have been going on for years and were known and at least tolerated by the French federation and cycling in general' (*Cycling Weekly*, 5 December 1998). Though Roussel might, perhaps, have been trying to shift some of the responsibility for the doping scandal on to others, there is no reason to doubt the accuracy of his statement. Given what we now know was the widespread and highly institutionalised practice of doping in cycling, it is difficult to imagine that many people within cycling had no knowledge of the nature and extent of doping in the sport, not least because the high level of mobility of riders from one team to another would ensure the rapid dissemination of such knowledge throughout the cycling community.

In this respect, the comments of a former professional rider, Nicolas Aubier, are particularly striking. Aubier made his comments in an interview which was published in the French newspaper *L'Equipe* (16 January 1997), as part of that paper's four day-long investigation into doping in cycling in 1997. Aubier said that, although most people involved in professional cycling were aware of the extent of doping in the sport, no one said anything publicly. Asked why, he explained:

> But why should they? Everyone profits from the system. The riders optimise their performance. The teams are more competitive and as a result more attractive to sponsors. Even you guys in the media . . . the slant is always about winning. Everyone knows exactly what's going on. No one says a word.
>
> (Quoted in Kimmage, 1998: 256)

Perhaps most striking, however, as an indication of the tolerance of doping, and of the associated hostility to outsiders who did not share this aspect of cycling culture, was the reaction of almost everyone involved in professional cycling – riders, team directors and race organisers – to the police investigation during the 1998 Tour de France. As we noted above, the riders staged an organised protest against the police searches of team hotels and vehicles. Manolo Saiz, the team director of the leading Spanish team, ONCE, declared: 'ONCE may never race in France again. Cycling is a family and it's heading for a divorce because the Tour has no respect for the riders anymore' (*The Times*, 30 July 1998). The reluctance of teams to race in France was still evident at the beginning of the 1999 season; the field in the Paris–Nice stage race, the first major stage race of the season, was reported to be 'one of the weakest in recent years as riders tried to avoid France and the French police'. Most top-ranking riders preferred to ride in the Tirreno–Adriatico stage race in Italy, which was held at about the same time and which, because of the riders' desire to avoid France, had 'probably the best field since the race began in 1966' (*Cycling Weekly*, 13 March 1999).

Most revealing, however, were the changes which were made to the route of the Tour of Spain in 1998 as a result of what happened in the Tour de France. The Tour of Spain – the Vuelta a España – is the third most important tour after the Tour de France and the Giro d'Italia, and in 1998 it was held some two months after the Tour de France. The original route of the Vuelta had included a brief incursion into France, but, following the Tour de France, the organisers of the Spanish race modified the route so that the race did not enter French territory. The organisers explained that this was 'out of respect for French justice and to avoid causing more tension' or, as *Cycling Weekly* (22 August 1998) put it, 'to make sure none of the teams get searched'. Equally revealing was the announcement by five Italian and two Dutch teams who were competing in the Vuelta that they would not travel to Spain via France. The two Dutch teams, one of which was the TVM team, took a much longer route which involved sending their bikes, team cars, buses and medical equipment via Dover, driving along Britain's south coast to Plymouth and then taking the ferry to Santander, while the Italian teams sent their logistic back-up on a ferry from Genoa to Barcelona (*Cycling Weekly*, 5 September 1998). The previous month, the Spanish Cycling Federation[2] had withdrawn its team from the Tour de France Féminin because they were concerned about possible checks by the French police, while the organisers of the Tour of Portugal, in which Festina had entered a team, had promised that there would be no police controls and 'just the normal doping tests' during the race (*Cycling Weekly*, 15 August 1998).

It is in the above context that we can begin to make sense of what is perhaps the most striking paradox of the doping scandal in the 1998 Tour de France. This paradox – which curiously has not been commented on by any of those who have written about the Tour – arises from the following considerations. First, although we cannot be sure about precisely how many riders in the Tour were using drugs, the police investigation established beyond all reasonable doubt that the practice of doping is widespread. Second, despite routine dope tests after each stage of the Tour, *not a single rider was excluded from the Tour as a result of failing a doping control carried out by the Tour organisers.* All of the riders who tested positive did so as a result of tests which were conducted following the police action, rather than as a result of tests which were carried out under the auspices of any authority within the world of professional cycling.

The Tour organisers, or the governing body of cycling, the Union Cycliste Internationale, might legitimately claim that one of the most widely used drugs, EPO, is not detectable (as we shall see in the next chapter, a high red blood cell count suggests but cannot prove the use of EPO) and therefore would not show up in dope tests. However, it is clear that riders were using several other drugs, for many of which effective tests have long been available. In this context, we might note that the Festina masseur whose arrest triggered off the 'Festina affair' was reported to be carrying supplies not only of EPO but also of synthetic testosterone and human growth hormone (*Cycling Weekly*, 25 July 1998). Similarly, when police raided the TVM team hotel during the Tour, they found steroids and masking agents (*Cycling Weekly*, 21 November 1998). Moreover, the police report which was sent to the French judge handling the TVM case indicated that each rider on the TVM team had tested positive for steroids and growth hormones, while three riders tested positive for amphetamines and one rider tested positive for marijuana (*Cycling Weekly*, 21 November 1998). The tests on the Festina riders, which were also conducted as a result of the police investigation, suggested – but could not conclusively prove – that eight of the nine riders had been using EPO, but four riders also tested positive for amphetamines (*Cycling Weekly*, 5 December 1998).

It is therefore important to emphasise that the revelations about doping in the 1998 Tour de France came about not as a result of the enforcement by the Tour organisers of the anti-doping regulations within cycling, but as a result of the enforcement by outside bodies – in this case the French police and customs officers – of French criminal law. An important lesson to be drawn from the 1998 Tour thus concerns the ineffectiveness – at least when judged in terms of the criteria which are conventionally used – of doping control within professional cycling. This point is made not with a view to suggesting that we should move further down the road towards criminalisation of doping in sport,[3] as Houlihan correctly noted:

> there was, and remains, an understandable reluctance to add to the burden of anti-drug policing by criminalising a new set of drugs and users especially when there was not the extensive association between sports-drug use and crimes such as smuggling, street crime and violence.
> (1999: 150–1)

Rather, the point is made in order to draw attention to the difficulties of enforcing conventional doping controls in a sport in which the particular characteristics of that sport – most notably, the extreme physical demands placed upon riders – have been associated with the development of a culture which involves the acceptance or the tolerance of doping. In the next chapter, we shall examine some recent developments in relation to doping policy within professional cycling which, it may be argued, do take into account some of the special characteristics of the sport and which have on this account won the acceptance of the riders themselves. These developments also represent an interesting shift away from more conventional – and in the context of cycling, generally unsuccessful – attempts to control the use of performance-enhancing drugs.

One final point needs to be made in relation to the above analysis. A consideration of the special characteristics of professional cycling suggests that, whatever might be decided in relation to the development of doping controls within the sport, some consideration needs to be given to the physical demands which are made upon professional cyclists. As we have noted, a major tour such as the Tour de France or the Giro d'Italia – and many professionals will race in both events – involves riders in racing for several hours a day for more than three weeks, often in scorching heat and through some of Europe's highest mountains. Moreover, most professionals will race on at least 100, and sometimes considerably in excess of 100, days a year. It is this punishing schedule which largely sustains the tolerance of doping within cycling and, if we are seriously concerned about controlling the use of drugs and, perhaps more importantly, if we are seriously concerned about the health of professional cyclists, then reducing the physical demands made upon cyclists ought to be the first priority. This could be done in a variety of ways: by limiting the length of the major tours, either in terms of the distance covered or in terms of the number of days racing; by increasing the number of rest days in major tours; or by reducing the number of days in the year on which cyclists race. A move in this direction would make it possible for riders who do not use drugs to compete more effectively, while it would also provide more time for riders to recover from one stage of a race and to prepare for the next without the aid of drugs.

One potential problem, however, might be the attitude of team sponsors. Writing about the pressure on riders to win races, Jeremy Whittle, in *The Times* (20 July 1998), argued that 'that pressure comes from sponsors, who expect to be represented in cycling's global shop window at all costs'. It is not clear that sponsors would welcome a reduction in the number of races in which their team competes, for the publicity which the team gains for the sponsor by riding (and, it is hoped, winning) races represents the sponsors' return on their often very substantial financial investment in the team.

Notwithstanding this possible difficulty, the governing body of cycling, the Union Cycliste Internationale, is showing signs of moving in the direction of reducing the demands made on riders. In the wake of the Tour de France scandal, the UCI announced, in August 1998, a proposal to limit the number of days on which a professional may be allowed to race. The figure, it was reported (*Cycling Weekly*, 22 August 1998) was likely to be between 90 and 120 days per year. Some people might argue that the upper figure may still be too high, though any move towards limiting the number of days on which professionals are allowed to race will represent a move towards creating the conditions in which cyclists may be able to become less dependent on drugs. The UCI also indicated that it was to consider changing the way races are ranked, in order to discourage riders from over-racing. Under the existing ranking system, both riders and teams are ranked; every event is awarded a set number of points, and riders and teams win points by winning races, or by finishing among the leading riders. Under the current arrangements, even some relatively small races carry ranking points, so that teams feel constrained to enter, and the racing is often intense. The UCI announced that, in future, it will put greater emphasis on major races, emphasising quality rather than quantity.

Even before the 1998 Tour de France, however, the UCI had introduced an important shift in policy in order to try to tackle some of the problems associated with the widespread use of performance-enhancing drugs in cycling and, in particular, some of the potentially serious health problems associated with the use of EPO. This policy development, as we shall see in the next chapter, involved a move away from the more traditional punitive orientation which has generally characterised anti-doping policies in sport. But can we afford to move away from the more traditional anti-doping policies? Have not such policies served us well in the past? In the next chapter, we examine some of these issues.

10 Doping control in sport
A critical analysis

As we briefly noted in Chapter 6, doping control in sport is a relatively recent phenomenon. The first compulsory Olympic drug-testing took place at the Winter Olympic Games at Grenoble in 1968, and in the thirty years since then anti-doping policy has been based almost exclusively on what might be described as a punitive or 'law and order' approach. How successful has that policy been in terms of controlling the use of performance-enhancing drugs in sport? Is it perhaps time to re-examine some of the fundamental assumptions underlying that policy? Should the governing bodies of sport be considering alternative approaches to the problems associated with the use of performance-enhancing drugs? And can those responsible for administering anti-doping policies in sport learn anything from drug-control policies within the wider society? These are some of the central questions that are raised in this chapter.

The development and implementation of policy, whether in sport or in any other area of social life, is a complex process which, almost inevitably, has unplanned consequences, and it is therefore important that we continually monitor policies with a view to asking whether or not those policies are achieving the desired ends (Dopson and Waddington, 1996). In order to monitor anti-doping policies in sport, it is necessary to ask a number of questions about how those policies are working, and the most basic question is: has current policy been effective? It is, of course, never easy to measure the effectiveness of social policy, not only because policies are likely to have a variety of both intended and unintended consequences but also because the criteria of effectiveness are often not clear and no systematic attempt is made to monitor effectiveness. This is the case in relation to anti-doping policy in sport. This policy, underpinned by what Coakley (1998b: 148) called the 'absolutist' or the 'it's either right or wrong' approach (see Chapter 5), is widely seen as so obviously 'right' that one hardly dares to ask what the goals of the policy are, or how effective the policy has been in achieving those goals. However, such questions must be asked if we hope to develop a more adequate policy in relation to doping in sport.

It is reasonable to assume that, as far as sports governing bodies are concerned, the central objective of their anti-drugs policy is to control the use by athletes of performance-enhancing drugs. How successful, then, has this policy been?

It is generally agreed that the widespread use of drugs in sport dates from the l960s. As we noted in Chapter 8, by 1968 an estimated one-third of the athletes in the US track and field team had used steroids at the pre-Olympic training camp (Todd, 1987: 95). By this time, performance-enhancing drugs had already come to be regarded as an essential aid to training and/or competition by many athletes, and the evidence suggests that, since then, their use has become even more widespread. In 1987, a three-part investigation into drug use in British sport, published by *The Times*, characterised the history of drug-taking among British athletes during the previous fifteen years as involving 'the spread from the throwing events to all the track and field disciplines' and 'the spread from international down towards club level and the involvement of youngsters'. *The Times* held that the spread from the heavy throwing events into other sports had begun in the 1970s and that by the mid-1980s, 'with increasingly sophisticated products, the athlete using drugs is as likely to be a long jumper as a hammer thrower and even the once sacrosanct middle- and long-distance events are not immune' (*The Times*, 16 December 1987). Support for a central thrust of *The Times*' analysis came the following year from Professor Arnold Beckett of the drugs-testing centre at King's College, London, who stated: 'Drugs are spreading into the lower level of sport, especially in American football, ice hockey and other track and field events. It is spreading to schoolkids and to people who want to do better than they ever did before. It is crazy. It even gets into fun runs' (Doust *et al.*, 1988). Shortly afterwards, Sir Arthur Gold, the Chairman of the British Olympic Committee, held that drug use in sport was 'more widespread and deep seated than most people realise', and he added that 'it isn't only the elite who use steroids but also people who want to move up from one low rung of the ladder to one slightly higher' (Gold, 1989: 10).

It is clear that, by the mid to late 1980s, the use of drugs was widespread in many sports. In her evidence to the US Senate Judiciary Committee Hearing on Steroid Abuse in America, chaired in April 1989 by Senator Joseph Biden, Jr, Pat Connolly, a coach of the US women's track and field team, estimated that of the fifty members of the team at the 1984 Olympics, 'probably 15 of them had used steroids. Some of them were medallists.' Asked by Senator Biden whether the number of athletes using steroids had increased by the time of the Seoul Olympics of 1988, Connolly replied, 'Oh, yes. Oh, yes, it went up a lot.' She estimated that 'At least 40 per cent of the women's team in Seoul had probably used steroids at some time in their preparation for the games' (cited in Dubin, 1990: 339).

A few months before those Seoul Olympics William Standish, the chief physician to the Canadian Olympic team, claimed that the ideal of a drug-free Olympics was no longer possible. He said:

> We have solid information that the use of drugs to enhance performance is really an epidemic. There is rampant use of anabolic steroids and other performance-enhancing drugs among young athletes. . . . I think we have to look at the traditional Olympic charter and understand that to have a clean Olympics is no longer possible.
>
> (*The Times*, 7 April 1988)

Prince Alexandre de Merode, the head of the International Olympic Committee's Medical Commission, suggested that 10 per cent or more of competitors at the Barcelona Olympics used drugs (cited in Coomber, 1993), though other informed insiders have indicated that doping is substantially more common than this. Following the positive drug test on Ben Johnson at the Seoul Olympics, a Soviet coach was quoted by the *New York Times* as saying that 90 per cent of elite sportsmen use drugs (Yesalis, 1993: 35), while Dr James Puffer, who at the time was chief physician to the US Olympic team, suggested that perhaps 50 per cent of elite athletes did so (Doust *et al.*, 1988).

The most systematic and reliable evidence on the extent of doping in elite sport is unquestionably that which was presented to the Dubin Commission of Inquiry in Canada. Dubin took evidence from no fewer than forty-six Canadian athletes who had used anabolic steroids, and he concluded:

> After hearing evidence and meeting with knowledgeable people from Canada, the United States, Australia, New Zealand, and elsewhere, I am convinced that the problem is widespread not only in Canada but also around the world. The evidence shows that banned performance-enhancing substances and, in particular, anabolic steroids are being used by athletes in almost every sport, most extensively in weightlifting and track and field.
>
> (Dubin, 1990: 336)

In relation to specific sports, Dubin concluded that

> the sport of weightlifting in Canada and elsewhere is riddled with the use of anabolic steroids. The related non-Olympic sport of powerlifting is similarly afflicted. Bodybuilding is another non-Olympic sport that . . . has been the subject of heavy steroid use among its participants.

Dubin also concluded that there was 'extensive use of anabolic steroids by Canadian athletes in the sprinting and throwing events' (1990: 337–8).

There is no evidence to suggest that the problem has lessened in the last few years. Anthony Millar, Research Director at the Institute of Sports Medicine in Sydney, Australia, has written of an 'epidemic of drug usage' in sport, and has suggested that the use of performance-enhancing drugs 'is widespread and growing not only in the athletic community but also among recreational athletes' (Millar, 1996: 107–8). In a survey of 448 British Olympic athletes, carried out in 1995, 48 per cent felt that drug use was a problem in international competition in their sport (in track and field, the proportion was 86 per cent). Nor did these elite British athletes feel that the problem was being effectively tackled by the existing system of doping controls; 23 per cent of athletes felt that drug use had increased over the previous twelve months compared with just 6 per cent who felt it had decreased (Sports Council, 1996a: 34). The most recent survey of the views of British elite athletes was carried out by the *Independent* in December 1998 as part of a week-long investigation into doping in sport. Across all sports, 54 per cent believed that up to 30 per cent of competitors in their sport were using performance-enhancing drugs, 5 per cent believed that between 30–60 per cent were doing so and 4 per cent believed that over 60 per cent of competitors were using drugs.

As in the earlier survey, there were substantial variations between sports. Not a single respondent from weightlifting (including powerlifting) or rugby league believed their sport was 'clean' and only 3 per cent of athletes did so. Among elite level swimmers, 65 per cent believed that the use of performance-enhancing drugs was 'widespread' in their sport. In some sports, a very high proportion of competitors actually admitted to using drugs. In weightlifting and powerlifting, for example, 20 per cent of respondents admitted using anabolic agents, while 10 per cent admitted using testosterone. In rugby league, 46 per cent of respondents indicated that they had been offered drugs by other players or professional dealers; 15 per cent of respondents admitted using testosterone and 15 per cent admitted using stimulants. In horse-racing, 35 per cent of jockeys admitted using diuretics (*Independent*, 9 December 1998). It is fairly safe to assume that in each of these cases, the data understate the real level of drug usage; almost certainly, even in an anonymous survey, some of those using perfor-mance-enhancing drugs would have been reluctant to have admitted to their use. It is also clear that drugs are widely used in other sport-related contexts. In a British survey of anabolic steroid use in 'hardcore' gyms (defined as gyms having predominantly heavy weight-training equipment, competitive bodybuilders and relatively few female members), over 29 per cent of gym users were currently using anabolic steroids (Lenehan *et al.*, 1996).

All the available evidence indicates very clearly that the pattern of drug use varies from one sport to another; the use of drugs appears to be particu-larly common in sports such as the heavy throwing events, weightlifting and cycling. In professional cycling, as we saw in the last chapter, the use of performance-enhancing drugs is now so widespread that it may be realistic to suggest that those who do not use drugs are in a minority, and perhaps even a small minority. Both because of the widespread use of drugs in cycling, but more particularly because of the characteristics of one of the drugs – EPO, which is widely used within the sport – cycling also raises some interesting questions in relation to anti-doping policy. These issues will be examined in more detail later in this chapter.

What, then, can we say about patterns of drug use in sport? As Coomber (1993) noted, spokespersons for bodies such as the International Olympic Committee (IOC) and the International Amateur Athletic Federation (IAAF) sometimes point to the relatively small numbers of athletes who provide positive drug tests at major events, such as the Olympic Games or the World or National Championships, as evidence that international sport is relatively drug-free. However, such data are, at best, an extremely poor – some would say so poor as to be virtually worthless – indication of the extent of drug use in sport, for it is widely acknowledged that those who provide positive tests simply represent the tip of a large iceberg.

For example, Sir Arthur Gold (1989: 10) argued that testing at major competitions – where most testing takes place – is 'a waste of time' because the only people who get caught are 'the careless or the ill advised', while in Canada the Dubin Commission concluded that 'many, many more athletes than those actually testing positive have taken advantage of banned substances and practices' and that 'positive test results represent only a small proportion of actual drug users' (Dubin, 1990: 349–50). Conclusive evidence in support of Dubin's view was provided, as we saw in the last chapter, by the total absence of riders in the 1998 Tour de France testing positive as a result of the doping tests imposed by the Tour organisers.

Why so few drug-using athletes get caught is not the central concern of this chapter, though it might be noted that several informed observers, including reputable sports journalists (Butcher and Nichols, *The Times*, 15–17 December 1987), senior sports physicians who have held major positions of responsibility (for example, Voy, 1991) and elite-level athletes (for instance, Kimmage, 1998) have all argued that senior sports administrators often collude with drug-using athletes to beat the testing system, while it is also clear that drug-using athletes are often able to beat the system by virtue of their access to expert advice from team doctors or other sports physicians.

It is not possible to arrive at any precise estimate of the extent of drug use in sport. Nevertheless, the following points can be made with a fair degree of confidence:

1 There has been a very substantial increase in the illicit use of performance-enhancing drugs by athletes since the early 1960s.

2 In athletics, the use of performance-enhancing drugs, which was originally concentrated in the heavy throwing events, has subsequently spread
to many other track and field events.
3 The use of performance-enhancing drugs has also spread from athletics,
weightlifting and cycling – the three sports in which drugs appear to
have been most frequently used in the 1960s – to almost all other sports.
4 Although the prevalence of drug use varies considerably from one sport
to another, it is clear that in many sports doping is widespread and that
in some – cycling is perhaps the clearest example – the likelihood is that
a majority, and perhaps a very large majority, of competitors are using
performance-enhancing drugs.

In the light of these conclusions, what can be said about the effectiveness of
the anti-doping policies which have, since the late 1960s, been followed by
the IOC and other sporting bodies? Any attempt to evaluate the effectiveness of existing anti-doping policy must begin by recognising two obvious
points. The first of these is that, from the time anti-doping regulations
were introduced in the 1960s, anti-doping policy has been based on a 'law
and order' approach in which the emphasis has been placed on the detection
and punishment of offenders. The second, equally clear point is that this
policy has failed to reduce the prevalence of doping in sport; indeed, it is
evident that the prevalence of doping has substantially increased over this
period, that the use of performance-enhancing drugs is now widespread,
and that their use has undergone a process of diffusion from a few sports
to many, and from elite-level sport to sport at somewhat lower levels. The
continued growth in the use of performance-enhancing drugs is one of the
considerations which lies behind some of the calls for current policy to be
changed. For example, Coomber, after reviewing some of the evidence
indicating that doping in sport is widespread, suggests that

> If the use of performance-enhancing drugs is common rather than
> anomalous, policy designed to deal with it should reflect this situation,
> not ignore, deny or underplay it. If the use of performance-enhancing
> drugs was uncommon then the existing policy of prohibition and
> punishment could be considered effective; as it is, it can only be con-
> sidered ineffective and inappropriate.
>
> (Coomber, 1993: 171)

Coomber suggests that in both the sporting and non-sporting worlds,
though for different reasons, the demand for prohibited drugs is likely to
continue and that 'it is difficult to see the use of performance-enhancing
drugs declining voluntarily' (1993: 172). He concludes: 'in recognition of
the continuing use of and experimentation with performance-enhancing
drugs by athletes, and the large numbers involved, prohibition should be

lifted' (1993: 176). In other words, Coomber argues that (1) present policy has been ineffective; (2) the use of drugs is both widespread and likely to continue to increase, and that therefore (3) we should accept the inevitable and allow their use. Recently Cashmore (1996: 170) argued that there is 'a practical and morally-sound case for legitimizing drugs in sport', though Cashmore's position is based on philosophical rather than on empirical, sociological arguments.

But is the continued growth in the use of performance-enhancing drugs unambiguous evidence, as Coomber seems to suggest, of the failure of existing policy? As Goode (1997) argued, this would be a legitimate conclusion only if we apply criteria of success or failure deriving from what he calls the 'hard' or 'strict' punitive, or 'law and order', approach. Adherents to this approach hold that detection and punishment is an effective deterrent, and that a given activity (in this case doping) can be reduced or eliminated by the enforcement of laws or rules. Judged in these terms, existing anti-doping policy has unquestionably failed. However, we might reach a different conclusion if we apply the rather different criteria implied by what Goode calls the 'soft' or 'moderate' 'law and order' approach. Advocates of this approach argue that, in the absence of the enforcement of laws or rules, a given behaviour – again in our case doping – would be more common than it is with law enforcement; the enforcement of laws or rules does not *reduce* the incidence of such behaviour so much as *contain* it. One might thus argue that, notwithstanding what has almost certainly been a substantial increase in the use of drugs in sport over the last four decades, that increase would have been even greater without the existing anti-drugs policy.

Though such an argument is necessarily a hypothetical one, there are some grounds for thinking it may be at least partially valid. In the survey of elite British athletes referred to earlier, 23 per cent felt that the existing drug-testing programme did not act as a deterrent against drug use, while 14 per cent felt that it 'certainly' was a deterrent, and a further 56 per cent felt it was 'likely' to act as a deterrent (Sports Council, 1996a: 18). This would suggest the probability that existing programmes have had some, albeit limited, deterrent effect. In the light of these considerations, Coomber's view – that 'anti-doping policy doesn't work' – appears too simplistic; a more adequate conclusion, which recognises some of the complexities of the situation, might be not that 'it doesn't work', but that 'it isn't working well'. This is in fact Goode's conclusion in relation to anti-drugs policies more generally in American society, and his words would seem to be equally appropriate in relation to anti-doping policy in sport. Goode (1997: 4) writes: 'Our present system of attempting to control drug abuse . . . is vulnerable to criticism; it isn't working well, it costs a great deal of money, it has harmful side effects and it is badly in need of repair.' But what kind of repair? Coomber and Cashmore suggest that we should end the prohibition on the use of drugs in sport. Is this an appropriate conclusion or, indeed, one which is within the realm of practical possibilities?

Coomber adopts this position largely because of what he sees as the failure of existing policy, while Cashmore bases his argument largely on moral and philosophical considerations. Neither gives any consideration to the *symbolic* aspects of rules though, perhaps particularly in the case of drugs, these are of major importance. We might recall here Durkheim's observations on the relationship between law and morality. Durkheim (1933: 81) pointed out that we are not offended by an action because it is against the law but rather, it is against the law because it offends against our sense of what is right and proper. There can be little doubt that Durkheim's analysis of the relationship between law and popular sentiment is correct in relation to the issue of drug use, whether inside or outside sport.

In this context, it is important to note that the ending of the ban on currently proscribed drugs in sport would, as Goode put it, 'send a message' – a *symbolic* message which, there can be no doubt, the vast majority of people within western societies would find unacceptable. It matters not that most people may have little understanding of the constraints on top athletes to use drugs; nor that their objections to the use of drugs may be, in large measure, emotional rather than rational ones; nor that popular attitudes towards drugs in sport have undoubtedly been 'contaminated' by the widespread public concern – some would say 'moral panic' – about the possession, sale and 'abuse' of controlled drugs in society more generally. What is important in this context is that a large majority of people in western societies are strongly opposed to the use of drugs in sport, the evidence of which, as we noted in Chapter 6, can be seen in the often highly emotive and almost always condemnatory treatment of 'drug cheats'. That the use of drugs in sport evokes such strong sentiments is a clear indication of its unacceptability among the general population.

It has often been observed that although sociology cannot tell us what we *should* do, it can tell us something about what we *can* do. That is, it can tell us something about the limits of what is practically possible. The proposal to end the ban on performance-enhancing drugs must be considered, at least for the foreseeable future, as one of the less realistic policy options. At a time when many western governments are struggling with what are seen as major problems of drug abuse in society more generally, the lifting of the ban on drugs in sport would almost certainly be seen by those in government – rightly or wrongly – as socially irresponsible. The likely outcome of such a policy decision would be strong governmental pressure to reimpose the ban, reinforced if necessary by the withdrawal of government funding for sport. Additionally, this would almost certainly be coupled with a flight from sport by private sponsors, who would not wish to be associated with an activity in which the use of drugs was openly embraced.

The policy advocated by Coomber and Cashmore requires a major injection of realism.

However, we are not faced with a simple polarity of either maintaining or lifting the ban on the use of performance-enhancing drugs, for there is a range of policy options between these extremes. In order to examine some of these other policy options, it is useful to examine developments in drug-control policy outside the sporting context.

There are many similarities between the use of drugs within and outside sport: the 'medicalization' of sport and of social life generally (Zola, 1972; Waddington, 1996); the overlap in the drugs used – particularly amphetamines and anabolic steroids – in the two contexts; and public concern about the use of drugs, whether for sporting or recreational purposes. However, in one important area, that of policy formation, there has been virtually no overlap.

This is a point to which Coomber (1996) has usefully drawn attention. He notes that many of the public health issues involved in the use of drugs in sport are not dissimilar to those involved in the use of drugs in a non-sporting context. Thus athletes 'may be using unsafe ways of administering their drugs, using unsafe drugs in unsafe ways, and [there] may even be unintentional transmission routes into the non-sporting world of sexually transmitted diseases such as HIV' (Coomber, 1996: 18). Outside the sporting context, public health authorities in many countries have sought to deal with problems of this kind by the development of *harm reduction* policies. Coomber describes the development of these policies in Britain as follows:

> With the advent of HIV/AIDS in the non-sporting world, drug policy . . . concerned itself with reducing the spread of HIV to the general population. This meant accessing one of the high-risk groups likely to spread the virus – injecting drug users – who had contracted high levels of infection due to needle-sharing practices. Access to this group, and introducing them to practices likely to reduce the spread of the virus . . . took priority over compelling these people to stop using drugs. Without access to non-judgemental help and real benefits (such as clean needles, and in some circumstances even access to drugs of choice), these users, who were not interested in stopping using drugs, would not have been accessed. A major policy decision was made that HIV represented a bigger threat to Public Health than drug use.
>
> (1996: 19)

Harm reduction includes a variety of strategies, with needle exchange schemes a central aspect of such policies. Rather than attempting to *eliminate* drug use – an unrealistic target – the goal is to reduce harm. Harm reduction policies are already well established in a number of countries, including The Netherlands, Switzerland and Britain (Goode,

1997: 81), while some aspects of US policy (for example, the methadone maintenance programmes for heroin addicts) might also be considered as a move away from traditional punitive policies.

However, within the sporting world, anti-drugs policy has been almost exclusively of the punitive, 'law and order' kind, and little thought has been given to the development of harm reduction policies. Coomber suggests that one reason for this is that those responsible for making and implementing anti-doping policy in sport 'do not, in general, work within the same parameters as those policy makers outside sport. . . . Drug policy in sport is seen as an issue that concerns sport and sporting authorities, and it has essentially isolated itself from considerations of how drug policy in sport relates to the world outside of it' (1996: 17). He adds:

> There are many lessons to be learned about drugs, drug users and methods of control from the non-sporting world but those who make policy about drugs in sport are not drug policy experts, they are sport administrators. Those that are drug experts are often in fact literally just that; they are chemists and are often equally unaware of *broader* policy issues. This is patently obvious in the continued approach to sporting drug policy. It is bereft of ideas (because it is bereft of broader drug policy knowledge and experience), and it is putting people in danger by being so.
>
> (1996: 18)

What, then, would a harm reduction policy in sport look like, and what might be the advantages of such a policy? This question is not an entirely hypothetical one, for there have recently been some small but important movements in sport towards harm reduction policies. Let us begin by examining some recent developments in professional cycling.

That cycling is the first sport to move towards harm reduction policies is not perhaps surprising and can be explained largely in terms of two considerations. First, as we saw in the last chapter, doping is extremely common in professional cycling; indeed, it is possible that doping is more widespread in cycling than in any other sport. In this sense, the failure of traditional anti-doping policies is perhaps more clear in cycling than in any other sport. Second, not only is doping widespread, but one of the drugs most widely used, EPO, carries very substantial health risks; indeed, EPO may well be the most dangerous, in health terms, of all the performance-enhancing drugs currently available.

As we noted previously, EPO substantially boosts the performance of endurance athletes by stimulating the production of red blood cells. However, although EPO has a valuable medical use for patients with thin blood, its use in healthy people can produce a dangerous thickening of the blood which can result in blood clots leading to heart failure. EPO came on to the market in Europe in 1987 and it was followed almost immediately by a sudden spate of deaths from heart failure among professional cyclists. Between 1987 and 1990, fourteen Dutch riders and four Belgians – all young and apparently healthy elite athletes – died suddenly. Joseph Eschbach, a haematologist at the University of Washington Medical School, Seattle, noted that 'Deaths have occurred at this rate only since EPO came on the market' (*Independent on Sunday*, 14 July 1991), and the overwhelming probability is that some, if not all, of these unexpected and unexplained deaths were associated with the use of EPO. That all the deaths occurred amongst Dutch and Belgian riders also suggests the establishment of an early EPO 'grapevine' and distribution network in Holland and Belgium, though the use of EPO is now commonplace among professional riders throughout Europe.

Concern about the widespread use of drugs within cycling and, probably more importantly, concern about the particular health threat posed by EPO, appears to have stimulated a rethink of anti-doping policy in cycling in much the same way that the particular health threat associated with HIV/AIDS stimulated the development of harm reduction policies in relation to drug control more generally. Hein Verbruggen, the president of the governing body of professional cycling, the Union Cycliste Internationale (UCI), announced in February 1997 a significant shift in anti-doping policy. Verbruggen was in no doubt about the ineffectiveness of traditional anti-doping policies:

> The fight against doping simply by controlling and punishing doesn't work. The cheats stay ahead. You catch one per cent, and most of those are due to stupid mistakes made when taking medicine which is on the list. It's a very unsatisfactory situation and besides, you never get the guys who are often responsible – the doctors or other people around the team who push the riders to use drugs. You can't get them because if a guy is positive, how can you prove that the doctor gave him the product? You can't.
>
> (*Cycle Sport*, April 1997: 30)

Verbruggen emphasised that the 'whole doping fight is pretty ineffective', and that 'the fight against drugs is unsatisfactory. We've gone from nowhere to nowhere.' He stated: 'What we have been doing – putting huge sums of money and effort into the fight against drugs – has not improved the situation: they [the cyclists] are only moving on to more sophisticated drugs' (*Cycle Sport*, April 1997: 28–31).

The new system introduced by the UCI involves the taking of blood samples from riders shortly before major races. Blood tests then determine the level of haematocrit – the amount of red blood cells – in a rider's blood and any rider with a haematocrit level which is considered to be dangerous to health (defined by the UCI as above 50 per cent) is not allowed to start that race or any other race until a further test has indicated that the rider's haematocrit level has dropped to within safe limits.

Verbruggen emphasised the non-punitive, harm reduction aspects of the new policy:

> For us, the blood test is a health test. The UCI medical commission has been thinking about it for years but it has been impossible because you need blood tests, and they can't be imposed. What we have dreamed of is doing the same thing in cycling as is done in a normal working relationship between employer and employee. There are certain things the employer is obliged to take care of: for example, ear protection if you are working somewhere with a lot of noise. . . . Where a guy works in a paint factory and is found to have too much lead in his blood, he is released from his job, and has to get better before he can come back. For years, we thought about making the teams responsible for the riders' health, as other employers are. . . . We're in a tough sport and we should control the health of our riders.
>
> (*Cycle Sport*, April 1997: 30)

Verbruggen emphasised that the test was not an anti-doping test as such, but a health test. Noting that the effect which one gets with EPO can also be obtained by altitude training or by using an oxygen chamber, Verbruggen stated:

> You can have long, intellectual discussions about why you have to forbid EPO but accept riders training at altitude, which has exactly the same effect. The bad thing is the risk, the danger. . . . You limit the risk by saying, 'Wait a moment, we're not going to worry if it's EPO, an oxygen chamber or altitude training, if your haematocrit level is over 50, you don't start.
>
> (*Cycle Sport*, April 1997: 30)

It might be noted that, as Verbruggen indicated, the UCI cannot compel riders to supply a blood sample. However, unlike the first doping tests in cycling, which were introduced in the 1960s and which were met with riders' strikes, the new health tests were brought in with the agreement of the riders and teams, a fact which is probably associated with the non-punitive character of the tests. However, it might be noted that, at a time when cycling has made an important shift away from traditional policies and towards harm reduction policies, the IOC still presses ahead with its traditional 'punitive' approach. Five months after the UCI announced its new policy, the IOC announced that it was seeking to develop a test to detect EPO, and a spokesperson for the IOC claimed that 'the door will certainly be closed' for EPO at the 2000 Olympic Games in Sydney (*Guardian*, 14 June 1997).

Another harm reduction scheme worthy of examination is that which has recently been started in County Durham in the North of England. In January 1994, the County Durham Health Authority began funding a mobile needle exchange scheme which was targeted at injecting drug users and which was designed in the first instance as part of a harm reduction policy in relation to the transmission of HIV infection. Somewhat to the surprise of the person organising the needle exchange scheme, Mark Harrison, it quickly became clear that a majority – Harrison estimates 60 per cent – of those using the scheme were bodybuilders who were using anabolic steroids. Some users of anabolic steroids had been attracted to the scheme because they had been unable to get medical help and advice from their regular physicians, some of whom had responded to requests for help in a hostile and heavily judgemental fashion and had refused to offer any advice until the bodybuilders stopped using steroids. With this evidence of unmet medical need in the area, County Durham Health Authority established, in early 1995, a 'drugs and sport' clinic.

The clinic has approximately 250 clients, most of whom are body-builders. It provides a confidential and non-judgemental service to users of anabolic steroids and other performance-enhancing drugs, and the policy goals of the clinic centre on harm reduction rather than cessation of drug use. New clients are given an initial assessment in relation to their pattern of drug use and sexual health (the latter mainly in respect of HIV trans-mission), followed by a physical examination which includes blood sample analysis for a red blood cell count and a lipid profile. In addition, clients are monitored for liver function. Clients are encouraged to ensure that the intervals between cycles of drug use are such as to minimise the health risks and are also given advice – for example, in relation to diet – which may help them to achieve their desired body shape with lower doses of drugs, or perhaps by using less dangerous drugs. A confidential counselling service is also provided for anabolic steroid users who experience side effects such as sexual dysfunction or aggression (Harrison, 1997; personal communication).

A somewhat similar scheme is run by an agency in Wirral, Merseyside, which also offers information and support, including monitoring of blood pressure, plasma cholesterol and liver function and HIV screening, for users of anabolic steroids. Other schemes are in operation in Nottingham and Cardiff, and an increasing number of agencies have workers in the field targeting anabolic steroid users (Korkia and Stimson, 1993: 112–13).

The increasing number of schemes of this kind differ in some respects from the 'health tests' now being carried out in cycling. In the first instance, these tests are, unlike those in cycling, not being carried out by a governing body of sport but by public health authorities. Second, whereas competitive cycling is a sport, competitive bodybuilding is more accurately described as a sport-like activity. Notwithstanding these differences, it is legitimate to ask what lessons can be learnt from such schemes. Should sporting bodies in general consider the adoption of schemes such as that recently initiated by the UCI in relation to EPO? Should consideration be given by sporting bodies to the development and funding of 'sport and drugs' clinics on the lines outlined above? What might be some of the consequences of a re-orientation on the part of sporting bodies towards harm reduction policies? And what might be some of the objections to such a shift in policy?

At the outset it should be acknowledged that a re-orientation of policy along these lines would be problematic. However, if we are honest we should also recognise that the issue of drug use and control is, as Goode pointed out, one where there may be no ideal solution and that it may well be that we are forced to accept 'the least bad of an array of very bad options' (Goode, 1997: ix).

One possible objection to a movement towards harm reduction policies might be that, based on the evidence of the 1998 Tour de France, such policies simply do not work. The new policy of the UCI was, as we noted earlier, introduced in 1997 and, little more than a year later, we were provided with conclusive evidence of the continued widespread use of doping in professional cycling. On this basis it might be suggested that the UCI policy has had no significant impact in terms of controlling the use of performance-enhancing drugs in cycling. Such a judgement would, however, be inappropriate. In this context, it is important to bear in mind that the UCI policy initiative was not designed as a 'catch-all' drugs test; indeed, as the president of the UCI consistently emphasised, it was a health check rather than a drugs test, and it was targeted specifically to tackle the health problems arising from the use of EPO.

The UCI policy thus had limited but clearly specified and practical objectives: not to prevent the use of EPO (an unrealistic objective, especially given the absence of a test to identify its use), but to control its use within relatively safe limits and, where those limits were exceeded, to exclude riders from racing until their red blood cell counts had decreased to within safe limits. Moreover, the evidence suggests that, in terms of these limited objectives, the policy has had a measure of success. In the first four months following the introduction of the UCI blood tests in February 1997, no fewer than ten riders were withdrawn from races because their red blood cell count was too high. Since then, there has been a steady stream of riders who have failed the test and who have as a consequence been excluded from races.

Since the 1998 Tour de France, the UCI blood test has continued to be used to good effect; just two months after the 1998 Tour de France, seven Italian riders were excluded from the Tour of Portugal after the blood test indicated that their haematocrit levels were above 50 per cent (*Cycling Weekly*, 22 August 1998), while in the first half of the 1999 season, a number of other riders have been similarly excluded from races because their red blood cell counts have been too high. The most spectacular exclusion to date has been that of Marco Pantani, who won both the Tour de

France and the Giro d'Italia in 1998, and who was excluded from the two final stages of the 1999 Giro d'Italia – a race in which he had an apparently unassailable lead – after a blood test showed he had a haematocrit level of 52 per cent (*Sunday Times*, 6 June 1999).

It might therefore be argued that whereas, as we noted previously and as the 1998 Tour de France indicated quite clearly, conventional doping tests in cycling have been conspicuously unsuccessful in terms of identifying those riders using performance-enhancing drugs, the UCI blood test has been significantly more effective in terms of identifying and excluding from racing those riders who have used EPO and whose health might be at risk as a consequence. Moreover, the reasons for the greater effectiveness of the UCI tests are not difficult to identify; they relate to the greater acceptability of health tests, as opposed to drug tests, among the riders and, partly for this same reason, to the fact that the relevant authorities within cycling are likely to find it easier to impose health checks rather than doping tests. I return to these issues towards the end of this chapter.

A second possible objection to harm reduction policies is that such policies, it might be argued, imply the condoning of the use of drugs. In response to possible objections of this kind, it might be noted that such arguments were also voiced when harm reduction policies, such as needle exchange schemes, were initially developed in relation to drug control policies more generally. Although such arguments are still occasionally heard, the case for needle exchange schemes has now generally been accepted in Britain, and such schemes have in recent years been funded by a Conservative Government which no one would accuse of having taken a 'soft' or permissive policy in relation to drug use in general. Thus the shift towards harm reduction policies is not incompatible with, and does not necessarily imply the dismantling of, more conventional forms of drug control. In Britain, for example, the development of needle exchange schemes has not been accompanied by any relaxation of laws relating to the possession or sale of controlled drugs such as marijuana, heroin or cocaine. In similar fashion, the adoption in cycling of a policy which is geared towards harm reduction does not mean that the UCI has dropped its opposition to doping. The president of the UCI pointed out that it had not abandoned doping controls and that its 'chief objective is to resolve the problem of doping in the long term', but he added that 'right now, we need to stop this torrent of EPO' (*Cycling Weekly*, 1 February 1997). Arguing that 'the fact is that concentrating on punishment doesn't solve the doping problem', Verbruggen emphasised that the new policy did not replace, but ran alongside, the more traditional anti-doping policy. The new policy, he pointed out, involved regulating health *and* doping and this was, he said, 'a much better approach' (*Cycle Sport*, April 1997: 30). In this sense, harm reduction policies do not send out the same – and to most people, unacceptable – symbolic message as would the 'legalisation' policy recommended by Coomber and Cashmore.

What health benefits might be associated with harm reduction policies? One obvious benefit associated with 'sport and drugs' clinics of the kind outlined above is that they provide what is clearly a much needed service to those using performance-enhancing drugs, whether in sport or other sport-related activities, not least in the fact that they provide qualified, confidential and non-judgemental medical advice which otherwise might be difficult to obtain. Though many drug-using athletes at the elite level undoubtedly receive qualified medical advice and monitoring (as we saw in Chapters 7 and 8), it may be the case that, even at the elite level, there are some drug-using athletes who do not receive such support. Moreover, it is clear that, below this level, there is a considerable unmet demand for medical support. A study carried out in British gyms indicated that users of anabolic steroids generally felt that most medical practitioners had little knowledge of their use and were unable to provide unbiased information on different drugs and their effects on health. The researchers found that 'the majority of AS [anabolic steroid] users would welcome medical involvement but are unable to get the supervision they would like' (Korkia and Stimson, 1993: 113).

Not surprisingly, medical practitioners were not an important source of advice for most users of anabolic steroids, the major sources of information being friends (35.8 per cent), followed by anabolic steroid handbooks (25.7 per cent) and dealers (20.2 per cent). There are undoubtedly health risks associated with this pattern of obtaining information; Korkia and Stimson (1993: 110–11) noted, for example, that steroid users would sometimes recommend doping practices different from those they used themselves (in order not to reveal their 'secret for success'), while some men may provide advice to women based on the men's own experiences, which could have serious consequences for female anabolic steroid users in terms of virilising effects. Again, the provision of specialist medical advice on a confidential and non-judgemental basis might have considerable benefits in terms of harm reduction.

Finally, it should be noted that athletes, including those who are using performance-enhancing drugs, are less likely to try to evade, and more likely to co-operate with, the administration of health tests than with tests which are imposed as part of a more punitive policy. That this is so is indicated by the fact that whereas the Tour de France cyclists protested vigorously against the doping investigation in the 1998 Tour de France, they have voluntarily co-operated in providing the blood samples required for the new UCI policy. And as we noted earlier, a significant number of riders have been excluded from races as a result of failing the UCI blood test. That so many riders have failed the test may be seen as an indication that the cycling authorities are more likely to impose, and riders more likely to accept, a short exclusion on health grounds than a longer ban on grounds of doping. For the authorities, the short-term exclusion on health grounds is much less likely to result in a potentially costly challenge in the courts, like that involving the American 400 metres runner 'Butch' Reynolds (Houlihan, 1994: 68–9) or the American swimmer Rick DeMont (Houlihan, 1999: 174), while for the riders, an exclusion on health grounds does not carry the same public stigma as a penalty imposed for doping. For these and for other reasons, it may be that the health tests now being used in cycling will prove not only to have benefits in terms of harm reduction, but that – and for some people this may be the bottom line – they may also prove to be a more effective way of controlling the use of drugs such as EPO than the 'law and order' approach which the IOC continues to pursue. An appropriately cautious conclusion in this extremely complex and difficult area might be to suggest that harm reduction schemes of this kind merit serious consideration and careful monitoring by all those concerned with the health of athletes.

11 Conclusion

By way of conclusion, it may be helpful to recapitulate some of the main themes of this book, and also to offer a few final thoughts on some of the issues which have been raised.

There is an extensive literature on what is the central focus of the first two chapters of this book; namely, the relationships between physical activity, exercise, sport and health. However, as was noted at the beginning of the first chapter, almost all of this literature has been written from a physiological perspective while very little has been written from a specifically sociological perspective. In seeking to develop such a perspective, I argued that it is important to differentiate clearly between the concepts of physical activity, exercise and sport, because these are very different kinds of social activities; they are associated with different networks of relationships and those who take part in them are likely to have very different orientations towards physical activity. As an illustration, it will be recalled that the Health Education Authority listed, among its recommended physical activities, gardening and DIY. However, keen gardeners or DIY enthusiasts, for whom their hobby constitutes their main form of physical activity, are likely to be involved in different networks of relationships – and will probably have very different attitudes towards physical activity – from those who regularly take part in aerobics or 'exercise to music' sessions, while non-competitive aerobics, in turn, involves the participants in a network of relationships which is very different from that which characterises competitive sport. These differences are of major importance but, as we noted earlier, the concepts of physical activity, exercise and sport have often been conflated, particularly by people within the sports lobby, who frequently claim for sport the health benefits associated with non-competitive physical activity or exercise. It is time to reject such sleight-of-hand, for it is intellectually dishonest and it provides a misleading basis for public policy.

In sociological terms, it is nonsense to conflate concepts as different as those of physical activity, exercise and sport. For example, no one would suggest that we could discover a great deal about the structure of modern competitive sport by focusing on the leisure-time activity of the gardener or the DIY enthusiast. By the same token, if we wished to find out something about the importance of gardening or DIY within the context of domestic relations, we would learn little of relevance from a study of competitive rugby, soccer or hockey. Of course, exercise and sport necessarily involve physical activity, but to conflate the concepts on this basis is like suggesting that there is no difference between the social relations of religion, politics and science since all three involve people in the articulation of ideas!

However, there is a second and, at least in the short term, more practical consideration why it is important to maintain a clear separation between the concepts of physical activity, exercise and health. This relates to the fact that these concepts not only refer to very different types of social activities, but that these *social* differences are also likely to be associated with very different consequences for the *health* of those who participate in them. Thus, whereas the public health case in favour of moderate-intensity physical activity has been made very clearly, the public health arguments in favour of competitive sport – and, in particular, team sports like those which have been at the centre of recent Government policy – are hardly persuasive.

The third chapter addressed issues relating to child abuse in sport, and it was noted that, on the whole, those involved in the administration of sport have been relatively slow to react to this problem. It was suggested that this slowness to react may perhaps have been associated with the common-sense perception of sport as a healthy activity and, within this context, it might have seemed for many people 'unthinkable' that anyone could deliberately abuse young children. The Women's Sports Foundation (1999) has recently made a similar point:

> Sport is one of the last social institutions to have recognised sexual abuse, perhaps because of the longstanding myths about sport as a separate and morally pure sphere of life. Whilst anti-racist and anti-sexist initiatives have been promoted for the past twenty years, and gender equity policies have been adopted by most modern sport organisations, policies for 'child protection' in sport are still relatively rare.

Donnelly and Sparks (1997) have drawn attention to a similar slowness to react on the part of sports administrators in Canada. They note that awareness and concern about sexual abuse have increased in the last twenty years, partly in response to the women's and subsequently the children's rights movements, and that in schools, youth groups and other institutional settings for children, policies have been developed to guard against those seeking sexual access to children. However, they add:

> But sport and other recreational settings have been very slow to respond to these changes. Sport organizations have, in general, continued to act as if such things could not occur in the pristine world of sport and, as in the case of fighting and other forms of violence,

behaved as if the laws of society were suspended in the world of sport. After all, adults touching children and adults touching each other is a necessary part of training and practice of many sports. The erotic elements of such touching has (*sic*) always been denied, as has recognition of the opportunities for private encounters and coercion that readily exist in sport.

(Donnelly and Sparks, 1997: 1)

In recent years, partly as a result of a series of high-profile prosecutions in relation to child sexual abuse, sports administrators have begun to put into place child protection policies. Many sports organisations, however, have still not implemented appropriate policies, and, until they do so, children in such organisations will be at risk. As was noted in Chapter 3, sports organisations for children are obvious targets for those who might seek sexually to exploit children. Such organisations offer access to large numbers of children in situations where their bodies, perhaps partly clothed or undressed, may be exposed to the gaze of others, and where it is often legitimate for some physical contact to take place in the course of coaching.

Of course, there are other institutional contexts in which adults might come into contact with children under broadly similar circumstances: schools and children's homes are obvious examples. It is, however, much more difficult for adults to gain access to such institutions; to become a teacher or residential social worker requires a lengthy period of training in the course of which the students' teachers are able to make a considered assessment of their abilities, personality and suitability for such work. This is not to suggest, of course, that schoolteachers or social workers never abuse young people in their care; the controls on entry to teaching and social work may help to minimise but cannot eliminate the risk of child abuse. By contrast, however, many sports clubs for young people provide, at the local level, almost open access to any adults who wish to become involved with children, for whatever reason. At the local level, British sport relies heavily on volunteers, and often all that is required to become involved in a local club for young people is little more than apparent enthusiasm and a willingness to give up one's spare time. No extended period of training is required. No formal qualifications are required. And no references are required from professional people who have supervised one's training. There are relatively few situations in which adults are not only given access to young children, but in which they are given authority over young children with so few checks on either their ability or their integrity.

Chapter 4 examined a rather different health-related issue in sport, this time focusing not on the health of children and young people but on the provision of medical care (including physiotherapy) to professional footballers. The most striking finding from the research reported in this chapter concerned the very considerable variation in the roles of the club doctor and the club physiotherapist from one club to another, while these roles may also change radically when there is a change of manager within a club, as happens very frequently. Underlying these variations and in relation to clinical decision-making there is in professional football no standardised framework in terms of which the respective rights and responsibilities of the club doctor, physiotherapist and manager are defined; rather, these relationships are negotiated individually between the participants involved on a club-by-club basis.

This situation is, in terms of the quality of care available to players, a matter of some concern. There is, in almost all aspects of medical care, a growing awareness of the need to monitor and evaluate the quality of care provided, and to identify and disseminate 'good practice'. In professional football, however, there has been almost no attempt to identify a good practice model in relation to the roles of the club doctor and physio-therapist. In some situations, the clinical autonomy of the club doctor and physiotherapist may be severely limited by the intervention – medical staff often, and for understandable reasons, preferred to call it the 'interference' – of the manager and it is difficult to see how such conditions can be con-ducive to good clinical practice, or to the long-term health of the players. In similar fashion, there is considerable variation in terms of how much, and what kind of, information is passed on to the manager by club medical staff, and some of these situations also constitute a cause for concern in terms of the ethical issues involved.

The whole of the second half of the book has been given over to a detailed consideration of what is considered by many people to be one of the most difficult problems confronting those involved in contemporary sport; namely, the use of performance-enhancing drugs. The situation in relation to anti-doping policy in sport is currently changing rapidly, partly because of the stimulus provided by the scandal surrounding the 1998 Tour de France, and within such a fluid situation it is difficult to predict the ways in which anti-doping policy might develop in the next few years. In this concluding section, I want briefly to consider the policy statement produced by the anti-doping conference held by the IOC at Lausanne in February 1999 before moving on to consider some of the issues raised in Houlihan's (1999) excellent book on doping, and in particular, to reflect upon two recent trends in anti-doping policy which Houlihan identifies.

The IOC's anti-doping conference, held in Lausanne from 4 to 6 February 1999, illustrated some of the problems involved in developing anti-doping policy. The conference, which was attended by representatives of National Olympic Committees, sports ministers from several (mainly European) governments and a large number of Olympic athletes, resulted in the Lausanne Declaration on Doping and Sports. The Declaration was hailed by the IOC president, Juan Antonio Samaranch, as 'a great victory for clean sport' (*Daily Telegraph*, 5 February 1999), though this view was not shared by most commentators or by many of those who took part in the conference.

The central policy initiative taken at the conference involved the decision to establish an independent, international Anti-Doping Agency, with the IOC contributing $25 million towards the cost of establishing the agency. Beyond this there was, however, little consensus among the delegates. A central problem concerned the question of which body should be responsible for leading this new agency. The then British Minister of Sport, Tony Banks, argued that a body such as the World Health Organisation should be responsible for co-ordinating the activities of the proposed agency, but most delegates felt that, since this was a problem within the world of sport, it should be the responsibility of sporting bodies to tackle the problem. The IOC might have seemed, to many people, the obvious organisation to head the proposed agency, but recent scandals concerning corruption at high levels of the IOC, particularly in relation to the bidding process for hosting the Olympic Games, meant that many delegates were reluctant to accept IOC leadership of the agency. Although it was known that the IOC president had hoped to head the agency, delegates refused to agree to this, with the British Sports Minister arguing that 'the chairing of the independent agency by President Samaranch would compromise it and that is something we would not be happy to accept'. The British Sports Minister, speaking on behalf of European Union ministers, also said that if the IOC wanted government help, it would have to drop its proposal to have representatives of pharmaceutical companies and sports manufacturers on the agency.

However, perhaps most criticism focused on the failure of the conference to agree on uniform suspensions for athletes using performance-enhancing drugs. The original proposal which was put to the conference was that all athletes who are found to have used drugs should be subject to a minimum two-year suspension, but the governing bodies of football (soccer), cycling and tennis refused to agree to this policy, and the original proposal was modified to allow for different sanctions under 'exceptional circumstances'. The British Sports Minister argued that this modification 'provided an enormous loophole' and that the Declaration 'has weakened rather than strengthened anti-doping initiatives'. As a result, he said, the British Government had reserved its position in relation to the Declaration and would come back with further proposals (*Guardian*, 5 February 1999). Within the United Kingdom, commentators were even more critical. Mihir Bose, writing in the *Daily Telegraph* (5 February 1999), held that the IOC had scored 'a spectacular own goal', while Duncan Peat, writing in the *Guardian* (4 February 1999), held that 'the IOC's much-hyped World Conference on Doping in Sport is doomed to failure'. Without overstating the case, it might be concluded that the Lausanne Declaration has left a great many issues unresolved, while there are clearly a great many political and organisational problems to be overcome before the proposed anti-doping agency can be established.

Moving away from the specific proposals of the Lausanne conference to more general issues concerning anti-doping policy, Houlihan has suggested that one of the major problems associated with anti-doping policy in sport is that 'there is little evidence of consistency and stability regarding objectives of sports anti-doping policy'. He adds: 'it must be asked whether the ultimate objective is the complete elimination of drug use in all sport, in certain sports, or only in sport at certain levels. Is the objective elimination or simply the containment of the extent of drug use?' (Houlihan, 1999: 98).

It is important to answer such questions, not least because, as we noted in Chapter 10, until they are answered it is difficult to know what criteria should be used in monitoring and measuring the success of anti-doping policy. As Houlihan goes on to note, given that the objectives of current anti-doping policy are not clearly defined, it is not altogether surprising that 'techniques for measuring progress towards policy objectives are poor, relying mainly on trends in the number of positive test results' (Houlihan, 1999: 103). However, as we noted earlier, the incidence of positive test results is a poor index – some would argue so poor as to be virtually useless – of the extent of drug use by athletes. There is clearly a pressing need to define more distinctly the objectives of anti-doping policy, and to specify more exactly the criteria for monitoring the success of that policy.

Houlihan also draws attention to two current trends in anti-doping policy, the relationship between which would seem to require some clarification. The first of these involves what was, as we have noted, one of the key areas of discussion at the IOC's Lausanne conference; namely, the attempt to harmonise anti-doping policies between different countries and sporting federations. In this context, Houlihan notes that,

> Given the multiplicity of sources of legitimate anti-doping regulation and the global nature of modern elite sport, it is important that there is maximum uniformity of regulations so that drug abusers are not able to exploit differences and inconsistencies between countries, domestic governing bodies and international federations. The clearest motives for harmonisation are first, equity of treatment of elite athletes and second, the increasing concern to prevent a successful legal challenge to the decisions of international federations.
>
> (1999: 154)

The problems that can arise from inconsistency between rule-making authorities were well illustrated by the cases of Katrin Krabbe and Martin Vinnicombe (Houlihan, 1999: 154–5).

However, the current emphasis on harmonisation of anti-doping policy is not without its problems. On the political level, the policy is (as we saw from the IOC's Lausanne conference) likely to generate opposition from some federations. As Houlihan has noted, it is 'possible to argue that progress towards harmonisation has been attained at the expense of the autonomy of sports federations' (1999: 168), and many federations will undoubtedly seek to maintain their autonomy. There is, though, another and rather different problem which is raised by the current emphasis on harmonisation; this relates to the question of whether it is appropriate to apply a single, undifferentiated anti-doping policy to all sports, irrespective of the particular characteristics of each sport.

As we saw in Chapter 10, the pattern of drug use varies considerably from one sport to another. In some sports, the use of performance-enhancing drugs is very common; as we have seen, this is the case in cycling, where the most widely used drugs are EPO, anabolic steroids and amphetamines. In weightlifting and powerlifting, the use of performance-enhancing drugs – particularly anabolic steroids – is also common. In other sports – for example, table tennis, netball and lacrosse – the use of performance-enhancing drugs appears to be relatively rare. In sports such as archery and shooting, those who do use performance-enhancing drugs are not likely to use those drugs favoured by endurance athletes, but are much more likely to use beta-blockers. In relation to professional soccer in England, Malcolm observed that the data 'would seem to indicate that what limited drug use there is in football does not involve performance-enhancing drugs, but rather that the drugs are essentially taken for recreational purposes' (1998: 17–18).

Given these very considerable variations in the pattern of drug use from one sport to another, it might be reasonable to suggest that what is required is not anti-doping policy, but anti-doping *policies*. Thus, rather than push for harmonisation of all aspects of anti-doping policy, it might be more appropriate to adopt a sport-by-sport approach, the central object of which would be to examine the pattern of drug use in each sport, and to try to understand the conditions – both in terms of the physiological demands and the pattern of social organisation characteristic of each sport – which give rise to a particular pattern of drug use, as the basis for developing an anti-doping policy which was appropriately tailored to each sport.

It might possibly be objected that such a policy would establish a new – and, it might be argued, a dangerous – principle of anti-doping policy: the principle that athletes in different sports might be treated differently in relation to anti-doping controls. Such a view is, however, mistaken; the principle that athletes in different sports might be subject to different controls is not a new one, for it is already established in the anti-doping regulations of the IOC and other sporting bodies.

As we noted in Chapter 6, there are certain drugs – for example, alcohol, marijuana and beta-blockers – which are not on the IOC list of banned drugs, but which are defined as drugs 'subject to certain restrictions', and different governing bodies of sport have different regulations in relation to these drugs. In this context, Houlihan (1999: 164) has pointed out that there are some minor variations in the anti-doping regulations from one sport to another, and that these variations 'often involve the specification of additional drugs that have a particular relevance to their sport', as in the case of the Fédération Internationale du Sport Automobile (FISA), which has added alcohol and marijuana to its list of banned substances. As Houlihan correctly argues, 'one sign of the growing maturity of the policy discussions is that sports federations are beginning to refine the IOC list to meet the specific character and problems of their own sport' (1999: 148).

It should also be noted that the development of policy which is more differentiated on a sport-by-sport basis would not, of itself, imply any softening of anti-doping policies; indeed, it might, as in motor sport, involve the imposition in one sport of sanctions which do not apply in other sports. In more general terms, however, the question being raised here is not whether anti-doping policy is 'hard' or 'soft', but whether it is *appropriate* to each sport, for policy which is not appropriate is hardly likely to be effective.

The relevance of this point can perhaps be illustrated if we revisit the policy involving 'health tests' for professional cyclists which, as we noted earlier, was introduced by the Union Cycliste Internationale in 1997. This policy does not apply to all sports; it was introduced in one specific sport in order to deal with a problem which, at that time, was specific to that sport (though there is evidence that EPO is now being used by athletes in other endurance sports). The policy was introduced with the consent of almost everyone involved in cycling, mainly because there was widespread agreement within the sport that this particular drug, which was widely used within cycling (though not at that time in other sports) posed a particular and serious threat to the health of riders. These particular circumstances, which at the time appeared not to apply within any other sport, were considered sufficient justification for the introduction of a policy that was unique to cycling because it was targeted at a problem which, at the time, was also unique to cycling.

It is important, therefore, that in the drive towards policy harmonisation, we do not lose sight of the value of differentiating anti-doping policy in such a way that it is appropriately tailored to the requirements of each sport. In this sense, it might be suggested that what is required is harmonisation along certain axes of policy, together with differentiation along other axes.

In several respects, harm reduction policies, such as the 'health tests' which were introduced in professional cycling in 1997 and the sports and drugs clinics outlined in Chapter 10, represent an interesting development and one which, it was argued earlier, merits further consideration by those concerned with the health of athletes. However, it is important to note that harm reduction policies of this kind have been designed to cope with particular problems – the health risks associated with the use by cyclists of EPO, and the non-availability of medical advice to bodybuilders and others who use anabolic steroids – and, in line with the argument in favour of more differentiated policies within sport outlined above, it is not suggested that harm reduction policies of this kind, even if they were wholly successful in meeting their objectives within cycling and in relation to bodybuilders, could provide an appropriate basis for dealing with the many, complex and varied problems involving drug use in sport. More specifically, in so far as these harm reduction policies have had any success – and certainly in cycling they seem to have been considerably more successful than conventional anti-doping policies in terms of controlling the use of drugs – that success appears to have been premised on three fundamental points.

The most basic of these is that the harm reduction policies and the health tests on which they are based – unlike, for example, conventional doping controls in cycling – have been accepted as legitimate by those at whom the tests are targeted. This legitimacy, in turn, appears to be based on two further considerations. The first of these is that the tests are seen as an appropriate response to what is recognised, not just by those responsible for organising the testing but, more importantly, by the drug-using athletes themselves, as a serious health concern; in the case of cycling, this was the serious threat to the health of cyclists posed by their use of EPO and, in the case of bodybuilders, it was their lack of access to specialised medical advice to help them to deal with what they recognised as the undesirable side effects of anabolic steroid use. Quite clearly, however, 'health tests' would be much less likely to be seen as legitimate if they were designed to identify the use of drugs which, in the eyes of many people, do not pose serious health problems; the use of marijuana would be an obvious example. A precondition for gaining the co-operation of athletes in relation to health tests would thus seem to be that the tests address what the athletes themselves recognise as a serious health concern.

The second basis on which the harm reduction policies have been accorded legitimacy by those at whom they are targeted is that they have been framed very clearly within a non-punitive health framework, rather than within a punitive anti-doping framework. It is clear that any movement away from this health framework towards a more conventional, punitive, anti-doping framework would almost certainly result in the withdrawal of co-operation by the athletes concerned.

It might be noted that some other organisations have recently adopted the policy of 'health tests' pioneered by the Union Cycliste Internationale. Following the 1998 Tour de France, the French Cycling Federation not only adopted, but even extended, the principle of health checks. All elite riders on French teams are now given an in-depth health check every three months in order to reveal and investigate physical changes. The results of the second of these health tests revealed that half of the riders in French teams (67 out of 135 on whom the tests were done) had been temporarily excluded from racing for a variety of reasons, principally abnormally high iron levels but also because of kidney problems and abnormal red blood cell counts. Speaking to *Le Monde*, the doctor to the French Federation, Armand Megret, stated that the results 'would seem to indicate abuse of substances of all kinds, but not necessarily illegal ones, like, for example, the excessive intake of iron. This can be dangerous, even after stopping taking these products' (*Cycling Weekly*, 5 June 1999).

A system of 'health checks' has also recently been introduced by the Italian Olympic Committee (CONI) as part of a programme entitled *Io non rischio la salute* (I'm not risking my health). These health tests, involving analysis of blood and urine samples, have been carried out on various Italian sportspeople, including footballers, athletes, rowers and basketball players (*Cycling Weekly*, 29 May 1999). However, it was reported that, unlike the blood tests which were introduced by the UCI, the CONI tests have met with some resistance and that six football teams in Serie A, including Juventus, have refused to take part in the tests. This report might, perhaps, lend some support to the argument above that harm reduction policies involving health tests may not be appropriate in all situations and that such policies can provide only one part – albeit a useful one – of a more differentiated policy in relation to the use of drugs in sport.

In conclusion, the problems associated with the use of drugs in sport are many and complex and it is not possible to provide any quick or easy solution. Indeed, in this particularly difficult policy area, it might be appropriate to recall once again the words of Goode to the effect that, in such policy areas, there may be no ideal solution and that it may well be that we are forced to accept 'the least bad of an array of very bad options' (Goode, 1997: ix).

Notes

Introduction

1 Some critics of figurational sociology have alleged that advocates of this approach claim to be able to offer 'objective' analyses of social processes. From what has been said, it should be clear that this was not Elias's position and, indeed, it is a position which he explicitly rejected. However, since some of his critics have misunderstood Elias's argument on this point, it may be useful to reiterate one of the arguments contained in his classic essay, 'Problems of involvement and detachment' (1956). Elias noted that sociologists, like everyone else, are members of many social groups outside their academic communities – families, political parties, sports clubs and so on – and they cannot cease to take part in, or to be affected by, the social and political affairs of their groups and their time. In this sense, they cannot be wholly detached. However, Elias goes on to note that there is at least one sense in which it would not be desirable, in terms of the development of sociology, for them to be wholly detached, even if this were possible. Thus, while one need not know, in order to understand the structure of a molecule, what it feels like to be one of its atoms, in order to understand the way in which human groups work, one needs to know, as it were from 'inside' how human beings experience their own and other groups, and one cannot know this without active participation and involvement. The problem for sociologists, then, is not the problem of how to be completely detached, but of how to maintain an appropriate balance between these two roles of everyday participant and scientific inquirer and, as members of a professional group, to establish in their work the undisputed dominance of the latter.

3 Health-related issues in child sport

1 I am very grateful to Professor William Upper, of Algonquin College, Ontario, who has kindly provided me with a great deal of information about recent developments in relation to child abuse in Canada.

4 Doctors' dilemmas

1 As Freidson (1960; 1970) noted in his seminal work on doctor–patient relationships, doctors are likely to be subject to a greater degree of client control in general practice (primary care) than in the situation of hospital practice.

5 Doping in sport

1 The use of androstenedione is also banned in the United States in the NFL though, rather curiously, it is not banned in baseball. However, the IOC has, since McGwire set his record, called for androstenedione to be banned in baseball. It might also be noted that since McGwire set his record, sales of androstenedione are reported to have quadrupled in the United States (*The Times*, 1 February 1999).

2 Similar situations may also – indeed, almost certainly will – arise outside of the sporting context. In 1997 it was reported that, following the introduction of drug tests in British prisons, some prisoners 'have already switched from cannabis to heroin because heroin flushed out of the bloodstream more quickly' (*Independent*, 18 June 1997).

6 The emergence of doping as a problem in modern sport

1 It is striking that athletes and sports administrators from countries such as Britain and the United States rarely, if ever, draw attention to the advantages which athletes from those countries enjoy by comparison with athletes from poorer developing nations. However, prior to the collapse of the communist regimes in the Soviet Union and East Germany, those involved in sport in the West would often complain that athletes from the eastern-bloc countries enjoyed 'unfair' advantages in terms of financial and other support which enabled them to train on a full-time basis.

7 Doping in sport

1 A very similar and equally misleading technological determinist argument in relation to a different area of social life is the suggestion that changing patterns of sexual behaviour during the past three decades can simply be explained in terms of the development of the contraceptive pill, without reference to other changes (for example, changes in gender relations and relations between the generations, in patterns of work and in leisure activities).

8 The other side of sports medicine

1 Patricia Vertinsky (1990) has documented late-nineteenth-century medical views concerning what kinds of physical activity were considered appropriate for girls and women. She notes that these views were used to justify practices which 'prescribed and/or delimited levels of physical activity and restricted sporting opportunities' for females (1990: 1). It is interesting to note that Tissié's concern with what he saw as the physiological dangers of over-exertion was not confined to women, but also related to men.

2 Todd (1987: 93) suggests that Ziegler obtained this information at the 1954 World Weightlifting Championships, whereas Voy (1991: 8) suggests that he obtained this information while acting as a member of the medical staff of the US team at the 1956 World Games in Moscow. Both authors agree about his subsequent role in the development and use of anabolic steroids.

3 Note Todd's clever play on words with his use of the phrase 'big arms race', which correctly locates the sporting competition between the United States and the Soviet Union in the context of the Cold War and superpower rivalry.

9 A case study of cycling and the 1988 Tour de France

1 However, Donohoe and Johnson (1986) suggested that Linton did not die during or close to competition, but in fact died many years later from typhoid.

2 In the women's Tour de France, teams are entered by national federations and not, as in the men's race, by sponsored trade teams.

3 In the context of the criminal law, it is important to differentiate between criminalising the supplying of drugs used in doping (as under French law) and criminalising the use by athletes of dope. Given the high level of public concern about crime, and the fact that police resources in most countries are already severely stretched, it is not realistic to suggest that police should become directly involved in doping controls in sport. Such a development would almost certainly be resisted by most people involved in sport, while most members of the general public would probably prefer scarce police resources to be concentrated on combating what most people would probably regard as more serious crime.

Bibliography

Alderson, J. and Crutchley, D. (1990) 'Physical education and the National Curriculum', in N. Armstrong (ed.), *New Directions in Physical Education*, vol. 1, *Human Kinetics*, pp. 37–62, Champaign, IL.

Allied Dunbar National Fitness Survey (1992) London, Health Education Authority, Sports Council and Department of Health.

Almond, L., Harrison, P. and Laws, C. (1996) 'Sport: raising the game: a physical education perspective', *British Journal of Physical Education*, 27 (3), 6–11.

American Academy of Orthopaedic Surgeons (1984) 'Pioneers in sports medicine', in *Athletic Training and Sports Medicine*, Chicago, pp. 3–5.

American College of Sports Medicine (1987) 'American College of Sports Medicine position stand on blood-doping as an ergogenic aid', *Medicine and Science in Sports and Exercise*, 19, 540–3.

—— (1990) 'Position stand: the recommended quantity and quality of exercise for developing and maintaining cardiorespiratory and muscular fitness in healthy adults', *Medicine and Science in Sports and Exercise*, 22, 265–74.

Anderson, R. and Bury, M. (eds) (1988) *Living with Chronic Illness: the Experience of Patients and their Families*, London, Hyman Unwin.

Armstrong, R. (1991) 'Anti-doping procedures and legal consequences: medical and ethical factors and conflicts of interest', in International Athletic Foundation, *International Symposium on Sport and Law: Official Proceedings*, Monte Carlo, Monaco, International Athletic Foundation, pp. 59–64.

Bagley, C. and King, K. (1990) *Child Sexual Abuse*, London and New York, Tavistock/Routledge.

Black, T. (1996) 'Does the ban on drugs in sport improve societal welfare?' *International Review for the Sociology of Sport*, 31(4), 367–84.

Blair, S. N., Paffenbarger, R. S., Clark, D. G., Cooper, K. H. and Gibbons, L. W. (1989) 'Physical fitness and all-cause mortality', *Journal of the American Medical Association*, 262 (17), 2395–401.

Botham, I. (1997) *The Botham Report*, London, CollinsWillow.

Bottomley, M. (1990) 'Athletics at an overseas venue: the role of the team doctor', in S. D. W. Payne (ed.), *Medicine, Sport and the Law*, Oxford, Blackwell, pp. 158–65.

Brackenridge, C. H. (1994) 'Fair play or fair game? Child sexual abuse in sport organisations', *International Review for the Sociology of Sport*, 29(3), 287–99.

British Medical Association (1992) *Cycling: Towards Safety and Health*, Oxford and New York, Oxford University Press.

Brown, T. C. and Benner, C. (1984) 'The nonmedical use of drugs', in W. N. Scott, B. Nisonson and J. A. Nicholas (eds), *Principles of Sports Medicine*, Baltimore, MD and London, Williams & Wilkins, pp. 32–9.

Canadian Association for the Advancement of Women and Sport and Physical Activity (CAAWS) (1998) *What Parents Can Do about Harassment and Abuse in Sport*, Gloucester, Ont., CAAWS.

Canadian Hockey Association (1997) *Speak Out! . . . Act Now! A Guide to Preventing and Responding to Abuse and Harassment for Sport Clubs and Associations*, Gloucester, Ont., Canadian Hockey Association.

Carrington, T. and Leaman, O. (1983) 'Work for some and sport for all', *Youth and Policy*, 1, 10–16.

Cashmore, E. (1996) *Making Sense of Sport*, 2nd edn, London, Routledge.

Clumpner, R. A. and Pendleton, B. B. (1981) 'The People's Republic of China', in J. Riordan (ed.), *Sport under Communism*, London, C. Hurst & Co., pp. 103–40.

Coakley, J. (1998a) 'Deviance and the normative structure of sports', in *MSc Sociology of sport distance learning material*, University of Leicester, Module 4, Unit 1, section 2, pp. 111–26.

—— (1998b) *Sport in Society*, 6th edn, Boston, MA, Irwin McGraw-Hill.

Coakley, J. and Hughes, R. (1994) 'Deviance in sport', in J. Coakley, *Sport in Society: Issues and Controversies*, 5th edn, St Louis, Mosby.

—— (1998) 'Deviance in sport', in J. Coakley, *Sport in Society: Issues and Controversies*, 6th edn, Boston, MA, Irwin McGraw-Hill, pp. 144–78.

Collings, A. F. (1988) 'Blood doping: how, why and why not', *Excel* (Canberra, Australia), 4(3), 12–16.

Colquhoun, D. (1991) 'Health based physical education, the ideology of healthism and victim blaming', *Physical Education Review*, 14(1), 5–13.

Colquhoun, D. and Kirk, D. (1987) 'Investigating the problematic relationship between health and physical education: an Australian study', *Physical Education Review*, 10(2), 100–9.

Coni, P., Kelland, G. and Davies, D. (1988) *AAA Drug Abuse Enquiry Report*, Amateur Athletics Association.

Coomber, R. (1993) 'Drugs in sport: rhetoric or pragmatism', *The International Journal of Drug Policy*, 4(4), 169–78.

—— (1996) 'The effect of drug use in sport on people's perception of sport: the policy consequences', *The Journal of Performance Enhancing Drugs*, 1(1), 16–20.

Cooper, D. M. (1993) *Child Abuse Revisited*, Buckingham and Philadelphia, Open University Press.

Corbin, C. B., Pangrazi, R. P. and Welk, G. J. (1994) 'Towards an understanding of appropriate physical activity levels for youth', *Physical Activity and Research Digest*, Series 1, no. 8, President's Council on Fitness and Sport, USA.

Cowan, D. A. (1994) 'Drug abuse', in M. Harries, C. Williams, W. D. Stanish and L. J. Micheli (eds), *Oxford Textbook of Sports Medicine*, New York, Oxford and Tokyo, Oxford University Press, pp. 314–29.

Cramer, R. B. (1985) 'Olympic cheating: the inside story of illicit doping and the US cycling team', *Rolling Stone*, 441, 25–6, 30.

Crawford, R. (1980) 'Healthism and the medicalization of everyday life', *International Journal of Health Services*, 10(3), 365–89.

—— (1984). 'A cultural account of "health": control, release, and the social body', in J. B. McKinley (ed.), *Issues in the Political Economy of Health Care*, New York and London, Tavistock, pp. 60–103.

Crawford, S. A. G. M. (1987) 'Pioneering women: recreational and sporting opportunities in a remote colonial setting', in J. A. Mangan and R. J. Park (eds), *From 'Fair Sex' to Feminism*; London, Frank Cass, pp. 161–81.

Cycle Sport, London, IPC Magazines Ltd.

Cycling Plus, Bath, Future Publications.

Cycling Weekly, London, IPC Magazines Ltd.

De Swaan, A. (1988) *In the Care of the State: Health Care, Education and Welfare in Europe and the USA in the Modern Era*, Cambridge, Polity Press.

Dealy, F. X., Jr. (1990) *Win at Any Cost: the Sell Out of College Athletics*, New York, Carol Publishing Group.

Department for Education and Employment (1999) 'Blunkett unveils proposals for National Curriculum from 2000', *DfEE News*, 13 May, London, DfEE.

Department of Education (Ireland) (1997) *Targeting Sporting Change in Ireland*, Dublin, Department of Education.

Department of Health (1992) *The Health of the Nation: a Strategy for Health in England*, London, HMSO.

Department of National Heritage (DNH) (1995) *Sport: Raising the Game*, London, DNH.

Dirix, A. (1988) 'Classes and methods', in A. Dirix, H. G. Knuttgen and K. Tittel (eds), *The Olympic Book of Sports Medicine*, Oxford, Blackwell, pp. 669–75.

Donnelly, P. (1993) 'Problems associated with youth involvement in high-performance sport', in B. R. Cahill and A. J. Pearl (eds), *Intensive Participation in Children's Sports*, Champaign, IL, Human Kinetics Publishers, pp. 95–126.

Donnelly, P. and Harvey, J. (1996) 'Overcoming Systematic Barriers to Active Living', Discussion paper prepared for Fitness Branch, Health Canada and Active Living Canada.

Donnelly, P. and Sparks, S. (1997) 'Child sexual abuse in sport', *Policy Options*, 18(3), 3–6.

Donohoe, T. and Johnson, N. (1986) *Foul Play: Drug Abuse in Sports*, Oxford, Blackwell Scientific Publications.

Dopson, S. and Waddington, I. (1996) 'Managing social change: a process-sociological approach to understanding organisational change within the National Health Service', *Sociology of Health and Illness*, 18(4), 525–50.

Dorrell, S. (1995) 'Sport in education', *RECMAN Conference*, 28 March.

Doust, D., Hughes, R. and Freman, S. (1988) 'Fallen heroes', *Sunday Times*, 2 October.

Dubin, The Hon. Charles L. (1990) *Commission of Inquiry into the Use of Drugs and Banned Practices Intended to Increase Athletic Performance*, Ottawa, Canadian Government Publishing Centre.

Dunning, E. (1986a) 'The dynamics of modern sport: notes on achievement-striving and the social significance of sport', in N. Elias and E. Dunning, *Quest for Excitement*, Oxford, Basil Blackwell, pp. 205–23.

—— (1986b) 'Sport as a male preserve: notes on the social sources of masculine identity and its transformation', in N. Elias and E. Dunning, *Quest for Excitement*, Oxford, Basil Blackwell, pp. 267–83.

—— (1990) 'Sociological reflections on sport, violence and civilization', *International Review for the Sociology of Sport*, 25(1), 65–82.

Dunning, E. and Sheard, K. (1979) *Barbarians, Gentlemen and Players*, Oxford, Martin Robertson.

Durkheim, E. (1933) *The Division of Labor in Society*, Glencoe, The Free Press.

Edwards, H. (1973) *Sociology of Sport*, Homewood, IL, Dorsey Press.

Elias, N. (1956) 'Problems of involvement and detachment', *British Journal of Sociology*, 7(3), 226–52.

—— (1978a) *What is Sociology?* London, Hutchinson.

—— (1978b) *The Civilizing Process*, Oxford, Basil Blackwell.

—— (1986a) 'The genesis of sport as a sociological problem', in N. Elias and E. Dunning, *Quest for Excitement*, Oxford, Basil Blackwell, pp. 126–49.

—— (1986b) 'An essay on sport and violence', in N. Elias and E. Dunning, *Quest for Excitement*, Oxford, Basil Blackwell, pp. 150–74.

—— (1987) *Involvement and Detachment*, Oxford, Basil Blackwell.

Elias, N. and Dunning, E. (1986) *Quest for Excitement*, Oxford, Basil Blackwell.

Elliott, P. N. C. (1996) 'Drug treatment of inflammation in sports injuries', in D. R. Mottram (ed.), *Drugs in Sport*, 2nd edn, London, E. & F. N. Spon.

Elston, M. A. (1991) 'The politics of professional power: medicine in a changing health service', in J. Gabe, M. Calnan and M. Bury (eds), *The Sociology of the Health Service*, London, Routledge.

English Sports Council (1997) *England, the Sporting Nation*, London, English Sports Council.

Eriksson, B. O., Mellstrand, T., Peterson, L. and Renström, P. (1990) *Sports Medicine*, Enfield, Middlesex, Guinness Publishing.

Fletcher, S. (1987) 'The making and breaking of a female tradition: women's physical education in England, 1880–1980', in J. A. Mangan and R. J. Park (eds), *From 'Fair Sex' to Feminism*, London, Frank Cass, pp. 145–57.

Freidson, E. (1960) 'Client control and medical practice', *American Journal of Sociology*, 65, 374–82.

—— (1970) *Profession of Medicine*, New York, Dodd, Mead & Company.

Gillham, B. (1994) *The Facts about Child Physical Abuse*, London and New York, Cassell.

Gledhill, N. (1982) 'Blood doping and related issues: a brief review', *Medicine and Science in Sport and Exercise*, 14, 183–9.

Gledhill, N. and Froese, A. B. (1979) 'Should research on blood-doping be continued?' *Modern Athlete and Coach*, 17(1), 23–5.

Gold, A. (1989) Interview in *Athletics Today*, 3(52) (28 December), 10–11.

Goldman, B. and Klatz, R. (1992) *Death in the Locker Room II*, Chicago, Elite Sports Medicine Publications.

Goode, E. (1997) *Between Politics and Reason: the Drug Legalization Debate*, New York, St Martin's Press.

Goudsblom, J. (1986) 'Public health and the civilizing process', *Millbank Quarterly*, 64(2), 181.

Guttmann, A. (1978) *From Ritual to Record*, New York, Columbia University Press.

—— (1988) *A Whole New Ball Game*, Chapel Hill and London, University of North Carolina Press.

—— (1992) *The Olympics: a History of the Modern Games*, Urbana and Chicago, University of Illinois Press.

Hanson, N. (1991) *Blood, Mud and Glory*, London, Pelham.

Harris, J. (1994) 'Young people's perceptions of health, fitness and exercise: implications for the teaching of health related exercise', *Physical Education Review*, 17(2), 143–51.

Harris, J. and Cale, L. (1997) 'Activity promotion in physical education', *European Physical Education Review*, 3(1), 58–67.

Health Education Authority (HEA) (1995) *Moving On: a Summary*, London, HEA.

—— (1996) *Promoting Physical Activity in Primary Health Care: Guidance for the Primary Healthcare Team*, London, HEA.

—— (1997) *Young People and Physical Activity: Promoting Better Practice*, London, HEA.

—— (1998) *Young and Active?* London, HEA.

Heil, J. (1993) 'Sport psychology, the athlete at risk and the sports medicine team', in J. Heil, *Psychology of Sport Injury*, Champaign, IL, Human Kinetics Publishers.

Herbert, D. L. and Herbert, W. G. (1991) 'Medico-legal issues', in R. C. Cantu and J. M. Lyle (eds), *ACSM's Guidelines for the Team Physician*, Philadelphia, Lea and Febiger, pp. 118–25.

Hicks, R. (1998) 'Arthritis and the professional footballer', *Football Decision* (December), pp. 22–3.

Hill, C. R. (1992) *Olympic Politics*, Manchester and New York, Manchester University Press.

Hoberman, J. (1992) *Mortal Engines*, New York, Free Press.

Hollmann, W. (1989) 'Sports medicine: present, past and future', in M. Kvist (ed.), *Paavo Nurmi Congress Book*, The Finnish Society of Sports Medicine, pp. 4–6.

Holloway, S. W. F. (1964) 'Medical education in England, 1830–1858: a sociological analysis', *History*, 49, 299–324.

Horan, F. T. (1990) 'Medical care in cricket', in S. D. W. Payne (ed.), *Medicine, Sport and the Law*, Oxford, Basil Blackwell, pp. 341–6.

Houlihan, B. (1991) *The Government and Politics of Sport*, London and New York, Routledge.

—— (1994) *Sport and International Politics*, London, Harvester Wheatsheaf.

—— (1999) *Dying to Win: Doping in Sport and the Development of Anti-Doping Policy*, Strasbourg, Council of Europe.

Hume, P. A. and Marshall, S. W. (1994) 'Sports injuries in New Zealand: exploratory analyses', *New Zealand Journal of Sports Medicine*, 22, 18–22.

Illich, I. (1975) *Medical Nemesis*, London, Calder & Boyars.

Jaques, R. and Brackenridge, C. (1999) 'Child abuse and the sports medicine consultation', *British Journal of Sports Medicine*, 33(4), 229–30.

Jarvie, G. (1985) *Class, Race and Sport in South Africa's Political Economy*, London, Routledge.

Joy, B. (1952) *Forward, Arsenal: the Arsenal Story, 1888–1952*, London, Phoen House.

Kennedy, K. W. (1990) 'The team doctor in Rugby union football', in S. D. W. Payne (ed.), *Medicine, Sport and the Law*, Oxford, Basil Blackwell, pp. 315–23.

Kew, F. (1997) *Sport: Social Problems and Issues*, Oxford, Butterworth-Heinemann.

Kimmage, P. (1990) *A Rough Ride: an Insight into Pro Cycling*, London, Stanley Paul.

—— (1998) *Rough Ride: Behind the Wheel with a Pro Cyclist*, London, Yellow Jersey Press.

Kirk, D. and Colquhoun, D. (1989) 'Healthism and physical education', *British Journal of Sociology of Education*, 10(4), 417–34.

Korbut, O. (1992) *My Story*, London, Sydney, Auckland, Johannesburg, Century.

Korkia, P. and Stimson, G. V. (1993) *Anabolic Steroid Use in Great Britain*, London, Centre for Research into Drugs and Health Behaviour.

Lancet (1988) 'Sports medicine – is there lack of control?' 2, 612.

Lapchick, R. (1989) 'For the true believer', in *Sport in Contemporary Society: an Anthology*, ed. D. Stanley Eitzen, 3rd edn, pp. 17–23.

Lenehan, P., Bellis, M. and McVeigh, J. (1996) 'A study of anabolic steroid use in the North West of England', *The Journal of Performance Enhancing Drugs*, 1(2), 57–70.

Lenskyj, H. (1987) 'Canadian women and physical activity, 1890–1930: media views', in J. A. Mangan and R. J. Park (eds), *From 'Fair Sex' to Feminism*, London, Frank Cass, pp. 208–31.

—— (1990) 'Power and play: gender and sexuality issues in sport and physical activity', *International Review for the Sociology of Sport*, 25(3), 235–43.

Long, J. and Sanderson, I. (1998) 'The social benefits of sport: where's the proof?', *Sport in the City: a Major International Conference*, 2–4 July, vol. 2, Loughborough University/Sheffield Hallam University/University of Sheffield, pp. 295–324.

Lynch, J. M. and Carcasona, C. B. (1994) 'The team physician', in B. Ekblom (ed.), *Handbook of Sports Medicine and Science: Football (Soccer)*, Oxford, Blackwell Scientific Publications, pp. 166–74.

Macauley, D. (1991) *Sports Medicine*, Northern Ireland: Quest Books (N.I.) for the Sports Council of Northern Ireland.

McIntosh, P. C. (1976) 'Sport in society', in J. G. P. Williams and P. N. Sperryn (eds), *Sports Medicine*, 2nd edn, London, Edward Arnold, pp. 1–6.

McLatchie, G. R. (1986) 'The organisation and teaching of sports medicine', in G. R. McLatchie (ed.), *Essentials of Sports Medicine*, Edinburgh, Churchill Livingstone, pp. 21–9.

McPherson, B. D., Curtis, J. E. and Loy, J. W. (1989) *The Social Significance of Sport*, Champaign, IL, Human Kinetics.

Malcolm, D. (1998) 'White lines, grass and the level playing field', in P. Murphy (ed.), *Singer and Friedlander's Review: 1997–98 Season*, London, Singer & Friedlander Investment Funds Ltd.

Mandell, R. D. (1987) *The Nazi Olympics*, Urbana and Chicago, University of Illinois Press.

Mangan, J. A. (1981) *Athleticism in the Victorian and Edwardian Public School*, Cambridge, Cambridge University Press.

Mangan, J. A. and Park, R. J. (eds) (1987) *From 'Fair Sex' to Feminism*, London, Frank Cass.

Mantell, M. (1997) 'EPO-scandal in the peloton', *Cycling Plus*, May, 38–9.

Mellion, M. B. and Walsh, W. M. (1990) 'The team physician', in M. B. Mellion, W. M. Walsh and G. L. Shelton (eds), *The Team Physician's Handbook*, Philadelphia, Hamley & Belfus.

Mennell, S. (1992) *Norbert Elias: an Introduction*, Oxford, Basil Blackwell.

Messner, M. (1990) 'When bodies are weapons: masculinity and violence in sport', *International Review for the Sociology of Sport*, 25(3), 203–18.

Millar, A. P. (1996) 'Drugs in sport', *The Journal of Performance Enhancing Drugs*, 1(3), 106–12.

Monnington, T. (1986) 'The politics of black African sport', in L. Allison (ed.), *The Politics of Sport*, Manchester, Manchester University Press, pp. 149–73.

Moore, J. (1991) 'Women can . . . and do', *Community Care* (April), 17–18.

Morris, J. N., Everitt, M. G., Pollard, R. and Chave, S. P. W. (1980) 'Vigorous exercise in leisure-time: protection against coronary heart disease', *The Lancet*, 6 December, 1207–10.

Mottram, D. R. (ed.) (1988) *Drugs in Sport*, London, E. & F.N. Spon.

—— (ed.) (1996) *Drugs in Sport*, 2nd edn, London, E. & F. N. Spon.

Murphy, P., Sheard, K. and Waddington, I. (2000, forthcoming) 'Figurational sociology and its application to sport', in J. Coakley and E. Dunning (eds), *A Handbook of Sport and Society*, London, Sage.

National Coaching Foundation (1997) *Guidance for National Governing Bodies on Child Protection Procedures*, Leeds, NCF.

Nelson, G. (1995) *Left Foot Forward*, London, Headline.

Nepfer, J. (ed.) (1994) *FIFA World Cup Report*, Zurich, FIFA.

Nevin, P. and Sik, G. (1998) *In Ma Head, Son*, London, Headline.

Newton, F. (1990) 'Medical hazards of water sports – and how to avoid them', in S. D. W. Payne (ed.), *Medicine, Sport and the Law*, Oxford, Basil Blackwell, pp. 299–309.

Nicholl, J. P., Coleman, P. and Brazier, J. E. (1994) 'Health and healthcare costs and benefits of exercise', *PharmacoEconomics*, 5(2), 109–22.

NSPCC/National Coaching Foundation (1995) *Protecting Children: a Guide for Sportspeople*, Leeds, National Coaching Foundation.

Nuzzo, N. A. and Waller, D. P. (1988) 'Drug abuse in athletes', in J. Thomas (ed.), *Drugs, Athletes and Physical Performance*, London and New York, Plenum Medical Book Co., pp. 141–67.

O'Leary, J. (1998) 'The regulation of drug use in sport', in S. Gardiner, F. Felix, M. James, R. Welch and J. O'Leary (eds), *Sports Law*, London, Cavendish, pp. 161–97.

On the Line (1990) 'Drugs, Lies and Finishing Tape', BBC2 TV, 24 January.

—— (1996) BBC Radio Five Live, 12 March.

Our Healthier Nation: a Contract for Health. A Consultation Paper (1998) Cm. 3852, London, The Stationery Office.

Paffenbarger, R. S., Hyde, R. T., Wing, A. L. and Hsieh, C-C. (1986) 'Physical activity, all-cause mortality, and longevity of college alumni', *New England Journal of Medicine*, 314(10), 605–13.

Pavelka, E. (1985) 'Olympic blood boosting: how American cyclists sweated blood – literally – to win', *Bicycling* (Emmaus, PA), April, pp. 32–9.

Penney, D. and Evans, J. (1994) 'It's just not (and not just) cricket', *The British Journal of Physical Education*, 25(3), 9–12.

—— (1997) 'Naming the game: discourse and domination in physical education and sport development in England and Wales', *European Physical Education Review*, 3(1), 21–32.

Percy, E. C. (1983) 'Sports medicine: its past, present and future', *Arizona Medicine*, 40, 789–92.

Pool, H. and Carnall, D. (1997) 'Sport is war minus the shooting!', *Guardian Education*, 18 February, pp. 10–11.

Reder, P., Duncan, S. and Gray, M. (1993) *Beyond Blame: Child Abuse Tragedies Revisited*, London and New York, Routledge.

Reijnen, J. and Velthuijsen, J.-W. (1989) 'Economic aspects of health through sport', *Proceedings of an International Conference: Sport – an Economic Force in Europe*, Lilleshall, UK, 20–22 November, pp. 76–90.

Riordán, J. (1977) *Sport in Soviet Society*, Cambridge, Cambridge University Press.

—— (1981) 'The USSR', in J. Riordan (ed.), *Sport under Communism*, London, C. Hurst & Company, pp. 13–53.

—— (1986) 'State and sport in developing societies', *International Review for the Sociology of Sport*, 21(4), 287–303.

—— (1991) *Sport, Politics and Communism*, Manchester, Manchester University Press.

—— (1994) 'The use of ergogenic aids in Eastern Europe: ethos and ethics', Paper presented to the 1994 IOC Sports Medicine Course (March), Hong Kong Sports Institute.

Roberts, K. (1996a) 'Youth cultures and sport: the success of school and community sport provisions in Britain', *European Physical Education Review*, 2(2), 105–15.

—— (1996b) 'Young people, schools, sport and government policies', *Sport, Education and Society*, 1(1), 47–57.

Roberts, R. and Olsen, J. (1989) *Winning is the Only Thing*, Baltimore, Johns Hopkins University Press.

Roderick, M. (1998) 'The sociology of risk, pain, and injury: a comment on the work of Howard L. Nixon II', *Sociology of Sport Journal*, 15, 64–79.

Rowley, S. (1986) *The Effect of Intensive Training on Young Athletes: a Review of the Research Literature*, London, The Sports Council.

Roy, S. and Irvin, R. (1983) *Sports Medicine: Prevention, Evaluation, Management and Rehabilitation*, Englewood Cliffs, NJ, Prentice-Hall.

Royal College of Physicians of London (1991) *Medical Aspects of Exercise*, London, Royal College of Physicians.

Ryan, A. J. (1989) 'Sports medicine in the world today', in A. J. Ryan and F. L. Allman, Jr., *Sports Medicine*, 2nd edn, San Diego, Academic Press, pp. 3–21.

Ryan, J. (1996) *Little Girls in Pretty Boxes*, London, Women's Press Ltd.

Sheard, K. and Dunning, E. (1973) 'The Rugby football club as a type of "male preserve": some sociological notes', *International Review of Sport Sociology*, 3–4(8), 5–24.

Simbler, S. (1999) 'Ibuprofen – sweets for athletes?', *News*, National Sports Medicine Institute of the United Kingdom Newsletter, 15, Summer, 27.

Smith, A. and Jacobson, B. (eds) (1988) *The Nation's Health*, London, King Edward's Hospital Fund for London.

Sperryn, P. N. (1983) *Sport and Medicine*, London, Butterworth.

Sports Council (1991) *Injuries in Sport and Exercise*, London, The Sports Council.

—— (1995) *Young People and Sport in England, 1994*, London, The Sports Council.

—— (1996a) *Doping Control in the UK: a Survey of the Experiences and Views of Elite Competitors, 1995*, London, Sports Council.

—— (1996b) *Report on the Sports Council's Doping Control Service, 1995–96*, London, Sports Council.

—— (1998a) Ethics and Anti-doping Directorate, *Annual Report, 1997–98*, London, UK Sports Council.

—— (1998b) *Competitors and Officials Guide to Drugs and Sport*, London, UK Sports Council.

Sports Council and Health Education Authority (1992) *Allied Dunbar National Fitness Survey*, London.

Stephens, T. (1988) 'Physical activity and mental health in the United States and Canada: evidence from four population surveys', *Preventive Medicine*, 17, 35–47.

Sugden, J. and Bairner, A. (1993) *Sport, Sectarianism and Society in a Divided Ireland*, Leicester, Leicester University Press.

Sullivan, S. N., Wong, C. and Heidenheim, P. (1994) 'Exercise related symptoms', *New Zealand Journal of Sports Medicine*, 22, 23–5.

Taylor, P. (1985) *The Smoke Ring*, London, Sphere Books.

Tittel, K. and Knuttgen, H. G. (1988) 'The development, objectives and activities of the International Federation of Sports Medicine', in A. Dirix, H. G. Knuttgen and K. Tittel (eds), *The Olympic Book of Sports Medicine*, Oxford, Basil Blackwell, pp. 7–12.

Todd, T. (1987) 'Anabolic steroids: the gremlins of sport', *Journal of Sport History*, 14, 87–107.

US Department of Health and Human Services (1996) *Physical Activity and Health: a Report of the Surgeon General, Executive Summary*, Department of Health and Human Services.

van Krieken, R. (1998) *Norbert Elias*, London, Routledge.

Verbruggen, H. (1997) 'The cheats stay ahead', Interview with William Fotheringham, *Cycle Sport*, April, 28–31.

Verroken, M. (1996) 'Drug use and abuse in sport', in D. R. Mottram (ed.), *Drugs in Sport*, 2nd edn, London, E. & F. N. Spon, pp. 18–55.

Vertinsky, P. (1987) 'Body shapes: the role of the medical establishment in informing female exercise and physical education in nineteenth-century North America', in J. A. Mangan and R. J. Park (eds) *From 'Fair Sex' to Feminism*, London, Frank Cass, pp. 256–81.

—— (1990) *The Eternally Wounded Woman*, Manchester and New York, Manchester University Press.

Videman, T. and Rytömaa, T. (1977) 'Effect of blood removal and autotransfusion on heart rate response to a submaximal workload', *Journal of Sports Medicine*, 17, 387–90.

Vinger, P. F. and Hoerner, E. F. (eds) (1982) *Sports Injuries: the Unthwarted Epidemic*, Littleton, MA, PSG Publishing Co. Inc.

Voy, R. (1991) *Drugs, Sport and Politics*, Champaign, IL, Leisure Press.

Waddington, I. (1984) *The Medical Profession in the Industrial Revolution*, Dublin, Gill & Macmillan.

—— (1996) 'The development of sports medicine', *Sociology of Sport Journal*, 13, 176–96.

Waddington, I., Malcolm, D. and Cobb, J. (1998) 'Gender stereotyping and physical education', *European Physical Education Review*, 4(1), 34–46.

Waddington, I., Malcolm, D. and Green, K. (1997) 'Sport, health and physical education: a reconsideration', *European Physical Education Review*, 3(2), 165–82.

Waddington, I. and Murphy, P. (1992) 'Drugs, sport and ideologies', in E. Dunning and C. Rojek (eds), *Sport and Leisure in the Civilizing Process*, Basingstoke, Macmillan, pp. 36–64.

—— (1998) 'Sport for all: some public health policy issues and problems', *Critical Public Health*, 8(3), 193–205.

Waddington, I., Roderick, M. and Parker, G. (1999) *Managing Injuries in Professional Football: the Roles of the Club Doctor and Physiotherapist*, Centre for Research into Sport and Society, University of Leicester.

Wadler, G. I. and Hainline, B. (1989) *Drugs and the Athlete*, Philadelphia, F. A. Davis.

Waitzkin, H. B. and Waterman, B. (1974) *The Exploitation of Illness in Capitalist Society*, New York, Bobbs-Merrill.

Weaver, S. (1985) 'Eyewitness: Tom Dickson, MD, describes procedures at the LA Olympics', *Bicycling* (Emmaus, PA), March, pp. 58–9.

Williams, G. (1996) 'Review essay: Irving Kenneth Zola (1935–94): an appreciation', *Sociology of Health and Illness*, 18(1), 107–25.

Williams, J., Dunning, E. and Murphy, P. (1989) *Hooligans Abroad*, 2nd edn, London, Routledge.

Williams, J. G. P. (1962) *Sports Medicine,* London, Edward Arnold.

Williams, J. G. P. and Sperryn, P. N. (eds) (1976) *Sports Medicine,* 2nd edn, London, Edward Arnold.

Williams, M. H. (1981) 'Blood doping: an update', *The Physician and Sportsmedicine,* 9(7), 59–64.

Williams, M. H., Lindhjem, M. and Schuster, R. (1978) 'The effect of blood infusion upon endurance capacity and ratings of perceived exertion', *Medicine and Science in Sports,* 10, 113–18.

Williams, S. J. and Calnan, M. (eds) (1996) *Modern Medicine: Lay Perspectives and Experiences*, London, UCL Press.

Wimbush, E. (1994) 'A moderate approach to promoting physical activity: the evidence and implications', *Health Education Journal*, 53, 322–36.

Women's Sports Foundation (1999) *Sexual Abuse in Sport – Recognition and Prevention: a Women's Sports Foundation Factsheet*, London, Women's Sports Foundation.

Yesalis, C. E. (ed.) (1993) *Anabolic Steroids in Sport and Exercise*, Champaign, IL, Human Kinetics.

Yorganci, I. (1992) 'Preliminary findings from a survey of gender relationships and sexual harassment in sport', in C. Brackenridge (ed.) *Body Matters: Leisure Images and Lifestyles*, Brighton, Leisure Studies Association.

Young, K. (1993) 'Violence, risk and liability in male sports culture', *Sociology of Sport Journal*, 10, 373–96.

Young, K. and White, P. (1995) 'Sport, physical danger, and injury: the experience of elite women athletes', *Journal of Sport and Social Issues*, 19(1), 45–61.

Young, K., White, P. and McTeer, W. (1994) 'Body talk: male athletes reflect on sport, injury, and pain', *Sociology of Sport Journal*, 11(2), 175–94.

Zola, I. (1972) 'Medicine as an institution of social control', *Sociological Review*, n.s., 20, 487–504.

Index